TONY ROSE MUSIC BUSINESS, CD PACKAGING, PRODUCTION, PROMOTION, PUBLICITY, MANAGEMENT & DISTRIBUTION CONSULTATION SERVICES

$2,000 - $4,000 with up to 500 CDs and up to 12 songs includes:

CD Packaging, CD Jackets, CD Duplication, CD Jewell boxes and CD Mastering with Record Business, Record Industry, Record Promotion, Record Publicity, Artist Management , CD Distribution Consultation Services.

Extra services:
Production, Producing & Engineering available!

Contact: Tony Rose - 602-743-7211
<u>amberbk@aol.com</u>

WWW.TONYROSEENTERPRISES.COM

QUALITY PRESS BOOK CONSULTATION SERVICES

WWW.QUALITYPRESS.INFO

QUALITY PRESS IS THE NATION'S LARGEST AFRICAN AMERICAN BOOK PACKAGER FOR SELF-PUBLISHERS

Contact Yvonne Rose for YOUR FREE CONSULTATION

602-743-7426 / amberbks@aol.com

Quality Press is a Book Packaging Company founded by Tony Rose, NAACP Image Award Winner for Outstanding Literature and Publisher of Amber Books. Under the Direction of Yvonne Rose, QP works with Self Published Authors specializing in books by, for and about African Americans and featuring all genres including, Children, Poetry, Self-help, Biographies, Non-fiction and Fiction. QP offers consultation and services in every aspect of Paperback, Hardcover and eBook Publishing, such as: Proofreading, Editing, Ghostwriting, Design/Formatting, Printing, Marketing Publicity, Promotions and Distribution. **Email Yvonne Rose at:** amberbks@aol.com for your free consultation or Call: 602-743-7426.

WWW.AMBERBOOKS.COM
WWW.QUALITYPRESS.INFO
WWW.AFRICANAMERICANPAVILION.COM

HOW TO BE

In the Entertainment Business

AND BECOME A
RECORD COMPANY, RECORD PRODUCER,
MUSIC PUBLISHER, PERSONAL MANAGER,
FILM PRODUCER, BOOK PUBLISHER

A Beginners Guide to Success

In the Music, Film, Television
and Book Publishing Industries

PLUS CONTRACTS

TONY ROSE

Amber Books
Phoenix
Los Angeles <> New York

How to Be in The Entertainment Business
and Become a
Record Company, Record Producer, Music Publisher, Personal Manager, Film Producer, Book Publisher
A Beginner's Guide to Success in the Music, Film, Television and Book Publishing Industries
By Tony Rose

Published by
Amber Books
An Imprint of Amber Communications Group, Inc.
1334 East Chandler Boulevard, Suite 5-D67
Phoenix, AZ 85048
Amberbk@aol.com
www.amberbooks.com
www.how2bebooks.com
www.tonyroseenterprises.com

Publisher's Note

The Publisher and Author shall have neither liability nor responsibility to any person or organization with respect to any loss or damage caused or alleged to be caused directly or indirectly by the information contained in this book. The purpose of this book is to educate, entertain and stimulate. This book is sold with the understanding that the Publisher and Author are not involved in offering legal, medical or psychological services. If any assistance is required, the services of a competent professional should be sought.

All Rights Reserved, including the right to reproduce the book, or any portion thereof, in any form without prior permission of the Publisher, except for the inclusion of brief quotations in a review.

Copyright 2016 © by Tony Rose
Paperback ISBN #: 978-1-937269-54-8
eBook ISBN #: 978-1-937269-55-5
Library of Congress Control Number: 2016937775

WWW.How2BEbooks.com
HOME OF THE $2.99 BOOK
Ebook Entertainment Series

RECORD PRODUCER

MUSIC PUBLISHER

RECORD COMPANY

PERSONAL MANAGER

FILM PRODUCER

BOOK PUBLISHER

EMAIL: AMBERBK@AOL.COM / CALL: 602-743-7211
WWW.AMBERBOOKS.COM / WWW.QUALITYPRESS.INFO
WWW.TONYROSEENTERPRISES.COM

WWW.TONYROSEENTERPRISES.COM

WELCOME TO
AMBER BOOKS
WORLD OF BOOKS AND MUSIC

WWW.TONYROSEENTERPRISES.COM

TABLE OF CONTENTS

1   HOW TO BE A RECORD COMPANY
1   What is a record company
6   How to start a record label
8   Record label organizations and operations
14   Record company contract - short version
25   Record company contract - long version
36   Recording contract (album deal - traditional royalties)
45   Exclusive artist recording contract
56   Blank deal memo recording contract
67   Master licensing contract
73   Ringtone licensing contract

79   HOW TO BE A RECORD PRODUCER
79   What is a record producer
87   Five-year production and distribution contract – (label distribution)
94   Record company and producer contract
96   Producer letter of agreement for artist
99   Producer / artist work made for hire contract
109 Promoter and artist contract
112 Booking contract for artist/ musicians
113 Music / dance re-mix work for hire-flat fee - (recording contract)
116 Artist release from a record company contract

119 HOW TO BE A MUSIC PUBLISHER
119 What is a music publisher
123 What does a music publisher do
126 How to start a music publishing company
129 Exclusive songwriting contract

146 HOW TO BE A PERSONAL MANAGER
146 What is a personal manager
150 Personal management contract (1)
157 Personal management contract (2)

160	Non-disclosure-non compete contract
162	Confidentiality agreement
166	Life rights acquisition agreement

176	**HOW TO BE A FILM PRODUCER**
176	What is a film producer
180	What are the responsibilities of a film producer
185	Joint venture film production contract
195	Film production partnership agreement
204	Film – television – theatrical – internet – intellectual properties partnership agreement

214	**HOW TO BE A BOOK PUBLISHER**
214	What is a book publisher
216	What is pod book publishing
216	What is traditional book publishing
217	Book publishing contract (1)
224	Book publishing contract (2)
227	What is electronic or digital book publishing
229	E-book licensing contract
234	How to self-publish an e-book
245	E-book publishing contract
247	Literary agency contract (1)
250	Literary agency contract (2)
255	Partnership agreement for book fairs and festivals
264	Book fair joint venture contract
279	About The Author

A BEGINNERS GUIDE TO SUCCESS

IN THE MUSIC, FILM, TELEVISION AND BOOK PUBLISHING INDUSTRIES

ONE

HOW TO BE A RECORD COMPANY

WHAT IS A RECORD COMPANY IN TODAYS WORLD

A **record label** is a brand or trademark associated with the marketing of music recordings and music videos. Often, a record label is also a publishing company that manages such brands and trademarks; coordinates the production, manufacture, distribution, marketing, promotion, and enforcement of copyright for sound recordings and music videos; conducts talent scouting and development of new artists ("artists and repertoire" or "A&R"); and maintains contracts with recording artists and their managers. The term "record label" derives from the circular label in the center of a vinyl record which prominently displays the manufacturer's name, along with other information.

Music industry

Within the music industry, most recording artists have become increasingly reliant upon record labels to broaden their consumer base, market their albums, and be both promoted and heard on video, MP3, radio, and television, with publicists that assist performers in positive media reports to market their merchandise, and make it available via stores and other media outlets. The Internet has increasingly been a way that artists avoid costs and gain new audiences, with the use of videos to sell their products.

Major versus independent record labels

Record labels may be small, localized, and "independent" ("indies"), or they may be part of a large international media group, or somewhere in between. As of now there are only three labels that can be referred to as "major labels". A "sub label" is a label that is part of a larger record company but trades under a different name.

Imprint

When a label is strictly a trademark or brand, not a company, then it is usually called an *imprint,* a term used for the same concept in publishing. An imprint is sometimes marketed as being a "project", "unit", or "division" of a record label company, even though there is no legal business structure associated with the imprint.

Major Labels

Major labels (Big Three)
1. Universal Music Group (part of EMI's recorded music division absorbed into UMG)
2. Sony Music Entertainment (EMI Music Publishing absorbed into Sony/ATV Music Publishing)
3. Warner Music Group (EMI's Parlophone and EMI/Virgin Classics labels absorbed into WMG in July 2013.

Record labels are often under the control of a corporate umbrella organization called a *Music Group.* A music group is typically owned by an international conglomerate "holding company", which often has non-music divisions as well. A music group controls and consists of music publishing companies, record (sound recording) manufacturers, record distributors, and record labels. The *Big Three* music groups control about 70% of the world music market, and about 80% of the United States music market. Record companies (manufacturers, distributors, and labels) may also comprise a *Record Group* which is, in turn, controlled by a music group. The constituent companies in a music group or record group are sometimes marketed as being *Divisions* of the group.

Independent Record Labels

Record companies and music publishers that are not under the control of the big three are generally considered to be *independent* (*indie*), even if they are large corporations with complex structures. The term *indie label* is sometimes used to refer to only those independent labels that adhere to independent criteria of corporate structure and size, and some consider an *indie* label to be almost any label that releases non-mainstream music, regardless of its corporate structure.

Vanity Labels

Vanity labels are labels that bear an imprint that gives the impression of an artist's ownership or control, but in fact represent a standard artist/label relationship. In such an arrangement, the artist will control nothing more than the usage of the name on the label, but may enjoy a greater say in the packaging of his or her work.

However, not all labels dedicated to particular artists are completely superficial in origin. Many artists, early in their careers, create their own labels which are later bought out by a bigger company. If this is the case it can sometimes give the artist greater freedom than if they were signed directly to the big label.

Relationship with Artists

A label typically enters into an exclusive recording contract with an artist to market the artist's recordings in return for royalties on the selling price of the recordings. Contracts may extend over short or long durations, and may or may not refer to specific recordings. Established, successful artists tend to be able to renegotiate their contracts to get terms more favorable to them.

A contract either provides for the artist to deliver completed recordings to the label, or for the label to undertake the recording with the artist. For artists without a recording history, the label is often involved in selecting producers, recording studios, additional musicians, and songs to be recorded, and may supervise the output of recording sessions. For established artists, a label is usually less involved in the recording process.

The relationship between record labels and artists can be a difficult one. Many artists have had albums altered or censored in some way by the labels before they are released—songs being edited, artwork or titles being changed, etc. Record labels generally do this because they believe that the album will sell better if the changes are made. Often the record label's decisions are prudent ones from a commercial perspective, but this typically frustrates the artists who feels that their art is being diminished or misrepresented by such actions.

In the early days of the recording industry, record labels were absolutely necessary for the success of any artist. The first goal of any new artist or band was to get signed to a contract as soon as possible. Most artists were so desperate to sign a contract with a record company that they usually ended up signing a bad contract, typically giving away the rights to their music in the process. To this day, standard recording contracts define record labels as the rights holders of the music that the contracts cover. Entertainment lawyers should be used to look over any contract before it is signed.

Through the advances of the Internet the role of labels is becoming increasingly diminished, as artists are able to freely distribute their own material through other sources. However, research shows that record labels still control most access to distribution.

New label strategies – The 360 Deals.

With the advancement of the computer and technology like Internet, leading to an increase in file sharing and direct-to-fan digital distribution, combined with music sales plummeting in recent years, labels and organizations have had to change their strategies and the way they work with artists. New types of deals are being made with artists called "multiple rights" or ***360 Deals*** with artists. These types of pacts give labels rights and percentages to artist's touring, merchandising, and endorsements. In exchange for these rights, labels usually give higher advancement payments to artists, have more patience with artist development, and higher percentages in CD sales. These ***360*** style deals are most effective when the artist is established and has a loyal fan base. For that reason, labels now have to be more relaxed with the development of artists because longevity is the key to these types of pacts.

A look at an actual ***360 Deal*** offered by Atlantic Records to an artist shows a variation of the structure. Atlantic's document offers a conventional cash advance to sign the artist, who would receive a royalty for sales after expenses were recouped. With the release of the artist's first album, however, the label has an option to pay an additional $200,000 in exchange for 30 percent of the net income from all touring, merchandise, endorsements, and fan-club fees. Atlantic would also have the right to approve the act's tour schedule, and the salaries of certain tour and merchandise sales employees hired by the artist. But the label also offers the artist a 30 percent cut of the label's album profits, if any, which represents an improvement from the typical industry royalty of 15 percent. A great book written to help you understand 360 deals is *Understanding and Negotiating 360 Ancillary Rights Deals: An Artist's Guide to Negotiating 360 Record Deals* by Kendall Minter – Legendary Entertain-ment Attorney, Kendall Minter, is the leading authority on Entertainment Law and 360 deals. He can be reached at - www.askmusiclawyer.com.

Resurgence of independent labels

As a result of the widespread use of home studios, consumer recording technology, and the Internet, independent labels began to become more commonplace. Independent labels are often artist-owned (although not always), with a stated intent often being to control the quality of the artist's output. Independent labels usually do not enjoy the resources available to the *big three* and as such will often lag behind them in market shares. Often independent artists manage a return by recording for a much smaller production cost of a typical big label release. Sometimes they are able to recoup their initial advance even with much lower sales numbers.

On occasion, established artists, once their record contract has finished, move to an independent label. This often gives the combined advantage of name recognition and more control over one's music along with a larger portion of royalty profits. Constant touring can result in noteworthy success for an act without significant major funding.

Some independent labels become successful enough that major record companies negotiate contracts to either distribute music for the label or in some cases, purchase the label completely.

Internet and digital labels

With the Internet now being a viable source for obtaining music, *Net Labels* have emerged. Depending on the ideals of the net label, music files from the artists may be downloaded free of charge or for a fee that is paid via PayPal or other online payment system. Some of these labels also offer hard copy CDs in addition to direct download. *Digital Labels* are the latest version of a *Net Label*. Whereas *net labels* were started as a free site, digital labels are more competition for the major record labels.

Open-source labels

The new century brings the phenomenon of *Open-Source* or *Open-Content* record label. These are inspired by the free software and open source movements and the success of **GNU/Linux**.

Publishers as labels

Some music publishing companies have begun undertaking the work traditionally done by labels. The publisher Sony/ATV Music, for example, leveraged its connections within the Sony family to produce, record, distribute, and promote albums under the dormant Sony-owned imprint, rather than waiting for a deal with another label.

TONY ROSE

HOW TO START A RECORD LABEL

DEFINE YOUR PLACE IN THE MUSIC INDUSTRY

What do you love the most? What music do you know inside and out? The most valuable currency in the music industry is passion.

No matter what kind of label you chose to start, make sure you're choosing something that you support 100%. Trends can come and go. If you're serious about making it last, pick music that you can stand behind long into the future.

Picture yourself sitting on your porch when you're retired. You've got your headphones on. You're reflecting on the fullness of your life and all your most cherished memories. What are you listening to? That's what you should be releasing. Whatever music is timeless to you.

FIGURE OUT YOUR FORMAT

'Which format is the best' is one of the most talked about issues among music labels these days.

It's like asking, what do I want for dessert. No matter what you choose you're having a tasty treat. But choosing just one is the most important part in the beginning. Juggling five different formats when you're starting out can be hard. Keep it simple.

The four most common formats are:
1. Limited Edition Cassette
2. Limited Edition Vinyl
3. Digital Only
4. CD

Even though these are the most common formats, your label does not have to be limited to them. It's hard to stand out in such a saturated industry. Feel free to be creative with your formats. Just like you'd be creative with your sundae toppings.

USE STREAMING PLATFORMS

164-billion songs were streamed last year in the US alone.

Streaming platforms such as SoundCloud, Bandcamp, and Discogs will give your small business the visibility it needs to thrive.

Platforms like these fall under the umbrella of distribution (which we will discuss later) but they also give you immediate visibility and listenability. If you want to say something to the masses, you're gonna need a megaphone.

DEFINE WHO WILL BE PRODUCING MUSIC ON YOUR LABEL

A label is a community. Do you get together on the weekend and play records with your friends who create music? Start a label.

Labels grow out of groups of like-minded individuals who want to give something back to music. Finding your core of artists is simple if you remember the idea of 'label as community.'

You're going to need new music. Lots of it. Foster your artists now and treat them like the stars of the future. Their music should always come first.

WRITING A BUSINESS PLAN

You'll need a business plan to template and outline how your business will operate.

It allows you to explore ways to get startup financing and get investors.

A good business plan will cover:
1. Name and Vision
2. Start-up Expenses
3. Products Offered
4. Market Analysis
5. Competition
6. Brand Strategy and Implementation
7. Revenue Forecast
8. Goals
9. Monthly Overhead

You're an entrepreneur now and a business plan is one of the best ways to get legit and find money immediately.

RECORD LABEL ORGANIZATION AND OPERATIONS

Remember that nowadays, many record companies are huge corporations that own a variety of record labels. For the most part, these companies are located in New York, Los Angeles or Nashville. These corporations usually consist of a parent company that owns more than one record label. In today's economy, most large record companies are actually huge conglomerates that own a variety of subsidiary record labels. Often, the subsidiary labels are each mini-companies operating under the umbrella of the larger corporation.

To describe the hierarchy of a record company, it's best to start at the top. The CEO (chief executive officer) is in charge of the business of the whole company. In addition, each label also has its own president. Under the president of the individual label, there are vice presidents in charge of different departments. Let's take a look at the departments that make up a major record label:

- **A&R** - The A&R (artists and repertoire) department is often considered the most glamorous department at a record label. This is because A&R is in charge of discovering new talent. A&R people work very hands-on with the artists that they "sign." (When a record label "signs" an artist, it simply means that the artist makes an exclusive contract with that record label.) They do everything from assisting with song selection to choosing the people that will produce the album to deciding where the album will be recorded. The people in this department work as the link between the recording artist and all the other departments of the record company.

- **Art Department** - This department is in charge of all the artwork that goes along with producing an album. This includes CD cover art, advertisements and displays at music stores.

- **Artist Development** - This department is responsible for planning the careers of the artists who are signed to the record label. It promotes and publicizes the artists over the course of their career. Many labels no longer have artist development departments. As record labels have come to see artists as products in recent years, some artist development departments have been renamed "Product Development." Many insist that this is because the emphasis in the current music business is to promote artists very heavily in the beginning of their career, as opposed to long-term planning. *If you don't want to be a "one-hit-wonder," pay close attention to how the record label views this aspect of career planning.*

- **Business Affairs** - This department deals with the business side of things. It takes care of bookkeeping, payroll and general finances.

HOW TO BE A RECORD COMPANY

- **Label Liaison** - This is usually one person, or small group of people, who serves as the liaison between the record company's distribution company (either an entirely separate division under the huge corporate umbrella or an outside company responsible for getting the CDs into the stores) and the record company. The label liaison also helps decide when to release an album (when the album goes on sale to the public) and makes sure it doesn't conflict with any of the other labels the record company owns.
- **Legal Department** - This department is responsible for all the contracts that are made between the company and the artist, as well as contracts between the record label and other companies. Any legal issues that arise (such as lawsuits between an artist and the company) go through this department.
- **Marketing Department** - This department creates the overall marketing plan for every album that the record company will release. It helps coordinate the plans of the promotion, sales and publicity departments.
- **New Media** - This department is in charge of dealing with the newer aspects of the music business, including producing and promoting music videos for the artist. In addition, this department is often responsible for helping an artist create a presence on the Internet. It deals with the new technologies in which artists can stream music and music videos through the Internet.
- **Promotion Department** - This department's main purpose is to make sure that an artist is being played on the radio. It must get an artist's new songs on the radio in order to ensure the future success of the record company. This department makes sure that all the other departments are communicating about the best way to sell the artist to the public. The promotion department also tries to get videos played on MTV or VH1 channels. This can be the responsibility of this department or in conjunction with the New Media department.
- **Publicity** - This group is responsible for getting the word out about a new or established artist. It arranges for articles to be written in newspapers and magazines. They also deal with radio and television coverage of an artist. Many artists also have their own independent publicists who help coordinate publicity with this department as well.
- **Sales** - This department oversees the retail aspect of the record business. It works with chains like Targets and Walmart's and other stores that sell music to get new albums onto retailers' shelves. The sales department often coordinates these efforts with the promotion and publicity departments.

Remember that any given record label may have a slightly different organization. As large companies buy up smaller record labels, the organization of record companies changes a great deal. Most record companies have their own Web sites where you can find what labels the company owns and what artists the company is promoting.

WHY SHOP FOR A LABEL

Record companies (known as record labels because albums have a label indicating which company produced it) take on a lion's share of the work of the music industry. They sign, develop, record, promote, publicize and sell music. Of course, all those things happen before the album ever gets into the store.

Record labels come in all sizes, from small independent labels run by one or two people to huge corporations made up of hundreds of people in dozens of departments. In fact, Billboard, the best known music industry publication, lists more than 2,000 record companies currently in operation. Music is big business. Successful records sell millions of copies and earn billions of dollars for the record companies.

THE GATEKEEPERS: A&R

The A&R department of a record label is often regarded as the gatekeepers of the record company. A&R departments have a powerful reputation because they have the all-important job of finding and nurturing the musical talent.

A&R stands for "artists and repertoire," but many musicians joke that A&R stands for "attitude and rejection." Without being noticed or discovered by A&R people, there is almost no way for an artist to get signed by a major record label. In times past, artists would send "unsolicited" demos (tapes that were not requested by the record company) to A&R departments, and the executives would listen to the tapes and hope to find the next big thing. Over time, so many artists were sending demos that it became impossible for A&R people to keep up. Because of this and other legal issues, labels, with a few exceptions, soon stopped listening to unsolicited material. Because it is so difficult for the average musician's demo tape to even make it to the desk of the powerful A&R execs, many people ask how A&R people go about finding talent.

If you ask A&R people, they will tell you that they are always completely inundated with new material. They often barely have time to listen to the numerous demo tapes given to them by friends, agents, managers, attorneys and other reliable sources. With only a few people serving as the gatekeepers and thousands of aspiring bands and singers out there, you can imagine how difficult it can be to break into the record industry.

What kind of talent A&R people look for and how they find is to first listen to demos given to them by their most trusted business sources and works their way down from there. Other executives, examine the music industry itself to see if there is a void in the market. Others may seek out a certain type of artist that they feel is doing a different kind of music than what is already in the stores.

It is also important to remember that when A&R executives discover and promote a particular artist, they are putting their own name on the line. If the artist fails, an A&R executive's job may be at stake. As this part of the recording industry becomes clearer, you can see how difficult it is for an average band without record industry contacts to "make it." The other thing to remember about this industry, though, is that while a lot bands get rejected, some still make it through the gates of A&R. When an artist is discovered by a record company, then the full machinery of the record label must begin the work of producing, promoting, marketing, distributing and selling the album.

THE BUSINESS OF MUSIC

Now that you understand how a record label is organized and what the A&R department does, it's time to take you through the steps a record company goes through when it decides to sign an artist. To understand this process, let's take a look at an "Act" we'll call "Act X," and a record label we'll call "For Example Records."

Before artists can be signed, they have to be discovered. Imagine, for this example, that Act X is discovered after an A&R representative from For Example Records goes to see Act X at a live show. Before the A&R person went to the show, he was given a demo tape by a trusted source and did his research on the band. At the club, he likes what he sees and now must convince the entire A&R staff to sign the band. When they are in agreement, the band is signed and the wheels go into motion.

Act X must now plan its album. The A&R director and producer decide on the concept of the album and select the songs that will be on the album. For Example Records gives Act X a budget, which is used for studio musicians, studio engineers and studio time. The A&R executive then coordinates a time for the band to begin recording the album. (In the past, record labels had their own "in-house" recording studios, but today most record labels use independent recording studios.)

As this is going on, the other departments of the record company are in full swing. A budget is allotted for advertising, art, publicity and promotion.

As graphic artists, designers and copywriters begin their work, the A&R department, as well as publicity, marketing and sales, decide on a release date for the album. The artist development department (along with other departments) plans the live performances, promotional tour and radio and TV appearances. The record company must make sure that there is promotion for Act X on the national, regional and local level (depending on how much money the label is willing to spend).

Near the time that the album will be released, the label's departments are working hard to secure press coverage and exposure for the band. All the machine's parts are working together to make sure that Act X's album will sell many copies, ensuring the success of everyone involved, from the artist to the radio stations to the CD stores.

This is just a sampling of some of the things that happen when a record label signs an artist. As you can tell, the music business is not just parties and hanging out with the stars. A record label must do a great deal of work to discover, sign, produce, promote, distribute and sell an album.

THE IMPORTANCE OF RADIO

While record companies represent a huge part of the music industry, the other huge part consists of radio stations. Record labels and radio stations must work together to succeed. Record labels must get radio stations to play the music of the artists they represent, and radio stations need a consistent flow of new material for their listeners. While record companies make their money by selling albums, radio stations make money by broadcasting advertisements. Radio stations need an audience of listeners so that advertisers will buy airtime. If record labels can deliver radio stations music that will get listeners, stations can sell airtime. In this way, everyone gets what they want. There is a process that both labels and radio stations go through before this can happen.

When record labels are about to release an album, they have their promotions and/or sales department try to get radio airplay for the album. In the history of the music industry, there have been a million ways record labels have tried to get their artists on radio stations. They have done everything from fly an artist to a station to do an interview to offer stations illegal money (called payola) to play an artist's music.

Often, radio stations and labels will work together to promote artists, like when a radio station hosts a concert or in-store record signing. It's important for both record label executives and radio station personnel to be aware of the current trends in music, keep track of an artist's success and keep up with changing radio formats. Good relationships between a record label and radio stations can mean that everyone will make money off of an artist's success.

MUSIC MOGULS VS THE INDEPENDENTS

As it became more and more difficult for bands to get signed by the huge record labels, independent record labels began to pop up. Independent record labels (also known as indies or garage labels) can be as large as some of the smaller corporate record companies or as small as one or two people. The reason that so few independent record labels succeed is due to the sheer amount of money, work and time it takes to run a record label.

Now that you understand the organization of a record label, you can see how difficult it would be to have to take on the job of A&R, artist development, marketing, publicity and sales with only a few people. The larger record companies succeed because they have the money and power to hire many people to do all these jobs. At an independent record label, it may be the same person who discovers the artist or band, calls the radio stations about getting airplay and arranges the artist's publicity. That is not to say that independent record labels cannot succeed, it just takes a lot more work.

The best way to succeed in the indie record label game is to specialize in either local music or genre music. These are two areas that the major record companies may ignore. In this way, independent labels succeed by bringing music to consumers that the major record labels don't release.

The Internet has also done a lot to promote the success of independent record labels. If they have trouble getting retail stores to carry their product, indie labels can sell albums over the Internet. The Internet has also been host to a variety of contests for music artists wherein the winner receives a record contract with an indie.

TONY ROSE

RECORD COMPANY AGREEMENT SHORT VERSION

Dated as of:

Artist:

Dear Gentlemen:

The following when countersigned by you, will constitute this the interim recording agreement between us and shall remain in full force and effect pending the execution of a more formal recording contract. This Agreement shall be binding upon you.

1. Recording Commitment.

(a) Initial Term: Album / singles

(b) Option Terms: Five (5) consecutive options for one (1) album each option period. Each option shall be deemed automatically exercised unless we notify You in writing, which such notice shall be sent to you not later than thirty (30) days prior to the expiration of the then current Term.

(c) Notwithstanding anything to the contrary set forth herein, the Recording Commitment applicable to this Agreement shall be the same as that set forth in the Distribution Agreement (as described below); provided however, in the event the Term of the Distribution Agreement should expire or be terminated prior to the delivery and release of at least six (6) albums, then we shall have a period of nine (9) months after the date of such termination or expiration to secure a new Distribution Agreement, as defined below. In the event we do not secure a New Distribution Agreement with the aforesaid nine (9) month period, then you shall have the right to terminate this Agreement upon written notice within thirty days thereafter. In the event we do secure a New Distribution Agreement, then this Agreement shall be extended so as to be co-terminus with the Term and the Recording Commitment of the New Distribution Agreement, provided however, in no event shall you be obligated to record more than six (6) albums in the aggregate.

(d) Notwithstanding the above, we shall have the right, in our sole discretion to manufacture, distribute, market, promote, sell or otherwise exploit single recordings and albums through independent distribution (as described below) prior to the execution of the Distribution Agreement.

2. Term.

(a) The Initial Term of this Agreement shall commence as of the date hereof and shall continue for a period ending on the date which is the sooner of (i) twelve (12) months after the date of Delivery of the masters constituting the album due for the initial contract Term; or (ii) nine (9) months after the initial commercial release of the first album.

(b) Each Option Period shall be exercised on or before the date which is the sooner of twelve (12) months after the Delivery of the immediately preceding Album, or nine (9) months after the initial commercial release in any country of the Territory of the immediately preceding Album, and shall expire on the date which is nine (9) months after the initial commercial release in any country of the Territory of the Album Delivered in fulfillment of the recording commitment for the applicable contract period.

(c) Each album due hereunder shall be recorded within four (4) months after the commencement of the applicable contract period unless we agree to extend said period, in writing.

(d) We shall have the right to suspend the running of the Term hereof, by written notice to you, in the event you should fail to timely deliver any particular album hereunder, or in the event you should breach this Agreement or default in the performance of any of your obligations hereunder. Provided, in the event such failure to timely deliver a particular album is not caused by your acts or omissions, then we shall not be entitled to suspend the Term. Any such suspension shall be for a period equal to the length of your breach, default or delay in delivery.

(e) You shall have the right upon written notice to terminate the Term of this Agreement in the event we have not secured a distribution or production agreement with an established U.S. or European major or substantial independent record company (the "Distribution Agreement") within twelve (12) months from the date hereof. For the purpose of this Agreement the term **Major Record Company** shall include Sony BMG, Universal, EMI, Warner

Music Group and any labels distributed, owned or controlled by such a major company. The term **Substantial Independent Record Company** shall be defined as a U.S. record distribution company or record label with at least $1,000,000 in average annual gross billings.

3. Territory. Worldwide.

4. Rights.

(a) You hereby acknowledge that we shall be the sole and exclusive owner of all master tapes, multi-track tapes, outtakes and all derivatives therefrom recorded pursuant to this Agreement (the "Masters"), in perpetuity, including the sound recording copyrights in and to all such master tapes and materials. We shall not have any rights to any masters recorded by you and paid for by you or a third party prior to the date hereof. We shall have the exclusive right to manufacture, distribute, sell, license, reproduce and otherwise exploit worldwide all such materials without any obligation to you, except as expressly set forth herein. We shall have the right, in our sole discretion, to grant to others the right to manufacture, distribute, sell and otherwise exploit the Masters.

(b) You grant us the right, exclusive during the Term hereof for the Territory and non-exclusive thereafter, to use your name (legal and professional), approved biographies and approved photographs and likenesses in connection with the marketing, promotion and sale of the Masters and all derivatives therefrom. You shall furnish us within ten (10) days after our request with biographical material and negatives for photographs. We shall also submit to you for your approval any materials and photographs which we wish to use hereunder. You shall have a period of five (5) business days to approve or disapprove or any such materials, failing which they shall be deemed approved.

(c) We shall have the right to assign this Agreement to any of our subsidiaries or affiliates, to any entity that acquires all or substantially all of our assets or capital stock, and to any third party major U.S. or European record distributor or to any third party substantial independent U.S. record company (as defined above). This Agreement is personal to you and as such may not be assigned except to a corporation or partnership owned solely by you and provided such entity and you execute and deliver such additional documents as we may require (i.e.: inducement letter and personal guarantee).

(d) You shall have the right to terminate this Agreement upon written notice to us in the event our company should file a petition in bankruptcy or should become insolvent or should be subject to the appointment of a receiver or trustee, or if ( ) should cease to be actively involved in the performance of this Agreement on behalf of our Company.

5. Advances.

In consideration of the rights granted to us hereunder and subject to your full and timely performance of your material obligations hereunder, we shall pay to you the following non-returnable advances, recoupable from royalties, excluding mechanical royalties, payable to you hereunder.

(a) In the event we should enter into the Distribution Agreement with a major U.S. record company then, with respect to the initial album, the sum of Twenty-Five Thousand ($25,000) Dollars, said sum shall be paid to You one-half (1/2) upon the full execution of the Distribution Agreement and the balance upon the Delivery to and acceptance by Company of the first album. In the event we should enter into the Distribution Agreement with a U.S. independent record company then, with respect to the initial album, the sum of Fifteen Thousand ($15,000) Dollars, said sum shall be paid to You one-half (1/2) upon the full execution of the Distribution Agreement and the balance upon the Delivery to and acceptance by Company of the first album.

(b) We shall pay to you additional advances for optional albums as provided below:

(Distribution)

Option: Albums	Independent	Major
First Option Album:	$20,000	- $35,000
Second Option Album:	$25,000	- $45,000
Third Option Album:	$30,000	- $55,000
Fourth Option Album:	$35,000	- $65,000
Fifth Option Album:	$40,000	- $75,000

Each such option album advance shall be paid:

(i) Fifty (50%) percent upon commencement of recording of each album; and

(ii) Fifty (50%) percent upon the completion, delivery and acceptance of the Masters constituting each album.

(c) We shall pay all recording costs for each album recorded hereunder. You NAME shall be responsible for any excess recording costs which are incurred as a result of your own acts or omissions. All recording costs shall be deemed to be advances recoupable from the record royalties payable to you pursuant to paragraph "6" hereunder.

(d) We shall be entitled to recoup all advances paid by us for the production of videos, fifty (50%) percent from record/audio royalties and one hundred (100%) percent from gross revenues derived from the commercial exploitation of such videos, if applicable. Notwithstanding the foregoing, in the event the Distribution Agreement should provide for recoupment of video production and exploitation costs utilizing a different manner of computation, then the provision set forth in the Distribution Agreement shall be deemed incorporated herein by reference and shall control.

(e) Fifty (50%) percent of all expenditures made by us or our licensees and distributor for the independent promotion, publicity and marketing of the Masters and records derived therefrom shall be recoupable from royalties payable to you under paragraph "6" below.

6. Royalties.

(a) Company shall pay to you all "inclusive royalties" as follows:

USNRC:
Net Sales: 0 - 500,000 Units   500,001 - 1M Units   1M+ Units

LP # 1	13%	13.5%	14%
LP # 2	13%	13.5%	14%
LP # 3&4	14%	14.5%	15%

LP # 5&6   15%   15.5%   16%
Singles (U.S.) 9%   10%   10%

For Sales outside of the U.S.A., we shall pay you the following royalties which shall be calculated as a percentage of the base U.S. royalties:

Canada: 85%
U.K. & Europe: 75%
Japan & Australia: 66-2/3%
Rest Of World: 50%

(b) Notwithstanding anything to the contrary set forth above with respect to royalties, the maximum amount of royalties which we shall be obligated to pay to you hereunder for record and video sales (including digital, electronic and all configurations)shall not be in excess of sixty five (65%) percent of the net royalties received by us pursuant to the Distribution Agreement.

(c) For the purpose of this Agreement the term "net royalties" shall be defined as the gross royalties payable to Company pursuant to the Distribution Agreement and/or any other direct license agreements less all recoupable costs including but not limited to recording costs, independent marketing costs, independent publicity costs, independent promotion costs, video production and exploitation costs, advances, featured fees, producer fees, sample clearance costs, legal fees, accounting fees, and any other direct and reasonable expenditures incurred by Company in connection with the recording of the Masters, the acquisition of rights and the delivery of the Masters.

(d) We shall have the right to establish a royalty reserve up to twenty-five (25%) percent for all albums and up to fifty (50%) percent for all singles sold, said reserve to be fully liquidated within four (4) semi-annual accounting periods from the date initially established. Notwithstanding the foregoing, in the event the royalty reserve policy established by our distributor should differ from that contained herein, the policy of our distributor shall control and be deemed incorporated herein.

7. **Accountings.**

1. We shall render royalty accounting statements to you semi-annually within ninety (90) days after June 30th and December 31st annually. Each

statement shall detail all sales of product derived from the Masters and shall be accompanied by the payment of royalties due, if any.

2. You shall have the right to inspect our books and records to verify the accuracy of ujjmall statements rendered to you hereunder upon written notice, given within eighteen (18) months from the date a particular statement is rendered. Your right of inspection shall be subject to at least thirty (30) days prior notice, shall be conducted at the office where our records are located and may only be conducted once within any given twelve (12) month period.

8. Creative Matters.

We shall consult with you with respect to all materials to be recorded hereunder and all producers to be retained (and the terms of their employment) for the recording of the Masters. We shall designate the studios to be used, in consultation with you. In the event of a dispute, our decision shall control. We shall consult with you with respect to album and single cover artwork.

9. Videos.

We agree to use our reasonable efforts to produce at least one (1) video for each album recorded hereunder. You and we shall mutually designate and agree upon the budget, the storyboard, director, producer and primary creative elements for each video produced hereunder. In the event of a dispute with respect to the producer or budget for any particular video, our decision shall control. We shall exclusively own all rights in and to each video recorded pursuant to this Agreement.

10. Mechanical Rates.

With respect to the Controlled Compositions, you agree to license said compositions to us or our distributor(s) for the United States and Canada at seventy-five (75%) percent of the minimum statutory rate in effect at the date of Delivery of the Master(s) embodying each such composition. We shall not be obligated to pay mechanical royalties in excess of the following rates: LPs - eleven (11) times; Eps - five (5) times; Singles - two (2) times; Maxi-Singles - three (3) times; the reduced Controlled Composition Mechanical Rate. Notwithstanding the foregoing, in the event the mechanical rates for Controlled Compositions which are set forth in the Distribution Agreement should differ from those set forth herein, then the terms set forth in the Distribution Agreement shall be deemed incorporated herein by reference and shall control.

11. Website.

Company shall have the perpetual right and may grant to others the right, subject to the terms and conditions hereof, without any liability to any Person to create, maintain and host websites. In the event that Company exercises its option to extend the Term of this agreement for an Option Period, then as of the date of such option exercise you shall automatically be deemed to have licensed to Company the exclusive right, coupled with a security interest and without any liability to any Person, during the Tern of this agreement to register, secure any registration renewals thereof, administer such registrations, control and use the Domain Names as Internet Addresses including, without limitation, the right to use such Domain Names in connection with Company Websites. During the Term of this agreement, Company will have the right to designate one (1) Company Website as the "official" Website (the "Official Website"), and neither you, nor any Person deriving any rights from you or shall designate any other Website as an "official" Website except as otherwise provided herein. In the event that (Name).com, (Name).net and/or (Name).org are not available to be used as the Domain Names in connection with the Official Website, you and Company will mutually approve the Domain name to be used in the United States in connection with the Official Website, provided that an inadvertent to so obtain your approval with you will not be deemed a breach of this agreement. Company's rights as described in the first sentence of this clause shall be exclusive during the term of this agreement and non-exclusive thereafter, except that, for the avoidance of doubt, such rights shall be exclusive in perpetuity with respect to utilizing and/or otherwise exploiting Masters, Videos and/or Artwork hereunder in connection with Websites. Fifty (50%) percent of all costs incurred by us in connection with the development, maintenance and hosting of each official website shall be deemed a recoupable advance hereunder.

12. Tour Support.

In the event we should request, or should we approve your request, that you undertake one or more promotional appearances and/or performances, including but not limited to in-store appearances, promotional live shows, media interviews and appearances at industry events, we shall make additional advances to you, recoupable from royalties payable to you hereunder, subject to a budget to be approved on a case-by-case basis, to cover or subsidize the approved costs of such appearances. We hereby pre-approve a per diem of fifty ($50.00) dollars per each appearance and travel day. In the event of a disagreement as to any particular line item or budget, our decision shall be final and shall control. We may, in our sole discretion, administer the payment of each tour support budget.

13. Passive Income Participation.

(a) In the event the ***Distribution Agreement*** should contain any so-called ***passive income provisions*** which grant certain rights to the Distributor to receive a share of income which you earn in connection with your activities in the entertainment industry (excluding records and music publishing), then you hereby grant to Company's Distributor, on a "pass through" basis as such necessary rights. Company shall be entitled to be paid and retain sums equivalent to an additional five (5%) percent of all such passive income streams as are paid to the Distributor, for Company's own account.

(b) In the event the Distribution Agreement does not contain any so-called "passive income or ***360*** provisions", then the following shall apply:

(i) If you enter into an agreement with any third party with respect to any entertainment industry activity that would normally fall outside of the scope of this agreement (i.e., an agreement not related to recording services) (each, an ***Ancillary Rights Agreement*** (including, without limitation, any agreement for acting services in motion pictures or television shows or services in connection with books, touring, endorsements, etc. [but specifically excluding music publishing]), you shall cause the applicable third party to pay Company directly an amount equal to fifteen percent (15%) of Ancillary Net Receipts in connection with any such ***Ancillary Rights Agreement.***

(ii) Company shall have the same rights to audit your books and records (and to bring an action against you) in connection with any ***Ancillary Rights Agreement*** as you have to audit Company's Books and Records pursuant to paragraph 7(b) herein below. As used herein, ***Ancillary Net Receipts*** shall mean all royalties, one-time payments, or other compensation received by or credited to you in connection with any ***Ancillary Rights Agreement***, less any actual and legitimate costs or expenses that you payor incur in connection with any such agreement (i.e., management fees, booking agent fees and legal fees).

14. Merchandising.

You hereby grant us the exclusive right of first refusal and last matching right to enter into license agreements regarding the exploitation of your merchandising right during the Term. In the event you should secure a bona fide written offer from a third party merchandising company to enter into an agreement pursuant to which – during the Term – you will grant rights to exploit your name and likeness in connection with the sale of goods, then you shall promptly provide us with a copy of said written offer and we shall have a period of thirty (30) days after our receipt of same to match the material terms and conditions, failing which you shall have the right to enter into an agreement with such third party on terms no less favorable then those contained in the offer. We shall have the exclusive right during the Term to exploit so-called ***bounce back merchandising*** derived from album cover photography. We shall maintain a separate non-cross collateralized account for all such sales and shall account to you on the same schedule as set forth in paragraph 7 above. We shall pay to you sixty (60%) percent of all of our net receipts derived therefrom. We shall have a period of thirty (30) days after receipt from you of a bona fide third party offer to exercise our last matching right.

15. Miscellaneous.

1. This Agreement shall be construed and interpreted in accordance with the laws of the State of Arizona.

2. This Agreement constitutes the entire understanding between the parties and may not be modified or amended except by a written document signed by all parties hereto.

3. In the event of the breach or default of any term or provision contained in this Agreement by either party, then the other party shall provide written notice specifying the details of such breach or default and shall have the right

to terminate this Agreement in writing in the event such breach or default is not cured within thirty (30) days after receipt of notice or unless the breaching party has not commenced to cure said breach if it is incapable of being fully cured within said thirty (30) day period.

4. The parties hereto agree that upon the execution of this Agreement, all prior recording agreements between the parties shall be deemed to be terminated and expired.

5. All notices intended to be given hereunder shall be in writing and shall be delivered in person, by certified or registered mail, return receipt requested, by Federal Express or DHL or by facsimile with proof of transmission/receipt.

YOU HEREBY ACKNOWLEDGE THAT WE HAVE ADVISED YOU OF YOUR RIGHT TO SEEK THE ADVICE OF INDEPENDENT LEGAL COUNSEL, SELECTED BY YOU, TO REPRESENT YOU IN THE NEGOTIATION OF THIS AGREEMENT.

Very truly yours,

By: _____

ACCEPTED AND AGREED TO:

Artist

HOW TO BE A RECORD COMPANY

RECORD COMPANY AGREEMENT LONG VERSION

Dated as of:
Artist:
Dear Gentlemen:

The following when countersigned by you, will constitute this the interim recording agreement between us and shall remain in full force and effect pending the execution of a more formal recording contract. This Agreement shall be binding upon you.

1. Recording Commitment.

(a) Initial Term: singles

(b) Option Terms: Five (5) consecutive options for one (1) album each option period. Each option shall be deemed automatically exercised unless We notify You in writing, which such notice shall be sent to you not later than thirty (30) days prior to the expiration of the then current Term.

(c) Notwithstanding anything to the contrary set forth herein, the Recording Commitment applicable to this Agreement shall be the same as that set forth in the Distribution Agreement (as described below); provided however, in the event the Term of the Distribution Agreement should expire or be terminated prior to the delivery and release of at least six (6) albums, then we shall have a period of nine (9) months after the date of such termination or expiration to secure a new Distribution Agreement, as defined below. In the event we do not secure a New Distribution Agreement with the aforesaid nine (9) month period, then you shall have the right to terminate this Agreement upon written notice within thirty days thereafter. In the event we do secure a New Distribution Agreement, then this Agreement shall be extended so as to be co-terminus with the Term and the Recording Commitment of the New Distribution Agreement, provided however, in no event shall you be obligated to record more than six (6) albums in the aggregate.

(d) Notwithstanding the above, we shall have the right, in our sole discretion to manufacture, distribute, market, promote, sell or otherwise exploit single recordings and albums through independent distribution (as described below) prior to the execution of the Distribution Agreement.

2. Term.

(a) The Initial Term of this Agreement shall commence as of the date hereof and shall continue for a period ending on the date which is the sooner of (i) twelve (12) months after the date of Delivery of the masters constituting the album due for the initial contract Term; or (ii) nine (9) months after the initial commercial release of the first album.

(b) Each Option Period shall be exercised on or before the date which is the sooner of twelve (12) months after the Delivery of the immediately preceding Album, or nine (9) months after the initial commercial release in any country of the Territory of the immediately preceding Album, and shall expire on the date which is nine (9) months after the initial commercial release in any country of the Territory of the Album Delivered in fulfillment of the recording commitment for the applicable contract period.

(c) Each album due hereunder shall be recorded within four (4) months after the commencement of the applicable contract period unless we agree to extend said period, in writing.

(d) We shall have the right to suspend the running of the Term hereof, by written notice to you, in the event you should fail to timely deliver any particular album hereunder, or in the event you should breach this Agreement or default in the performance of any of your obligations hereunder. Provided, in the event such failure to timely deliver a particular album is not caused by your acts or omissions, then we shall not be entitled to suspend the Term. Any such suspension shall be for a period equal to the length of your breach, default or delay in delivery.

(e) You shall have the right upon written notice to terminate the Term of this Agreement in the event we have not secured a distribution or production agreement with an established U.S. or European major or substantial independent record company (the "Distribution Agreement") within twelve (12) months from the date hereof. For the purpose of this Agreement the term "major" record company shall include Sony BMG, Universal, EMI, Warner

Music Group and any labels distributed, owned or controlled by such a major company. The term "substantial independent record company" shall be defined as a U.S. record distribution company or record label with at least $1,000,000 in average annual gross billings.

3. Territory. Worldwide.

4. Rights.

(a) You hereby acknowledge that we shall be the sole and exclusive owner of all master tapes, multi-track tapes, outtakes and all derivatives therefrom recorded pursuant to this Agreement (the "Masters"), in perpetuity, including the sound recording copyrights in and to all such master tapes and materials. We shall not have any rights to any masters recorded by you and paid for by you or a third party prior to the date hereof. We shall have the exclusive right to manufacture, distribute, sell, license, reproduce and otherwise exploit worldwide all such materials without any obligation to you, except as expressly set forth herein. We shall have the right, in our sole discretion, to grant to others the right to manufacture, distribute, sell and otherwise exploit the Masters.

(b) You grant us the right, exclusive during the Term hereof for the Territory and non-exclusive thereafter, to use your name (legal and professional), approved biographies and approved photographs and likenesses in connection with the marketing, promotion and sale of the Masters and all derivatives therefrom. You shall furnish us within ten (10) days after our request with biographical material and negatives for photographs. We shall also submit to you for your approval any materials and photographs which we wish to use hereunder. You shall have a period of five (5) business days to approve or disapprove or any such materials, failing which they shall be deemed approved.

(c) We shall have the right to assign this Agreement to any of our subsidiaries or affiliates, to any entity that acquires all or substantially all of our assets or capital stock, and to any third party major U.S. or European record distributor or to any third party substantial independent U.S. record company (as defined above). This Agreement is personal to you and as such may not be assigned except to a corporation or partnership owned solely by you and provided such entity and you execute and deliver such additional documents as we may require (i.e.: inducement letter and personal guarantee).

(d) You shall have the right to terminate this Agreement upon written notice to us in the event our company should file a petition in bankruptcy or should become insolvent or should be subject to the appointment of a receiver or trustee, or if ( ) should cease to be actively involved in the performance of this Agreement on behalf of our Company.

5. Advances.

In consideration of the rights granted to us hereunder and subject to your full and timely performance of your material obligations hereunder, we shall pay to you the following non-returnable advances, recoupable from royalties, excluding mechanical royalties, payable to you hereunder.

(a) In the event we should enter into the Distribution Agreement with a major U.S. record company then, with respect to the initial album, the sum of Twenty-Five Thousand ($25,000) Dollars, said sum shall be paid to You one-half (1/2) upon the full execution of the Distribution Agreement and the balance upon the Delivery to and acceptance by Company of the first album. In the event we should enter into the Distribution Agreement with a U.S. independent record company then, with respect to the initial album, the sum of Fifteen Thousand ($15,000) Dollars, said sum shall be paid to You one-half (1/2) upon the full execution of the Distribution Agreement and the balance upon the Delivery to and acceptance by Company of the first album.

(b) We shall pay to you additional advances for optional albums as provided below:

(Distribution)

Option Albums	Independent	Major
First Option Album:	$20,000	$35,000
Second Option Album:	$25,000	$45,000
Third Option Album:	$30,000	$55,000
Fourth Option Album:	$35,000	$65,000
Fifth Option Album:	$40,000	$75,000

Each such option album advance shall be paid:

HOW TO BE A RECORD COMPANY

(i) Fifty (50%) percent upon commencement of recording of each album; and

(ii) Fifty (50%) percent upon the completion, delivery and acceptance of the Masters constituting each album.

(c) We shall pay all recording costs for each album recorded hereunder. You shall be responsible for any excess recording costs which are incurred as a result of your own acts or omissions. All recording costs shall be deemed to be advances recoupable from the record royalties payable to you pursuant to paragraph "6" hereunder.

(d) We shall be entitled to recoup all advances paid by us for the production of videos, fifty (50%) percent from record/audio royalties and one hundred (100%) percent from gross revenues derived from the commercial exploitation of such videos, if applicable. Notwithstanding the foregoing, in the event the Distribution Agreement should provide for recoupment of video production and exploitation costs utilizing a different manner of computation, then the provision set forth in the Distribution Agreement shall be deemed incorporated herein by reference and shall control.

(e) Fifty (50%) percent of all expenditures made by us or our licensees and distributor for the independent promotion, publicity and marketing of the Masters and records derived therefrom shall be recoupable from royalties' payable to you under paragraph "6" below.

6. Royalties.

(a) Company shall pay to you all "inclusive royalties" as follows:

USNRC and Jamaica:

Net Sales:	0 - 500,000 Units	500,001 - 1M Units	1M+ Units
LP #1	13%	13.5%	14%
LP #2	13%	13.5%	14%
LP #3&4	14%	14.5%	15%
LP #5&6	15%	15.5%	16%
Singles (U.S.)	9%	10%	10%

For Sales outside of the U.S.A., we shall pay you the following royalties which shall be calculated as a percentage of the base U.S. royalties:

Canada:	85%
U.K. & Europe:	75%
Japan & Australia:	66-2/3%
Rest Of World:	50%

(b) Notwithstanding anything to the contrary set forth above with respect to royalties, the maximum amount of royalties which we shall be obligated to pay to you hereunder for record and video sales (including digital, electronic and all configurations)shall not be in excess of sixty five (65%) percent of the net royalties received by us pursuant to the Distribution Agreement.

(c) For the purpose of this Agreement the term "net royalties" shall be defined as the gross royalties payable to Company pursuant to the Distribution Agreement and/or any other direct license agreements less all recoupable costs including but not limited to recording costs, independent marketing costs, independent publicity costs, independent promotion costs, video production and exploitation costs, advances, featured fees, producer fees, sample clearance costs, legal fees, accounting fees, and any other direct and reasonable expenditures incurred by Company in connection with the recording of the Masters, the acquisition of rights and the delivery of the Masters.

(d) We shall have the right to establish a royalty reserve up to twenty-five (25%) percent for all albums and up to fifty (50%) percent for all singles sold, said reserve to be fully liquidated within four (4) semi-annual accounting periods from the date initially established. Notwithstanding the foregoing, in the event the royalty reserve policy established by our distributor should differ from that contained herein, the policy of our distributor shall control and be deemed incorporated herein.

7. Accountings.

1. We shall render royalty accounting statements to you semi-annually within ninety (90) days after June 30th and December 31st annually. Each

statement shall detail all sales of product derived from the Masters and shall be accompanied by the payment of royalties due, if any.

2. You shall have the right to inspect our books and records to verify the accuracy of all statements rendered to you hereunder upon written notice, given within eighteen (18) months from the date a particular statement is rendered. Your right of inspection shall be subject to at least thirty (30) days prior notice, shall be conducted at the office where our records are located and may only be conducted once within any given twelve (12) month period.

8. Creative Matters.

We shall consult with you with respect to all materials to be recorded hereunder and all producers to be retained (and the terms of their employment) for the recording of the Masters. We shall designate the studios to be used, in consultation with you. In the event of a dispute, our decision shall control. We shall consult with you with respect to album and single cover artwork.

9. Videos.

We agree to use our reasonable efforts to produce at least one (1) video for each album recorded hereunder. You and we shall mutually designate and agree upon the budget, the storyboard, director, producer and primary creative elements for each video produced hereunder. In the event of a dispute with respect to the producer or budget for any particular video, our decision shall control. We shall exclusively own all rights in and to each video recorded pursuant to this Agreement.

10. Mechanical Rates.

With respect to the Controlled Compositions, you agree to license said compositions to us or our distributor(s) for the United States and Canada at seventy-five (75%) percent of the minimum statutory rate in effect at the date of Delivery of the Master(s) embodying each such composition. We shall not be obligated to pay mechanical royalties in excess of the following rates: LPs - eleven (11) times; Eps - five (5) times; Singles - two (2) times; Maxi-Singles - three (3) times; the reduced Controlled Composition Mechanical Rate. Notwithstanding the foregoing, in the event the mechanical rates for

Controlled Compositions which are set forth in the Distribution Agreement should differ from those set forth herein, then the terms set forth in the Distribution Agreement shall be deemed incorporated herein by reference and shall control.

11. Website.

Company shall have the perpetual right and may grant to others the right, subject to the terms and conditions hereof, without any liability to any Person to create, maintain and host websites. In the event that Company exercises its option to extend the Term of this agreement for an Option Period, then as of the date of such option exercise you shall automatically be deemed to have licensed to Company the exclusive right, coupled with a security interest and without any liability to any Person, during the Tern of this agreement to register, secure any registration renewals thereof, administer such registrations, control and use the Domain Names as Internet Addresses including, without limitation, the right to use such Domain Names in connection with Company Websites. During the Term of this agreement, Company will have the right to designate one (1) Company Website as the "official" Website (the "Official Website"), and neither you, nor any Person deriving any rights from you or shall designate any other Website as an "official" Website except as otherwise provided herein. In the event that (Name).com, (Name).net and/or (Name).org are not available to be used as the Domain Names in connection with the Official Website, you and Company will mutually approve the Domain name to be used in the United States in connection with the Official Website, provided that an inadvertent to so obtain your approval with you will not be deemed a breach of this agreement. Company's rights as described in the first sentence of this clause shall be exclusive during the term of this agreement and non-exclusive thereafter, except that, for the avoidance of doubt, such rights shall be exclusive in perpetuity with respect to utilizing and/or otherwise exploiting Masters, Videos and/or Artwork hereunder in connection with Websites. Fifty (50%) percent of all costs incurred by us in connection with the development, maintenance and hosting of each official website shall be deemed a recoupable advance hereunder.

12. Tour Support.

In the event we should request, or should we approve your request, that you undertake one or more promotional appearances and/or performances, including but not limited to in-store appearances, promotional live shows, media interviews and appearances at industry events, we shall make additional advances to you, recoupable from royalties payable to you hereunder, subject to a budget to be approved on a case-by-case basis, to cover or subsidize the approved costs of such appearances. We hereby pre-approve a per diem of fifty ($50.00) dollars per each appearance and travel day. In the event of a disagreement as to any particular line item or budget, our decision shall be final and shall control. We may, in our sole discretion, administer the payment of each tour support budget.

13. Passive Income Participation.

(a) In the event the Distribution Agreement should contain any so-called "passive income provisions" which grant certain rights to the Distributor to receive a share of income which you earn in connection with your activities in the entertainment industry (excluding records and music publishing), then you hereby grant to Company's Distributor, on a "pass through" basis as such necessary rights. Company shall be entitled to be paid and retain sums equivalent to an additional five (5%) percent of all such passive income streams as are paid to the Distributor, for Company's own account.

(b) In the event the Distribution Agreement does not contain any so-called "passive income or 360 provisions", then the following shall apply:

(i) If you enter into an agreement with any third party with respect to any entertainment industry activity that would normally fall outside of the scope of this agreement (i.e., an agreement not related to recording services) (each, an "Ancillary Rights Agreement') (including, without limitation, any agreement for acting services in motion pictures or television shows or services in connection with books, touring, endorsements, etc. [but specifically excluding music publishing]), you shall cause the applicable third party to pay Company directly an amount equal to fifteen percent (15%) of Ancillary Net Receipts in connection with any such Ancillary Rights Agreement.

(ii) Company shall have the same rights to audit your books and records (and to bring an action against you) in connection with any Ancillary Rights

Agreement as you have to audit Company's Books and Records pursuant to paragraph 7(b) herein below. As used herein, "Ancillary Net Receipts shall mean all royalties, one-time payments, or other compensation received by or credited to you in connection with any Ancillary Rights Agreement, less any actual and legitimate costs or expenses that you pay or incur in connection with any such agreement (i.e., management fees, booking agent fees and legal fees).

14. Merchandising.

You hereby grant us the exclusive right of first refusal and last matching right to enter into license agreements regarding the exploitation of your merchandising right during the Term. In the event you should secure a bona fide written offer from a third party merchandising company to enter into an agreement pursuant to which – during the Term – you will grant rights to exploit your name and likeness in connection with the sale of goods, then you shall promptly provide us with a copy of said written offer and we shall have a period of thirty (30) days after our receipt of same to match the material terms and conditions, failing which you shall have the right to enter into an agreement with such third party on terms no less favorable then those contained in the offer. We shall have the exclusive right during the Term to exploit so-called "bounce back merchandising" derived from album cover photography. We shall maintain a separate non-cross collateralized account for all such sales and shall account to you on the same schedule as set forth in paragraph 7 above. We shall pay to you sixty (60%) percent of all of our net receipts derived therefrom. We shall have a period of thirty (30) days after receipt from you of a bona fide third party offer to exercise our last matching right.

15. Miscellaneous.

1. This Agreement shall be construed and interpreted in accordance with the laws of the State of _____.

2. This Agreement constitutes the entire understanding between the parties and may not be modified or amended except by a written document signed by all parties hereto.

3. In the event of the breach or default of any term or provision contained in this Agreement by either party, then the other party shall provide written notice specifying the details of such breach or default and shall have the right to terminate this Agreement in writing in the event such breach or default is not cured within thirty (30) days after receipt of notice or unless the breaching party has not commenced to cure said breach if it is incapable of being fully cured within said thirty (30) day period.

4. The parties hereto agree that upon the execution of this Agreement, all prior recording agreements between the parties shall be deemed to be terminated and expired.

5. All notices intended to be given hereunder shall be in writing and shall be delivered in person, by certified or registered mail, return receipt requested, by Federal Express or DHL or by facsimile with proof of transmission/receipt.

YOU HEREBY ACKNOWLEDGE THAT WE HAVE ADVISED YOU OF YOUR RIGHT TO SEEK THE ADVICE OF INDEPENDENT LEGAL COUNSEL, SELECTED BY YOU, TO REPRESENT YOU IN THE NEGOTIATION OF THIS AGREEMENT.

Very truly yours,

By: _____

ACCEPTED AND AGREED TO:

Artist

_____

TONY ROSE

RECORDING CONTRACT AGREEMENT
(ALBUM DEAL-TRADITIONAL ROYALTY)

This AGREEMENT (hereinafter referred to as the "Agreement") is made effective this _____ day of _____, 201__ by and between _____, located at _____ (hereinafter referred to as the "Artist") and _____, located at _____ (hereinafter referred to as the "Company").

WITNESSETH:

In consideration of the respective covenants contained herein, the parties hereto, intending to legally bound hereby, agree as follows:

1. Engagement.

A. Company hereby engages Artist and Artist hereby accepts such engagement as a musical artist in connection with the production of commercially satisfactory master recordings (the "Masters") comprising one (1) Album, as herein defined, entitled "_____ ALBUM". Artist shall record masters for Company hereunder in a recording studio selected by Company at such times and with such individual Artist(s) as Company may designate, subject to the approval of Artist. However, in the event of a dispute between Artist and Company with regard to such Artist, Company's decision shall prevail, so long as it is not unreasonable. The Masters recorded by Artist hereunder shall consist of Artist's newly recorded studio performances of material selected or approved by Company and not previously recorded by Artist. Each such Master shall be commercially satisfactory in Company's reasonable opinion. Upon the request of Company, Artist shall re-record any selection until a commercially satisfactory master shall have been obtained.

B. For the purposes of this Agreement, Artist shall be deemed to have completed recording a master when Company shall be in actual receipt of such master completed, fully edited, mixed and equalized, commercially satisfactory to Company and ready for Company's manufacture of records therefrom, together with all consents, approvals, licenses and permissions.

C. Company shall pay for all Recording Costs associated with the recording and production of the Masters hereunder, which Recording Costs shall be fully recoupable out of any sums due Artist hereunder. Company shall also pay the costs incurred in the preparation of commercial units of phonorecords derived from the Masters, including but not limited to costs associated with the creation and preparation of cover art, graphics, designs, credits, layout, mockups, printer fees, inks, films, special containers, shrinkwrap, and the like. All such costs paid by Company shall be deemed advances against and recoupable by Company out of all royalties becoming payable to Artist pursuant to this Agreement. Any creative material so prepared and paid for by Company shall be the sole property of Company.

2. Ownership of Masters. All Masters recorded by Artist hereunder, from the inception of the recording thereof and all reproductions derived therefrom, together with the performances embodied thereon, shall be the property of Company for the world free from any claims whatsoever by Artist or any person deriving any rights or interest from Artist. Each such master (referring only to the sound recordings as opposed to the underlying musical works) shall be considered a "work made for hire" for Company; if any such master is determined not to be a "work made for hire" it will be deemed transferred to Company by this Agreement, together with all rights in it.

A. Without limiting the generality of the foregoing, Company and its designee(s) shall have the exclusive, perpetual, and unlimited right to all the results and proceeds of the uninhibited exploitation of the Masters throughout the Territory, including, but not limited to:

(i) The right to manufacture, advertise, sell, lease, license, distribute or otherwise use or dispose of, in any or all fields of use by any method now or hereafter known, records embodying the Masters delivered hereunder, upon such terms and conditions as Company may elect, or at its discretion to refrain therefrom;

(ii) The right to use, reproduce, print, publish or disseminate in any medium, and to permit others to do the same, Artist's name (including any professional name now or hereafter adopted by Artist), photos, likeness, and biographical material concerning Artist in all connections which relate in any manner to the Masters or Company, including, without limitation, in the marketing, sale or other exploitation of records, and as news or other information, in connection with Company's business;

(iii) The right to perform the records publicly and to permit public performances thereof by means of radio broadcast, television or any other method now or hereafter known, and to synchronize such performances with visual images.

(iv) The right to license the Masters to third parties for use on a flat-fee and/or royalty basis.

(v) To include the Masters on compilations with masters by other Artists, Artists, and/or Artists.

B. All the rights herein granted to Company hereunder shall be for the Universe (the "Territory").

C. Artist acknowledges that the sale of records is speculative and agrees that the judgment of Company with regard to any matter affecting the sale, distribution and exploitation of such records shall be binding and conclusive upon Artist. Nothing contained in this Agreement shall obligate Company to make, sell, license, or distribute recordings manufactured from masters recorded hereunder.

3. Advances. Upon execution of this Agreement, Company shall pay Artist the sum of $_____ US Dollars. All monies paid to Artist, on behalf of Artist, or at the request of Artist, other than royalties payable pursuant to Paragraph 5 of this Agreement, shall constitute advances to Artist and shall be fully recoupable by Company from any monies payable under this or any Agreement between Company and Artist.

4. Re-Recording Restriction. (a) Artist shall not perform any selection recorded hereunder, or any portion thereof, for the purpose of making records for anyone other than Company for a period of five (5) years after the initial date of release of the respective record containing such selection.

5. Royalties. Conditioned upon Artist's full and faithful performance of each and all of the terms hereof, Company shall pay Artist the following royalties in respect of records sold subject to this Agreement, provided first that Company in then in a fully recouped position in accordance with the provisions of this Agreement:

A. A royalty of fifteen (15%) percent of the wholesale list price in the country of manufacture on ninety (90%) percent of all exploitation of the Masters licensed hereunder, after full recoupment of the advance to Artist described in paragraph 3.

B. As to records not consisting entirely of masters recorded and/or delivered hereunder, the royalty rate otherwise payable to Artist hereunder with respect to sales of any such record shall be prorated by multiplying such royalty rate by a fraction, the numerator of which is the number of Masters recorded and/or delivered hereunder embodied on such record and the denominator of which is the total number of masters embodied thereon.

C. Company shall have the right to include or to license others to include any one or more of the Masters in promotional records on which such masters and other recordings are included, which promotional records are designed for promotional uses or sale at or slightly above the cost of manufacture. No royalties shall be payable on sales of such promotional records.

D. Notwithstanding anything to the contrary contained herein, Artist shall not be entitled to receive or earn any monies in respect of any exploitation of the Masters for which Company is not entitled to receive or does not earn a royalty or credit.

E. Any royalties becoming payable under any other agreement to any other Artist, engineer, Artist, or other contributor for contributions to the creation of the Masters shall be shared equally by Company and Artist and shall be deducted "off the top" before the calculation of net receipts. Company shall pay the royalty directly to the Artist, engineer, Artist, or other contributor who so contributed.

F. Notwithstanding anything to the contrary contained in this Agreement, it is specifically understood and agreed that no royalties shall be payable to Artist hereunder unless and until Company has recouped all Recording Costs incurred in connection with the Masters hereunder.

G. Royalties in respect of sales of records outside the United States shall be computed in the same national currency as Company is accounted to by its licensees and shall be paid to Artist at the same rate of exchange as Company is paid. It is understood that such royalties will not be due and payable until payment thereof is received by Company in the United States of America.

H. As to Masters embodying performances of Artist together with the after the date upon which Company notifies Artist that it denies the validity of the objection.

6. Audits. Artist shall have the right at Artist's sole cost and expense to appoint a Certified Public Accountant who is not then currently engaged in an outstanding audit of Company to examine Company's books and records as same pertain to sales of records subject hereto as to which royalties are payable hereunder, provided that any such examination shall be for a reasonable duration, and shall take place at Company's offices during normal business hours on reasonable prior written notice and shall not occur more than once in any calendar year. Artist may examine Company's books and records with respect to a particular statement only once.

7. Notices. All notices to either party may be served upon that party personally or sent postage prepaid by registered or certified mail, return receipt requested to the party at its address first above written.

8. Suspension. Company reserves the right to suspend the operation of this Agreement for the duration of any of the following contingencies, if such contingency materially hampers performance of its obligations under this Agreement or its normal business operations: Act of God, fire, catastrophe, labor dispute, acts of government, its agencies or officers, any order, regulation, ruling or action of any labor union or association of Artists, musicians, composers or employers affecting Company, or the industry in which it is engaged, delays in delivery of materials and supplies, or any other cause beyond Company's control.

9. Warranties & Indemnification.
A. Artist warrants and represents that Artist is under no disability, restriction or prohibition, whether contractual or otherwise, with respect to Artist's right to execute this Agreement and perform its terms and conditions.

B. Artist warrants and represents that Company shall not be required to make any payment of any nature for, or in connection with, the rendition

Artist's services or the acquisition, exercise or exploitation of rights by Company pursuant this Agreement, except as specifically provided herein;

C. Artist warrants and represents that no materials, or any use thereof, will violate any law or infringe upon or violate the rights or any third party. "Materials," as used in this subparagraph 9(C) shall include:

(i) all musical compositions and other material contained on masters subject hereto,

(ii) all sound recordings of any nature delivered by Artist to Company,

(iii) each name used by Artist, in connection with masters recorded hereunder, including the project name, and

(iv) all other materials, ideas, other intellectual properties or elements furnished or selected by Artist and used in connection with any masters recorded hereunder or the packaging, sale, distribution, advertising, publicizing, or other exploitation thereof.

D. Artist agrees to and does hereby indemnify, save and hold Company harmless from any and all loss and damage (including reasonable attorneys' fees) arising out of, connected with or as a result of any inconsistency with, failure of, or breach by Artist of any warranty, representation, agreement, promise, undertaking or covenant contained in this Agreement. Upon the making or filing of any such claim, action or demand, Company and its respective licensees (as applicable) shall be entitled to withhold from any amounts payable under this Agreement such amounts as are reasonably related to the potential liability in issue, unless and until Artist posts a suitable undertaking or bond by a reputable bonding company satisfactory to Company and its respective licensees (as applicable) in the sum equal to the amount of Artist's potential liability hereunder (including reasonable legal fees and legal costs).

10. Miscellaneous. This Agreement sets forth the entire agreement between the parties. No modification, amendment, waiver, termination or discharge of this Agreement shall be binding unless contained in a writing signed and dated by the party sought to be bound. No waiver of any term or condition of this Agreement in any instance shall be deemed or construed as a waiver of such term or condition for the future, or of any subsequent breach thereof. Should any provision of this Agreement be adjudicated as void, invalid or inoperative, such provision shall be deemed stricken from this Agreement, and the remainder of the provisions shall continue in full force and effect, binding on both parties, as if the void, invalid or inoperative provision had not been contained herein. No breach of this Agreement by either party shall be deemed material unless within thirty (30) days after the non-breaching party learns of such breach, that party serves written notice thereof on the breaching party specifying the nature thereof and the breaching party fails to cure such breach, if any, within sixty (60) days after receipt of such notice. This Agreement shall be deemed to have been made in the State of New York and its validity, construction, performance and breach shall be governed by the laws of the State of _____ applicable to agreements made and to be wholly performed therein. The courts located in the City of _____ shall have exclusive jurisdiction over all disputes between Company and Artist pertaining to this Agreement and all matters related thereto.

11. Definitions. For purposes of this Agreement:

A. The words "master recording" or "master" shall mean the equivalent of a seven (7) inch, 45 r.p.m. single-sided original recording of sound (whether or not coupled with a visual image and whether on magnetic recording tape, film, lacquer or acetate disc, or any other substance or material now known or unknown), which is intended for use in the production and manufacture of phonograph records. Company shall not be required to accept delivery of any master recording which is less than three (3) minutes in playing time.

B. "Records", "phonograph records", "recordings" and "derivatives" mean all forms of reproductions, now or hereafter known, manufactured or sold primarily for home use, school use, juke box use or use on means of transportation, embodying sound alone or sound coupled with visual images.

C. "Recording Costs" - mean all amounts representing direct expenses paid or incurred by Company in connection with the production and recording of finished, commercially satisfactory Masters under this agreement. Recording Costs include, without limitation, travel, rehearsal, and equipment rental and cartage expenses, costs of materials, advances to Artists, transportation costs, hotel and living expenses approved by Company, per-diems, studio and engineering charges in connection with Company's facilities and personnel or otherwise, all costs and expenses of obtaining rights to all samples of Masters, selections and other materials embodied in Masters hereunder (including, without limitation, all advances, license fees, reasonable attorney's fees and clearing house fees), all fees and other sums payable to side Artists and other creative contributors, including without limitation any AFM and AFTRA payments, all costs of mastering, remastering, remixing and/or "sweetening" and all costs of lacquer, copper, and other equivalent masters.

D. "Single" - the equivalent of a CD disc configuration, a twelve (12) inch vinyl record, a maxi-cassette or cassingle; or the equivalent in non-vinyl configurations, which contains recordings of not more than four (4) Controlled Compositions and does not constitute an LP.

E. "Album" – a record of not less than 35 minutes of playing time. Multiple sets which consist of more than one (1) Album intended to be released, packaged and sold together for a single overall price shall be deemed to be the equivalent of one (1) Album for the purposes of this Agreement, but shall not be recorded hereunder without Company's prior written consent.

F. "Controlled Composition" - All compositions embodied on a Master recorded hereunder which are written or owned, in whole or in part by Artist or any entity owned (in whole or in part) or controlled by Artist.

IN WITNESS WHEREOF, the parties hereto have executed this Agreement on the day and year first above written.

AGREED TO AND ACCEPTED:

BY:
"ARTIST"

_____
(an authorized signatory)

BY:
"COMPANY"

_____
(an authorized signatory)

TONY ROSE

Schedule A
(The "Album")

1. _____

2. _____

3. _____

4. _____

5. _____

6. _____

7. _____

8. _____

9. _____

10. _____

INITIAL HERE:

BY:
"ARTIST"

_____
(an authorized signatory)

BY:

_____
(an authorized signatory)

HOW TO BE A RECORD COMPANY

EXCLUSIVE ARTIST RECORDING AGREEMENT

XYZ RECORD COMPANY
ADDRESS

Dated as of: _____
NAME
ADDRESS

Dear_____:

This letter shall confirm the material terms of the exclusive artist recording agreement ("Agreement") between NAME/ADDRESS (hereinafter "ARTIST" or "you"), and COMPANY NAME /ADDRESS (hereinafter "COMPANY" or "us") as follows:

1. ENGAGEMENT: COMPANY hereby engages ARTIST to perform as a recording artist exclusively for Company and ARTIST agrees, during the Term (as defined below) of this Agreement, to perform exclusively for COMPANY throughout the world ("Territory") for the purpose of making Master Recordings (as defined below) intended for the manufacture and sale of records.

2. TERM:
The "Term" of this Agreement shall commence on the date of this Agreement as set forth above and shall continue for five years from the Agreement commencement date.

3. DELIVERY OBLIGATION:
During each calendar year of the Term, ARTIST shall record and Deliver Master Recordings to COMPANY, technically and commercially satisfactory, in COMPANY's reasonable judgment, for the manufacture and sale of records. ARTIST shall Deliver one album per Term comprised of no fewer than six (6) Master Recordings, each Master Recording being not less than four minutes in length (collectively or individually referred to herein as "Album"). For the 201 calendar year, ARTIST shall Deliver his first Album

within _____ months of execution of the Agreement. The foregoing recording(s) are sometimes referred to herein as the "Minimum Recording Commitment" with respect to the term period applicable thereto. Following 2013, the Minimum Recording Commitment for each period shall be Delivered (or, "Deliver" as the verb context may indicate) to COMPANY no later than DATE following the commencement of each calendar year of the contract. The Minimum Recording Commitment for each period of the Term will be deemed Delivered to COMPANY when ARTIST has submitted to COMPANY and COMPANY has accepted:

(a) Satisfactory Master Recordings in the format specified by COMPANY for the production of parts necessary for the mastering of the recordings and the manufacture of records ("Masters" or "Master Recordings");

(b) All label copy information (e.g., the timing, title, and any other information specified by COMPANY that is to appear on labels and/or liners of records containing those Masters);

(c) All mechanical licenses for each composition embodied in the Masters;

(d) All "sideman" agreements, producer agreements and any other required third party clearances;

(e) A "sampling" clearance documents; and

(f) All other documents reasonably required by COMPANY for it to enjoy the full benefit of rights granted hereunder throughout the 'Territory in perpetuity.

4. OWNERSHIP RIGHTS AND PROMOTION:

(a) ARTIST and COMPANY shall be the joint owners of each Master Recording, each owning a fifty percent (50%) interest therein. Accordingly, ARTIST hereby irrevocably assigns to COMPANY fifty percent (50%) of the copyright interest in each and every Master Recording; and ARTIST hereby grants to COMPANY an irrevocable power of attorney to execute for ARTIST, in ARTIST's name, all documents necessary to make the assignment.

(b) Without limiting COMPANY's rights above, COMPANY shall have the exclusive right, throughout the Territory and in perpetuity, to:

(i) manufacture, distribute, transmit, promote, advertise, sell, lease, license or otherwise commercially exploit records containing the Masters in all media now known or hitherto devised;

(ii) use ARTIST's name, photograph, likeness and/or biography in connection with promotion, advertising and trade, including the exploitation of records, as news or information and in general goodwill advertising, including the right to create, develop or use any of the foregoing in or in connection with website(s), Facebook, twitter and/or any other form of social media, whether interactive or non-interactive, now known or hereafter developed;

(iii) license any or all of COMPANY's rights under this Agreement to third parties, as COMPANY deems advisable in its reasonable judgment;

(iv) publicly perform the Masters and to permit the public performance thereof by means of radio, internet, television or cable broadcast, or otherwise;

(v) or otherwise use the Masters in any or all fields of use upon such terms and conditions as Company may approve, or to refrain therefrom; and all such rights may be transferred to, and exercised by firms owned or controlled by or affiliated with Company or by unrelated third parties.

(c) In COMPANY's sole discretion, COMPANY shall have the right to register and own domain names containing ARTIST's name and/or similar derivations thereof and to own, create, host and maintain one or more official ARTIST websites ("ARTIST website(s)") and/or other websites and hyperlinks connected therewith, for purposes of marketing, promotion, sales, distribution, and other commercial exploitation under this Agreement. ARTIST also grants to COMPANY and COMPANY's Licensees at no cost an irrevocable license under copyright to reproduce, distribute and perform each ARTIST Composition or any portion thereof for use on an ARTIST website(s). ARTIST will supply COMPANY, at COMPANY's request, with website material for possible inclusion on ARTIST website(s), including, without limitation, transcripts of all published interviews of ARTIST, transcripts of all articles relating to ARTIST, photographs, and other similar materials. COMPANY and ARTIST shall work in cooperation to determine the appropriate content for the ARTIST website(s). ARTIST will be available, at COMPANY request, for promotional activity regarding ARTIST Website(s).

5. RECORDING PROCEDURE:

ARTIST shall be responsible for carrying out and completing the studio recording process necessary to create the Master Recordings. This includes, but is not limited to arranging for and scheduling the requisite studio time; recording and mixing the Master Recordings; obtaining the services of any required engineers, producers, arrangers, and sidemen; and paying all the expenses associated with any of the foregoing, such that ARTIST shall Deliver fully mixed Master Recordings to COMPANY. COMPANY shall pay for all Album artwork and the mastering costs for the Master Recordings. All COMPANY expenses shall be fully deductible "off the top" and recoupable by COMPANY prior to the distribution of royalties to ARTIST.

6. ROYALTIES:

(a) COMPANY will pay ARTIST a royalty equal to thirty percent (30%) of the Net Amount Actually Received by COMPANY through the sale or licensing of the records in physical configurations, and COMPANY will pay ARTIST a royalty equal to fifty percent (50%) of the Net Amount Actually Received by COMPANY through the sale or licensing of the records in DEMD formats. DEMD means any transmission, distribution, dissemination or making available of recordings (or the digitized content thereof) including, but not limited to, distribution via telephone (including, without limitation, ring tones, ring backs, realtones, push ringers, pictones, voicetones and text messages), satellite, broadcast, wireless, cable and/or the internet (by any method or means), whether or not a direct or indirect charge is made.

For purposes of this paragraph, the term "Net Amount Actually Received" shall mean the actual United States dollar amount received in the United States by COMPANY less all mastering, artwork, manufacturing, printing, distribution, and promotional expenses (all of the foregoing being referred to as "COMPANY expenses") which COMPANY shall be entitled to recoup in their entirety "off the top" from first dollars received.

(b) COMPANY shall be entitled to maintain a single account with respect to all records and compositions recorded under this Agreement.

(c) In the event that ARTIST renders services pursuant hereto on Master Recording(s) that contain the recorded performances of other royalty artists signed to Company, then, in that event, the COMPANY expenses incurred by COMPANY incident to said recordings shall be recouped from each royalty artist proportionally. The amount of recoupable costs to be recouped from ARTIST's royalty account in that event shall be computed by multiplying the total recoupable recording costs by a fraction, the numerator of which shall be ARTIST's royalty percentage and the denominator of which shall be the total royalty percentage of all royalty artists performing on said recordings.

(d) ARTIST shall receive 20 promotional albums per year, per album; and the ARTIST also shall be entitled to purchase CDs from COMPANY at a discount price to be determined by COMPANY.

7. CO-PUBLISHING:

(a) ARTIST and his publishing designee (hereinafter collectively referred to as "the Publishing Designee") hereby irrevocably assign, convey and set over to COMPANY an undivided fifty percent (50%) interest in the worldwide copyright (and all renewals and extensions thereof) and all other rights in and to each composition that is embodied in a Master Recording subject to this Agreement which is written, in whole or in part or owed and/or controlled, directly or indirectly by ARTIST ("ARTIST Composition"). For purposes of this Clause, "COMPANY" shall be deemed to refer to COMPANY and/or its publishing designee. For purposes of copyright registration, ARTIST's interest shall be registered as NAME and COMPANY's interest shall be registered as NAME.

(b) (i) COMPANY shall have the exclusive rights of administration of all rights in and to each such ARTIST Composition throughout the Territory for the term of copyright (and all renewals and extensions thereof), and COMPANY shall be entitled to exercise any and all rights with respect to the control and administration of the ARTIST Composition(s), including without limitation, the sole right to grant licenses, collect all income and to use the name, likeness and biographical material of each composer, lyricist and songwriter hereunder in connection with each applicable ARTIST Composition for the full term of copyright (including all renewals and extensions thereof) in and to each ARTIST Composition; and

(ii) Without limiting the generality of the foregoing, BMI, SESAC or ASCAP ("the Society") shall be authorized and directed to pay the publisher's share of performance fees collected by the Society with respect to public performances of ARTIST Compositions directly to COMPANY or its publishing affiliate NAME, and directly to ARTIST or his publishing affiliate, NAME, for each of their respective publisher shares of the public performance income; and neither COMPANY nor ARTIST shall look to the other for payment of such shares of public performance royalties as are the responsibility of the applicable Society to collect.

(c) ARTIST represents and warrants that each ARTIST Composition represented by ARTIST to be an original is original and does not infringe upon or violate the rights of any other person and that ARTIST has the full and unencumbered right, power and authority to grant to COMPANY all of the rights herein granted to COMPANY. For those Master Recordings which contain compositions which are cover songs, ARTIST shall inform COMPANY in writing that they are non-public domain cover songs, and COMPANY and ARTIST shall mutually decide at that time whether or not to include them on an Album to be released by COMPANY and/or how to allocate the expense of the compulsory mechanical royalty that must be paid for their use.

(d) From all royalties earned and received by COMPANY in the United States from the exploitation of the ARTIST Compositions(s) throughout the World (the "Gross Receipts"), COMPANY shall pay ARTIST fifty percent (50%) of the net publishing receipts. The net publishing receipts are the Gross Receipts minus all costs incurred by COMPANY in connection with the exploitation, administration and protection of the ARTIST Compositions. If ARTIST co-writes an ARTIST Composition with another person(s), the other person(s) shall receive his/her/their share of any publishing income and copyright interest from ARTIST's fifty percent (50%) share, not COMPANY's.

(e) Any assignment made of the ownership or copyright in, or right to license the use of, any ARTIST Compositions referred to in this Agreement shall be made subject to the provisions hereof. The provisions of this paragraph 7 are accepted by ARTIST on ARTIST's own behalf and on behalf of any other owner of any Artist Compositions or any rights therein (provided that nothing herein shall require ARTIST to cause an unaffiliated third party co-writer to convey to COMPANY any portion of an ARTIST Composition composed by such unaffiliated third party co-writer).

(f) ARTIST shall execute and deliver to COMPANY any documents which COMPANY may require to vest in COMPANY and/or COMPANY's designee(s), the copyright and other rights herein granted to COMPANY in respect of each ARTIST Composition. If ARTIST shall fail to promptly execute such document, ARTIST hereby irrevocably grants to COMPANY a power of attorney to execute such document in ARTIST's name.

8. ACCOUNTING:

HOW TO BE A RECORD COMPANY

(a) COMPANY will compute ARTIST's royalties as of each June 30th and December 31st for the prior six (6) months for each six-month period in which there are sales or returns of records or any other transactions on which royalties are payable to ARTIST. On the next September 30th or March 31st COMPANY will send ARTIST a statement covering those royalties and will pay ARTIST any royalties which are due after deducting unrecouped COMPANY expenses or other sums which are recoupable hereunder. COMPANY may maintain royalty reserves against anticipated returns or credits pursuant to subparagraph 9(d) below.

(b) COMPANY will pay ARTIST royalties only on those sales of records or licenses for which COMPANY actually receives payment. If COMPANY is unable to receive any payments in the United States in U.S. dollars, COMPANY will, at ARTIST's written request, deposit ARTIST's share thereof in a foreign depository of ARTIST's choosing at ARTIST's expense, and such deposit shall be deemed in full satisfaction of COMPANY's obligation to ARTIST with respect to such royalties.

(c) COMPANY will keep books and records which report sales of records and any other transactions on which royalties are payable to ARTIST. ARTIST may engage a certified public accountant to inspect those books and records during normal business hours at the place where such records are normally kept to check the accuracy of COMPANY's statements, but ARTIST may do so only once for any particular statement and only within one (1) year after the date when COMPANY is required to send ARTIST that statement. ARTIST must give COMPANY at least fifteen (15) days' notice of ARTIST's wish to inspect the books and records. ARTIST may object to any statement by giving COMPANY specific written notice within two (2) years after the date when COMPANY is required to send ARTIST that statement, but if ARTIST does not do so within that year the statement will be final and ARTIST will no longer have any right to object. ARTIST will not have any right to sue COMPANY in connection with any statement or royalty accounting unless ARTIST commences suit within that two (2) year period.

(d) COMPANY shall have the right to retain, as a reserve against charges, credits, or returns, twenty-five percent (25%) of the royalties earned hereunder for such particular semi-annual period; and a reserve shall be liquidated with respect to records sold by us hereunder as of the end of four (4) semi-annual accounting periods after the period in which such reserve was initially established.

9. WARRANTIES AND REPRESENTATIONS: ARTIST warrants and represents that: ARTIST has the right to enter into and perform this Agreement; ARTIST is under no disability with respect to his right to or his ability to completely perform all of the terms and conditions of this Agreement; ARTIST has the right to use his professional name, and grants to Company the right to use and allow others to use said name in connection with records subject hereto, and Company's use of such name in accordance with the terms hereof will not infringe upon the rights of any third party; COMPANY will not be required to make any payments in connection with the rights granted to it or exploited by it pursuant to this Agreement except as specifically set forth herein; except as set forth elsewhere in this Agreement, ARTIST will not record or perform any services for the purpose of making, promoting or marketing records for any entity or person except COMPANY; and no materials, including Master Recordings, ARTIST Compositions, names used by ARTIST or other musical and artistic elements furnished by ARTIST and used in connection with records made and distributed by COMPANY, will violate any law or infringe any person or entity's rights, including but not limited to copyright, trademark, privacy and defamation laws. ARTIST agrees to be available from time to time, at Company's request and expense, whenever the same will not unreasonably interfere with ARTIST's other professional activities, to appear for photography, poster and cover art, etc., under the direction of Company or its nominees and to appear for interviews with representatives of the communications media and Company's publicity personnel and to perform other reasonable promotional services.

10. INDEMNIFICATION: ARTIST will at all times indemnify COMPANY against any claims, damages, costs and expenses (including reasonable attorneys' fees) arising out of any breach or alleged breach by ARTIST of any warranty, representation or agreement in this Agreement. COMPANY will not withhold monies otherwise payable to ARTIST in an amount exceeding ARTIST's potential liability to COMPANY, as determined in COMPANY's reasonable business judgment. ARTIST shall promptly inform COMPANY of any such claims.

11. FORCE MAJEURE: If for any reason whatsoever the ability of ARTIST to perform shall become impaired or if ARTIST shall refuse, neglect, or be unable to comply with any of his obligations hereunder, or if as a result of an Act of nature, accident, fire, labor controversy, riot, civil commotion, act of public enemy, law, enactment, rule, order, or act of any government or governmental instrumentality, failure or technical facilities, failure or delay of transportation facilities, illness or incapacity, or other cause of a similar or dissimilar nature not reasonably within the control of COMPANY or which COMPANY could not by reasonable diligence have avoided, COMPANY (or its distributors and/or licensees) is/are hampered in the recording, manufacture, distribution, transmission or sale of records commercially impractical. Such suspension shall be for the duration of any such event or contingency (except for a maximum of six (6) months for each such an event of "force majeure" applicable only to COMPANY individually and not other record companies), and, unless COMPANY notifies ARTIST to the contrary in writing, the Term hereof, shall be automatically extended by such number of days as equal the total number of days of any such suspension. In the event that ARTIST's ability to perform as a recording ARTIST shall become impaired for more than six (6) months or ARTIST shall refuse, neglect, or be unable to comply with any of his obligations hereunder, then COMPANY shall have the right, at its election, and in addition to any other rights or remedies which COMPANY may have in such event, to terminate this contract upon written notice to ARTIST and shall thereby be relieved of any and all obligations hereunder except COMPANY's obligations with respect to masters produced hereunder embodying ARTIST's performances prior to such termination.

12. EXPIRATION OR TERMINATION:

(a) Upon the expiration or termination of this Agreement neither COMPANY nor ARTIST shall have any further obligations to the other, except that COMPANY shall continue to account to ARTIST for royalties due, if any, and all of ARTIST's warranties and representations shall survive and ARTIST's indemnity of COMPANY shall continue.

(b) ARTIST shall not re-record any composition recorded for COMPANY under this Agreement for a period of five (5) years following the release of the last recording embodying that composition by COMPANY, or two (2) years following the expiration of this Agreement or, if applicable, the final day of the re-recording restriction period set forth in Company's agreement with its distributor, whichever is later. Should ARTIST violate such re-recording restrictions, Company may, in addition to any other right or remedy which it may have on account of such breach, terminate its obligation to pay ARTIST any royalties earned with respect to any such composition which was improperly re-recorded by ARTIST.

13. INJUNCTIVE RELIEF:

ARTIST acknowledges that ARTIST's services are unique and that COMPANY would not be adequately compensated by money damages for the loss of those services, and COMPANY will be entitled to seek injunctive relief to enforce this Agreement

14. MISCELLANEOUS:

(a) All notices to COMPANY or to ARTIST shall be sent to their respective addresses on page one and may be given only by personal delivery or overnight courier with a signed receipt or certified or registered mail, return receipt requested. Notices will be considered to have been given when they are personally delivered, deposited with the courier or mailed, according to the method used.

(b) If ARTIST believes that COMPANY is in breach of any of its obligations, ARTIST shall send COMPANY a specific notice and COMPANY shall have a reasonable period of not less than thirty (30) days in which to cure the breach, if any. ARTIST shall not have the right to terminate this Agreement or recover any damages from COMPANY unless COMPANY fails to so cure a material breach of which it was given notice.

(c) This is the entire agreement between COMPANY and ARTIST and it supersedes all prior agreements or understandings, written or oral. Any amendment or modification must be in writing and must be signed by both COMPANY and ARTIST. Any waiver of rights by COMPANY in any one instance shall not be a waiver of its rights in the future and any immediate failure to enforce its rights shall not be deemed a waiver by COMPANY. Clause headings are used only for convenience and have no meaning or effect. If any part of this Agreement shall be determined to be invalid or unenforceable by a court of competent jurisdiction or by any other legally constituted body having the jurisdiction to make such determination, the remainder of this Agreement shall remain in full force and effect provided that the part of this Agreement thus invalidated or declared unenforceable is not essential to the intended operation of this Agreement.

(d) This Agreement shall inure to the benefit of and be binding upon the successors, permitted assigns and representatives of the parties hereto. COMPANY may, at its election, assign this Agreement or any of its rights hereunder provided that such assignee of COMPANY agrees to be bound by all of the terms and conditions of this Agreement. ARTIST shall not have the right to assign this Agreement.

(e) This Agreement shall be governed by the laws of the State of _____ STATE applicable to contracts entered into and performed in Arizona. COMPANY and ARTIST agree that any action related to this Agreement may only be brought in the state or federal courts located in STATE.

(f) ARTIST agrees to sign any additional documents, including tax forms required for payments to be made to ARTIST, which COMPANY may reasonably require. This Agreement does not constitute a joint venture or partnership, but the parties hereto are independent contractors.

(g) Whenever ARTIST's approval is required pursuant to any provision of this Agreement, such approval shall be deemed given to COMPANY if, after ten (10) days written notice to ARTIST by COMPANY that such approval or consent is required, ARTIST fails to respond in writing.

(h) ARTIST has been advised to obtain independent legal counsel prior to executing this Agreement and has either done so or has knowingly opted to forego obtaining such independent legal advice.

If you agree with the terms and conditions above, please indicate your acceptance by signing below.

Sincerely,

NAME
By: _____

ACKNOWLEDGED, AGREED AND ACCEPTED:
_____
NAME

TONY ROSE

BLANK DEAL MEMO RECORDING AGREEMENT

Dated as of: _____

NAME AND ADDRESS

_____

_____

Dear _____:

The following when countersigned by you, will constitute this the interim recording agreement between us and shall remain in full force and effect pending the execution of a more formal recording contract. This Agreement shall be binding upon you.

1. Recording Commitment.
  (a) Initial Term: One (1) album; plus
  (b) Option Terms: Five (5) consecutive options for one (1) album each option period. Each option shall be deemed automatically exercised unless We notify You in writing, which such notice shall be sent to you not later than thirty (30) days prior to the expiration of the then current Term.
  (c) Notwithstanding anything to the contrary set forth herein, the Recording Commitment applicable to this Agreement shall be the same as that set forth in the Distribution Agreement (as described below); provided however, in the event the Term of the Distribution Agreement should expire or be terminated prior to the delivery and release of at least six (6) albums, then we shall have a period of nine (9) months after the date of such termination or expiration to secure a new Distribution Agreement, as defined below. In the event we do not secure a New Distribution Agreement with the aforesaid nine (9) month period, then you shall have the right to terminate this Agreement upon written notice within thirty days thereafter. In the event we do secure a New Distribution Agreement, then this Agreement shall be extended so as to be co-terminuous with the Term and the Recording Commitment of the New Distribution Agreement, provided however, in no event shall you be obligated to record more than six (6) albums in the aggregate.

(d) Notwithstanding the above, we shall have the right, in our sole discretion to manufacture, distribute, market, promote, sell or otherwise exploit single recordings and albums through independent distribution (as described below) prior to the execution of the Distribution Agreement.

2. Term.

(a) The Initial Term of this Agreement shall commence as of the date hereof and shall continue for a period ending on the date which is the sooner of (i) twelve (12) months after the date of Delivery of the masters constituting the album due for the initial contract Term; or (ii) nine (9) months after the initial commercial release in Jamaica of the first album.

(b) Each Option Period shall be exercised on or before the date which is the sooner of twelve (12) months after the Delivery of the immediately preceding Album, or nine (9) months after the initial commercial release in any country of the Territory of the immediately preceding Album, and shall expire on the date which is nine (9) months after the initial commercial release in any country of the Territory of the Album Delivered in fulfillment of the recording commitment for the applicable contract period.

(c) Each album due hereunder shall be recorded within four (4) months after the commencement of the applicable contract period unless we agree to extend said period, in writing.

(d) We shall have the right to suspend the running of the Term hereof, by written notice to you, in the event you should fail to timely deliver any particular album hereunder, or in the event you should breach this Agreement or default in the performance of any of your obligations hereunder. Provided, in the event such failure to timely deliver a particular album is not caused by your acts or omissions, then we shall not be entitled to suspend the Term. Any such suspension shall be for a period equal to the length of your breach, default or delay in delivery.

(e) You shall have the right upon written notice to terminate the Term of this Agreement in the event we have not secured a distribution or production agreement with an established U.S. or European major or substantial independent record company (the "Distribution Agreement") within twelve (12) months from the date hereof. For the purpose of this Agreement the term "major" record company shall include Sony BMG, Universal, EMI, Warner Music Group and any labels distributed, owned or controlled by such a major company. The term "substantial independent record company" shall be defined as a U.S. record distribution company or record label with at least $1,000,000 in average annual gross billings.

3. **Territory.** Worldwide.

4. **Rights.**

(a)   You hereby acknowledge that we shall be the sole and exclusive owner of all master tapes, multi-track tapes, outtakes and all derivatives therefrom recorded pursuant to this Agreement (the "Masters"), in perpetuity, including the sound recording copyrights in and to all such master tapes and materials. We shall not have any rights to any masters recorded by you and paid for by you or a third party prior to the date hereof. We shall have the exclusive right to manufacture, distribute, sell, license, reproduce and otherwise exploit worldwide all such materials without any obligation to you, except as expressly set forth herein. We shall have the right, in our sole discretion, to grant to others the right to manufacture, distribute, sell and otherwise exploit the Masters.

(b)   You grant us the right, exclusive during the Term hereof for the Territory and non-exclusive thereafter, to use your name (legal and professional), approved biographies and approved photographs and likenesses in connection with the marketing, promotion and sale of the Masters and all derivatives therefrom. You shall furnish us within ten (10) days after our request with biographical material and negatives for photographs. We shall also submit to you for your approval any materials and photographs which we wish to use hereunder. You shall have a period of five (5) business days to approve or disapprove or any such materials, failing which they shall be deemed approved.

(c)   We shall have the right to assign this Agreement to any of our subsidiaries or affiliates, to any entity that acquires all or substantially all of our assets or capital stock, and to any third party major U.S. or European record distributor or to any third party substantial independent U.S. record company (as defined above). This Agreement is personal to you and as such may not be assigned except to a corporation or partnership owned solely by you and provided such entity and you execute and deliver such additional documents as we may require (i.e.: inducement letter and personal guarantee).

(d)   You shall have the right to terminate this Agreement upon written notice to us in the event our company should file a petition in bankruptcy or should become insolvent or should be subject to the appointment of a receiver or trustee, or if **(NAME)** should cease to be actively involved in the performance of this Agreement on behalf of our Company.

5. **Advances.**

In consideration of the rights granted to us hereunder and subject to your full and timely performance of your material obligations hereunder, we shall pay to you the following non-returnable artist advances, recoupable from royalties, excluding mechanical royalties, payable to you hereunder.

(a) In the event we should enter into the Distribution Agreement with a major U.S. record company then, with respect to the initial album, the sum of Twenty-Five Thousand ($25,000) Dollars, said sum shall be paid to You one-half (1/2) upon the full execution of the Distribution Agreement and the balance upon the Delivery to and acceptance by Company of the first album. In the event we should enter into the Distribution Agreement with a U.S. independent record company then, with respect to the initial album, the sum of Fifteen Thousand ($15,000) Dollars, said sum shall be paid to You one-half (1/2) upon the full execution of the Distribution Agreement and the balance upon the Delivery to and acceptance by Company of the first album.

(b) We shall pay to you additional advances for optional albums as provided below:

(Distribution) Option Albums	Independent	Major
First Option Album	$20,000	$35,000
Second Option Album	$25,000	$45,000
Third Option Album	$30,000	$55,000
Fourth Option Album	$35,000	$65,000
Fifth Option Album	$40,000	$75,000

Each such option album advance shall be paid:

(i) Fifty (50%) percent upon commencement of recording of each album; and

(ii) Fifty (50%) percent upon the completion, delivery and acceptance of the Masters constituting each album.

(c) We shall pay all recording costs for each album recorded hereunder. You shall be responsible for any excess recording costs which are incurred as a result of your own acts or omissions. All recording costs shall be deemed to be advances recoupable from the record royalties payable to you pursuant to paragraph "6" hereunder.

(d) We shall be entitled to recoup all advances paid by us for the production of videos, fifty (50%) percent from record/audio royalties and one hundred (100%) percent from gross revenues derived from the commercial exploitation of such videos, if applicable. Notwithstanding the foregoing, in the event the Distribution Agreement should provide for recoupment of video production and exploitation costs utilizing a different manner of computation, then the provision set forth in the Distribution Agreement shall be deemed incorporated herein by reference and shall control.

(e) Fifty (50%) percent of all expenditures made by us or our licensees and distributor for the independent promotion, publicity and marketing of the Masters and records derived therefrom shall be recoupable from royalties' payable to you under paragraph "6" below.

6. Royalties.

(a) Company shall pay to you all "inclusive royalties" as follows:

USNRC and Jamaica:

Net Sales	0 - 500,000 Units	500,001 - 1M Units	1M+ Units
LP #1	13%	13.5%	14%
LP #2	**13%**	**13.5%**	**14%**
LP #3&4	14%	14.5%	15%
LP #5&6	15%	15.5%	16%
Singles (U.S. & JAM)	9%	10%	10%

For Sales outside of the U.S.A. and Jamaica, we shall pay you the following royalties which shall be calculated as a percentage of the base U.S. and Jamaica royalties:

Canada:	85%
U.K. & Europe:	75%
Japan & Australia:	66-2/3%

Rest of World: 50%

(b) Notwithstanding anything to the contrary set forth above with respect to royalties, the maximum amount of royalties which we shall be obligated to pay to you hereunder for record and video sales (including digital, electronic and all configurations) shall not be in excess of sixty-five (65%) percent of the net royalties received by us pursuant to the Distribution Agreement.

(c) For the purpose of this Agreement the term "net royalties" shall be defined as the gross royalties payable to Company pursuant to the Distribution Agreement and/or any other direct license agreements less all recoupable costs including but not limited to recording costs, independent marketing costs, independent publicity costs, independent promotion costs, video production and exploitation costs, artist advances, featured artist fees, producer fees, sample clearance costs, legal fees, accounting fees, and any other direct and reasonable expenditures incurred by Company in connection with the recording of the Masters, the acquisition of rights and the delivery of the Masters.

(d) We shall have the right to establish a royalty reserve up to twenty-five (25%) percent for all albums and up to fifty (50%) percent for all singles sold, said reserve to be fully liquidated within four (4) semi-annual accounting periods from the date initially established. Notwithstanding the foregoing, in the event the royalty reserve policy established by our distributor should differ from that contained herein, the policy of our distributor shall control and be deemed incorporated herein.

7. Accountings.

(a) We shall render royalty accounting statements to you semi-annually within ninety (90) days after June 30th and December 31st annually. Each statement shall detail all sales of product derived from the Masters and shall be accompanied by the payment of royalties due, if any.

(b) You shall have the right to inspect our books and records to verify the accuracy of all statements rendered to you hereunder upon written notice, given within eighteen (18) months from the date a particular statement is rendered.

Your right of inspection shall be subject to at least thirty (30) days prior notice, shall be conducted at the office where our records are located and may only be conducted once within any given twelve (12) month period.

8. Creative Matters.

We shall consult with you with respect to all materials to be recorded hereunder and all producers to be retained (and the terms of their employment) for the recording of the Masters. We shall designate the studios to be used, in consultation with you. In the event of a dispute, our decision shall control. We shall consult with you with respect to album cover artwork

9. Videos.

We agree to use our reasonable efforts to produce at least one (1) video for each album recorded hereunder. You and we shall mutually designate and agree upon the budget, the storyboard, director, producer and primary creative elements for each video produced hereunder. In the event of a dispute with respect to the producer or budget for any particular video, our decision shall control. We shall exclusively own all rights in and to each video recorded pursuant to this Agreement.

10. Mechanical Rates.

With respect to the Controlled Compositions, you agree to license said compositions to us or our distributor(s) for the United States and Canada at seventy-five (75%) percent of the minimum statutory rate in effect at the date of Delivery of the Master(s) embodying each such composition. We shall not be obligated to pay mechanical royalties in excess of the following rates: LPs - eleven (11) times; Eps - five (5) times; Singles - two (2) times; Maxi-Singles - three (3) times; the reduced Controlled Composition Mechanical Rate. Notwithstanding the foregoing, in the event the mechanical rates for Controlled Compositions which are set forth in the Distribution Agreement should differ from those set forth herein, then the terms set forth in the Distribution Agreement shall be deemed incorporated herein by reference and shall control.

11. Website.

Company shall have the perpetual right and may grant to others the right, subject to the terms and conditions hereof, without any liability to any Person to create, maintain and host Artist websites. In the event that Company exercises its option to extend the Term of this agreement for an Option Period, then as of the date of such option exercise you shall automatically be deemed to have licensed to Company the exclusive right, coupled with a security interest and without any liability to any Person, during the Tern of this agreement to register, secure any registration renewals thereof, administer such registrations, control and use the Artist Domain Names as Internet

Addresses including, without limitation, the right to use such Artist Domain Names in connection with Company Artist Websites. During the Term of this agreement, Company will have the right to designate one (1) Company Artist Website as the "official" Artist Website (the "Official Artist Website"), and neither you, Artist, nor any Person deriving any rights from you of Artist shall designate any other Artist Website as an "official" Artist Website except as otherwise provided herein. In the event that **(Artist's Name).com, (Artist's Name).net** and/or **(Artist's Name).org** are not available to be used as the Artist Domain Names in connection with the Official Artist Website, you and Company will mutually approve the Artist Domain name to be used in the United States in connection with the Official Artist Website, provided that an inadvertent to so obtain your approval with you will not be deemed a breach of this agreement. Company's rights as described in the first sentence of this clause shall be exclusive during the term of this agreement and non-exclusive thereafter, except that, for the avoidance of doubt, such rights shall be exclusive in perpetuity with respect to utilizing and/or otherwise exploiting Masters, Videos and/or Artwork hereunder in connection with Websites. Fifty (50%) percent of all costs incurred by us in connection with the development, maintenance and hosting of each official artist website shall be deemed a recoupable advance hereunder.

12. Tour Support.

In the event we should request, or should we approve your request, that you undertake one or more promotional appearances and/or performances, including but not limited to in-store appearances, promotional live shows, media interviews and appearances at industry events, we shall make additional advances to you, recoupable from royalties payable to you hereunder, subject to a budget to be approved on a case-by-case basis, to cover or subsidize the approved costs of such appearances. We hereby pre-approve a per diem of fifty ($50.00) dollars per each appearance and travel day outside of Jamaica. In the event of a disagreement as to any particular line item or budget, our decision shall be final and shall control. We may, in our sole discretion, administer the payment of each tour support budget.

13. Passive Income Participation.

(a) In the event the Distribution Agreement should contain any so-called "passive income provisions" which grant certain rights to the Distributor to receive a share of income which you earn in connection with your activities in the entertainment industry (excluding records and music publishing), then you hereby grant to Company's Distributor, on a "pass through" basis as such necessary rights. Company shall be entitled to be paid and retain sums equivalent to an additional five (5%) percent of all such passive income streams as are paid to the Distributor, for Company's own account.

(b) In the event the Distribution Agreement does not contain any so-called "passive income or 360 provisions", then the following shall apply:

(i) If you enter into an agreement with any third party with respect to any entertainment industry activity that would normally fall outside of the scope of this agreement (i.e., an agreement not related to Artist's recording services) (each, an "Ancillary Rights Agreement') (including, without limitation, any agreement for Artists acting services in motion pictures or television shows or services in connection with books, touring, endorsements, etc. [but specifically excluding music publishing]), you shall cause the applicable third party to pay Company directly an amount equal to fifteen percent (15%) of Ancillary Net Receipts in connection with any such Ancillary Rights Agreement.

(ii) Company shall have the same rights to audit your books and records (and to bring an action against you) in connection with any Ancillary Rights Agreement as you have to audit Company's Books and Records pursuant to paragraph 7(b) herein below. As used herein, "Ancillary Net Receipts shall mean all royalties, one-time payments, or other compensation received by or credited to you or Artist in connection with any Ancillary Rights Agreement, less any actual and legitimate costs or expenses that you payor incur in connection with any such agreement (i.e., management fees, booking agent fees and legal fees).

14. Merchandising.

You hereby grant us the exclusive right of first refusal and last matching right to enter into license agreements regarding the exploitation of your merchandising right during the Term. In the event you should secure a bona fide written offer from a third party merchandising company to enter into an agreement pursuant to which – during the Term – you will grant rights to exploit your name and likeness in connection with the sale of goods, then you shall promptly provide us with a copy of said written offer and we shall have a period of thirty (30) days after our receipt of same to match the material terms and conditions, failing which you shall have the right to enter into an agreement with such third party on terms no less favorable then those contained in the offer. We shall have the exclusive right during the Term to exploit so-called "bounce back merchandising" derived from album cover photography. We shall maintain a separate non-cross collateralized account for all such sales and shall account to you on the same schedule as set forth in paragraph 7 above. We shall pay to you sixty (60%) percent of all of our net receipts derived therefrom. We shall have a period of thirty (30) days after receipt from you of a bona fide third party offer to exercise our last matching right.

15. Miscellaneous.

(a) This Agreement shall be construed and interpreted in accordance with the laws of the State of _____.

(b) This Agreement constitutes the entire understanding between the parties and may not be modified or amended except by a written document signed by all parties hereto.

(c) In the event of the breach or default of any term or provision contained in this Agreement by either party, then the other party shall provide written notice specifying the details of such breach or default and shall have the right to terminate this Agreement in writing in the event such breach or default is not cured within thirty (30) days after receipt of notice or unless the breaching party has not commenced to cure said breach if it is incapable of being fully cured within said thirty (30) day period.

(d) The parties hereto agree that upon the execution of this Agreement, all prior recording agreements between the parties shall be deemed to be terminated and expired.

(e) All notices intended to be given hereunder shall be in writing and shall be delivered in person, by certified or registered mail, return receipt requested, by Federal Express or DHL or by facsimile with proof of transmission/receipt.

TONY ROSE

YOU HEREBY ACKNOWLEDGE THAT WE HAVE ADVISED YOU OF YOUR RIGHT TO SEEK THE ADVICE OF INDEPENDENT LEGAL COUNSEL, SELECTED BY YOU, TO REPRESENT YOU IN THE NEGOTIATION OF THIS AGREEMENT.

Very truly yours,

(COMPANY NAME)

By: _____

ACCEPTED AND AGREED TO:

_____

p/k/a "_____"
Artist

HOW TO BE A RECORD COMPANY

MASTER LICENSING AGREEMENT

LICENSING AGREEMENT

This Agreement is made and entered into effective this ____ day of _____, 20___ by and between NAME_____ (collectively "Licensor"), and COMPANY NAME AND ADDRESS (lICENSEE);

WHEREAS, Licensor owns and or controls all rights in and to the master recordings ("Masters") including, but not limited to the musical and other performances embodied therein, listed on Schedule "A", attached hereto

WHEREAS, Licensee wishes, on a non-exclusive basis to license the Masters for worldwide distribution and licensing

The parties hereto agree as follows:

1. TERM: The term of this Agreement ("Term") shall be 7 years, commencing upon execution of this Agreement by both parties. The Term will automatically renew for an additional 1 year unless written notice is given to the other party no less than 90 days prior to the end of the current term.

2. TERRITORY: The territory for which Licensee is licensing the rights to Masters is the world.

3. GRANT OF RIGHTS: Licensor hereby grants to Licensee on a non-exclusive basis, all rights in and to the Masters in such formats, forms, and versions including the musical and other performances embodied therein; Licensee shall have the non-exclusive right to authorize the use of the Masters in any medium now know or in after devised, including, but not limited to:

(a) Secure the digital distribution of the Masters;
(b) Manufacture, sell, distribute, license to 3rd parties.
(c) Secure the synchronization licensing for film, television, DVD or all other audio-visual uses;
(d) The right to use or authorize others to use the group name, voice, and or likeness of artists contained in the Masters, in conjunction with any licenses issued hereunder;
(e) The right to use or authorize others to use the album artwork created for use with the Masters; and

(f) The right to collect all Gross Revenue or Net Revenue (as defined below) on our mutual behalf earned from any use of the Master(s) during the Term, regardless of whether such monies are received during the Term or after the Term.

4. LICENSOR'S OBLIGATIONS: Upon execution of this Agreement, Licensor shall furnish licensee with the following materials:

(a) All documentation providing proof of ownership of Masters and album artwork, where applicable.

(b) A Completion of Schedule A. In the event additional Masters become subject to this Agreement, Schedule A may be amended from time to time;

(c) Digital files of all Masters. If digital files of the Masters are not available, Licensor shall deliver audio copies in CDR format of each Master. Each Master delivered hereunder shall be subject to licensee's technical approval before commercially used.

(d) Album artwork corresponding to all Masters, if available.

5. CONSIDERATION: In consideration of the rights granted herein, Licensee shall pay to Licensor the following sums:

(a) Digital Distribution: Licensee shall pay to Licensor a sum equal to 50% percent of Net Revenue, derived from the sale of Masters hereunder. Net Revenue shall be Gross Revenue minus any commissions from 3rd party (such as digital store), and all mechanical royalties payable to publishers, publishing administrators, writers and co-writers of musical compositions identified. From licensor's 50% share of Net Revenue, Licensor shall pay (i) all royalties due to Artists, individual producers, performers, engineers, and any other persons engaged in connection with the creation of the Masters; (ii) any necessary union fees arising by the exploitation of the Masters (iii) any other fees, or monies due and or payable with respect to the artwork, metadata, trademarks and logos provided by Licensor to licensee. All additional delivery fees and processing costs will be borne by Licensee.

(b) Third Party Master Licenses (including Synchronization Licenses): With respects to Masters licensed for use in CDs, motion pictures, television, internet, or in any audio-visual devices, Licensor shall receive an amount equal to 50% percent of Gross Revenue actually received by licensee. Gross Revenue specifically excludes any and all writers' or publishers' shares that are paid directly to the applicable writers and publishers by the respective licensing party. Moreover, Gross Revenue does not include any fees that may be paid to third party agents for securing any synchronization licenses. From licensor's 50% share of Gross Revenue, Licensor shall pay (i) all royalties due to Artists, individual producers, performers, engineers, and any other persons engaged in connection with the creation of the Masters; (ii) any necessary union fees arising by the exploitation of the Masters.

6. ACCOUNTING

(a) Within sixty (60) days following the close of each calendar quarter ("Accounting Period"), Licensee shall render reasonably detailed accountings as to royalties payable to Licensor for the preceding Accounting Period. Licensee shall only be required to account and pay with respect to amounts actually received by Licensee. In the event the amount shown due by any accounting to Licensor that is due under this Agreement is less than Twenty-Five Dollars ($25.00), the obligation to pay such amount shall be carried over to the next accounting period when the aggregate amount due to Licensor is Twenty-Five Dollars ($25.00) or more, at which time such amount shall be paid. If any law or regulation requires the withholding of any taxes levied on the royalties payable under this Agreement, Licensee shall have the right to deduct such taxes from the amount otherwise payable to Licensor and make payment of same to the proper taxing authority. Except for the foregoing, each party shall be responsible for any taxes that are levied on it in connection with its obligations under this Agreement.

(b) Upon sixty (60) days prior written notice to Licensee, a certified public accountant on Licensor's behalf, shall have the right, once each year, during ordinary business hours, to inspect and audit such of Licensee business books and records solely regarding the Masters in this agreement as may reasonably be necessary for Licensor to verify the accuracy of any royalty statement rendered by Licensee within the eighteen (18) month period immediately preceding the date of the inspection. The information contained in a royalty statement shall be conclusively deemed correct and binding upon Licensor, resulting in the loss of all further audit rights with respect to such statement, unless specifically challenged by written notice from Licensor within eighteen (18) months from the date such royalty statement was delivered by Licensee. Licensor and its auditor shall keep all information learned as a result of such audit in strict confidence. The cost of such an audit will be borne by Licensor and audits shall not interfere unreasonably with Licensee business activities.

7. WARRANTIES AND REPRESENTATIONS

Licensee warrants and represents that:

(a) It has the full right, power and authority to enter into and fully perform this Agreement and to consummate the transactions contemplate hereby;

(b) In the operation of is business, it shall not infringe any patent, copyright, trade secret or other proprietary right of any third party or violate any law (including, without limitation, any federal law or regulation).

Licensor warrants and represents that:

(a) It has the full right and power to enter and fully perform this Agreement, and to consummate the transaction contemplated hereby;

(b) The execution, delivery and performance of this Agreement shall not constitute a breach or default under any contract or agreement to which Licensor is a party or by which Licensor is bound or otherwise violate the rights of any third party;

(c) The use by Licensee hereunder of the Masters shall not infringe on any patent, copyright, trade secret or other proprietary right of any third party or violate any law (including, without limitation, any federal law or regulation).

8. INDEMNIFICATION

(a) Licensee shall defend, indemnify and hold harmless Licensor, and its directors, officers, employees, agents, successors and assigns, from and against all third-party claims relating to any breach by Licensee of its representations, warranties and or covenants as set forth herein, which claim has resulted in a final judgment or has been settle with the prior written consent of Licensor.

(b) Licensor shall defend, indemnify and hold harmless Licensee , and its directors, officers, employees, agents successors and assigns, from and against (i) all third-party claims relating to any breach by Licensor of its representations, warranties and or covenants hereunder, (ii) any third-party claims relating to or resulting from an actual infringement by a Master and/or Composition of any copyright of a third party; and (iii) any third-party claims made by a songwriter, recording artists, record producers or others who performed on, rendered services for or granted rights in connection with the Master(s) seeking payment of a share of royalties paid by Licensee to Licensor hereunder, which claim has resulted in a final judgment or has been settle with the prior written consent of Licensee .

9. ASSIGNMENT.

(a) Licensee may assign this Agreement to any third party or to any subsidiary, affiliated or controlling corporation or to any party owning or acquiring a substantial portion of the assets or stock of Licensee.

(b) Licensor may assign this Agreement to any third party or to any subsidiary, affiliated or controlling corporation or to any party owning or acquiring a substantial portion of the assets or stock of Licensor, provided that Licensee does not exercise its option to purchase the Masters.

10. MISCELLANEOUS. This Agreement contains the entire understanding of the parties hereto relating to the subject matter hereof and cannot be changed or terminated except by written instrument signed by both parties hereto.

(a) This Agreement has been entered in STATE, and the validity, interpretation and legal effect of this Agreement shall be governed by the laws of the COUNTRY AND STATE, applicable to contracts entered into and to be wholly performed therein with respect to the determination of any claim, dispute or disagreement that may arise out of the interpretation, performance or breach of this Agreement.

(b) If any provision herein shall be deemed or declared unenforceable, invalid or void by a court of competent jurisdiction, the same shall not impair any of the other provisions contained herein which shall be enforced in accordance with their respective terms.

(c) Nothing in this Agreement shall be construed as creating a partnership, joint venture, or agency relationship between the parties, or as authorizing either party to act as agent for the other.

11. Right of First Refusal. In the event that Licensor wishes to sell to an independent third party any or all of the Masters and/or Compositions listed on Schedule A, Licensor shall first offer the Masters and/or Compositions to Licensee on the same terms and conditions as offered to such third party, whereby Licensee shall have the right to match the monetary terms of such third party offer within 30 days of Licensee receipt of Licensor's written notice to Licensee. If Licensee does not accept such offer within said 30-day period, Licensor shall be free to accept such third party offer.

This Agreement shall not become effective until executed by both parties.

LICENSEE:
By: _____   By: _____
    An authorized signatory   An authorized signatory

TONY ROSE

Print Authorized signatory name   Print Authorized signatory name
_____   _____
     Phone Number/ Email   Phone Number/ Email

Fed Tax ID # _____

SCHEDULE "A"

MASTER RECORDING   ARTIST   WRITER
PUBLISHER

SCHEDULE "B"

AUDIO MASTER METADATA

ALBUM TITLE
UPC
ALBUM ARTIST
ALBUM P LINE
ALBUM C LINE
RELEASE DATE (M/D/Y)
LABEL
TRACK # (SEQUENCE)
TRACK ARTIST
TRACK TITLE
DESCRIPTION
TIMING
YEAR
RECORDING DATE
TRACK P LINE
ISRC CODE
WRITER(S)
LOCAL PUBLISHER(S)
U.S. PUBLISHER(S) [IF KNOWN]
GENRE
LINER NOTES (IF APPLICABLE)
WORLDWIDE RIGHTS (Y/N)
IF NO, SPECIFY RESTRICTION

HOW TO BE A RECORD COMPANY

RINGTONES LICENSING AGREEMENT

LICENSING AGREEMENT

This Agreement is made and entered into effective this _____ day of _____, 20___ by and between (collectively "LICENSOR") of ADDRESS., and LICENSEE, ADDRESS;

WHEREAS, Licensor created the master recordings ("Masters") including, but not limited to the musical and other performances embodied therein, listed on Schedule "A", attached hereto

WHEREAS, Licensee wishes, on a non-exclusive basis to license the Masters for worldwide distribution and licensing

The parties hereto agree as follows:

1. TERM: The term of this Agreement ("Term") shall be 2 years, commencing upon execution of this Agreement by both parties. The Term will automatically renew for an additional 1 year unless written notice is given to the other party no less than 90 days prior to the end of the current term.

2. TERRITORY: The territory for which Licensee is licensing the rights to Masters is the world.

3. GRANT OF RIGHTS: Licensor hereby grants to Licensee the non-exclusive right (a) to sell, and commercially distribute and transmit ringtones, and (b) to commercially license use of the Masters for audiovisual purposes including film, television, commercial advertisements, webisodes, plays, DVDs, streaming, and other home and commercial audiovisual uses, in such formats, forms, and versions including the musical and other performances embodied therein; and (c) to collect all Gross Revenue or Net Revenue (as defined below) on our mutual behalf earned from any permitted use of the Master(s) by Licensee during the Term, regardless of whether such monies are received during the Term or after the Term.

4. LICENSOR'S OBLIGATIONS: Upon execution of this Agreement, Licensor shall furnish Licensee with the following materials:

(a) A Completion of Schedule A. In the event additional Masters become subject to this Agreement, Schedule A may be amended from time to time;

(b) Digital files of all Masters. If digital files of the Masters are not available, Licensor shall deliver audio copies in CDR format of each Master. Each Master delivered hereunder shall be subject to Licensee technical approval before commercially used.

5. CONSIDERATION: In consideration of the rights granted herein, Licensee shall pay to Licensor the following sums:

(a) Ringtones: Licensee shall pay to Licensor a sum equal to 50% percent of Net Revenue, derived from the uses permitted hereunder. Net Revenue shall be Gross Revenue minus any commissions paid to 3rd parties (such as digital store), and all mechanical royalties payable to publishers, publishing administrators, writers and co-writers of musical compositions identified. From Licensor's 50% share of Net Revenue, Licensor shall pay (i) all royalties due to Artists, individual producers, performers, engineers, and any other persons engaged in connection with the creation of the Masters; (ii) any necessary union fees arising by the exploitation of the Masters (iii) any other fees, or monies due and or payable with respect to the artwork, metadata, trademarks and logos provided by Licensor to Licensee. All additional delivery fees and processing costs will be borne by Licensee.

(b) Master Use Licenses: With respect to Masters licensed for use in film, television, commercial advertisements, webisodes, plays, DVDs, streaming, and other home and commercial audiovisual uses, Licensor shall receive an amount equal to 50% percent of Gross Revenue actually received by Licensee. Gross Revenue specifically excludes any and all writers' or publishers' shares that are paid directly to the applicable writers and publishers by the respective licensing party. Moreover, Gross Revenue does not include any fees that may be paid to third party agents for securing any synchronization licenses. From Licensor's 50% share of Gross Revenue, Licensor shall pay (i) all royalties due to Artists, individual producers, performers, engineers, and any other persons engaged in connection with the creation of the Masters; (ii) any necessary union fees arising by the exploitation of the Masters.

6. ACCOUNTING:

(a) Within sixty (60) days following the close of each calendar quarter ("Accounting Period"), Licensee shall render reasonably detailed accountings as to royalties payable to Licensor for the preceding Accounting Period. Licensee shall only be required to account and pay with respect to amounts actually received by Licensee. In the event the amount shown due by any accounting to Licensor that is due under this Agreement is less than Twenty-Five Dollars ($25.00), the obligation to pay such amount shall be carried over to the next accounting period when the aggregate amount due to Licensor is Twenty-Five Dollars ($25.00) or more, at which time such amount shall be paid. If any law or regulation requires the withholding of any taxes levied on the royalties payable under this Agreement, Licensee shall have the right to deduct such taxes from the amount otherwise payable to Licensor and make payment of same to the proper taxing authority. Except for the foregoing, each party shall be responsible for any taxes that are levied on it in connection with its obligations under this Agreement. Under no circumstances shall Licensee be permitted to cross-collateralize any sums payable to Licensor under this Agreement with any other agreement(s) between Licensor and Licensee or to otherwise deduct from any sums owed to Licensor under this Agreement in connection with any other agreement.

(b) Upon sixty (60) days prior written notice to Licensee, a certified public accountant on Licensor's behalf, shall have the right, once each year, during ordinary business hours, to inspect and audit such of Licensee business books and records solely regarding the Masters in this agreement as may reasonably be necessary for Licensor to verify the accuracy of any royalty statement rendered by Licensee within the eighteen (18) month period immediately preceding the date of the inspection. The information contained in a royalty statement shall be conclusively deemed correct and binding upon Licensor, resulting in the loss of all further audit rights with respect to such statement, unless specifically challenged by written notice from Licensor within eighteen (18) months from the date such royalty statement was delivered by Licensee. Licensor and its auditor shall keep all information learned as a result of such audit in strict confidence. The cost of such an audit will be borne by Licensor and audits shall not interfere unreasonably with Licensee business activities.

7. WARRANTIES AND REPRESENTATIONS:
Licensee warrants and represents that:

(a) It has the full right, power and authority to enter into and fully perform this Agreement and to consummate the transactions contemplate hereby;

(b) In the operation of is business, it shall not infringe any patent, copyright, trade secret or other proprietary right of any third party or violate any law (including, without limitation, any federal law or regulation.

Licensor warrants and represents that:

(a) It has the full right and power to enter and fully perform this Agreement, and to consummate the transaction contemplated hereby;

(b) The execution, delivery and performance of this Agreement shall not constitute a breach or default under any contract or agreement to which Licensor is a party or by which Licensor is bound or otherwise violate the rights of any third party;

(c) The use by Licensee hereunder of the Masters shall not infringe on any patent, copyright, trade secret or other proprietary right of any third party or violate any law (including, without limitation, any federal law or regulation).

8. INDEMNIFICATION:

(a) Licensee shall defend, indemnify and hold harmless Licensor, and its directors, officers, employees, agents, successors and assigns, from and against all third-party claims relating to any breach by Licensee of its representations, warranties and or covenants as set forth herein, which claim has resulted in a final judgment or has been settle with the prior written consent of Licensor.

(b) Licensor shall defend, indemnify and hold harmless Licensee, and its directors, officers, employees, agents successors and assigns, from and against (i) all third-party claims relating to any breach by Licensor of its representations, warranties and or covenants hereunder, (ii) any third-party claims relating to or resulting from an actual infringement by a Master and/or Composition of any copyright of a third party; and (iii) any third-party claims made by a songwriter, recording artists, record producers or others who performed on, rendered services for or granted rights in connection with the Master(s) seeking payment of a share of royalties paid by Licensee to Licensor hereunder, which claim has resulted in a final judgment or has been settle with the prior written consent of Licensee.

9. MISCELLANEOUS: This Agreement contains the entire understanding of the parties hereto relating to the subject matter hereof and cannot be changed or terminated except by written instrument signed by both parties hereto.

(a) This Agreement has been entered in CITY AND STATE, and the validity, interpretation and legal effect of this Agreement shall be governed by the laws of CITY AND STATE, applicable to contracts entered into and to be wholly performed therein with respect to the determination of any claim, dispute or disagreement that may arise out of the interpretation, performance or breach of this Agreement.

(b) If any provision herein shall be deemed or declared unenforceable, invalid or void by a court of competent jurisdiction, the same shall not impair any of the other provisions contained herein which shall be enforced in accordance with their respective terms.

(c) Nothing in this Agreement shall be construed as creating a partnership, joint venture, or agency relationship between the parties, or as authorizing either party to act as agent for the other.

This Agreement shall not become effective until executed by both parties.

LICENSEE:

By: _____   By: _____
　　An authorized signatory　　　　An authorized signatory

_____   _____
Print Authorized signatory name　Print Authorized signatory name

_____   _____
　　Phone Number/ Email　　　　　Phone Number/ Email

　　Fed Tax ID # _____

SCHEDULE "A"

MASTER RECORDING
   ARTIST -
   WRITER(S) -
     PUBLISHER -

SCHEDULE "A"
MASTER RECORDING
   ARTIST -
   WRITER(S) -
     PUBLISHER -

SCHEDULE "B"
AUDIO MASTER METADATA
ALBUM TITLE -
ALBUM TITLE -
UPC
ALBUM ARTIST -
ALBUM ARTIST -
ALBUM P LINE
ALBUM C LINE
RELEASE DATE (M/D/Y)
LABEL
TRACK # (SEQUENCE)
TRACK ARTIST
TRACK TITLE
DESCRIPTION
TIMING
YEAR
RECORDING DATE
TRACK P LINE
ISRC CODE
WRITER(S)
LOCAL PUBLISHER(S)
U.S. PUBLISHER(S) [IF KNOWN]
GENRE
LINER NOTES (IF APPLICABLE)
WORLDWIDE RIGHTS (Y/N)

HOW TO BE A RECORD COMPANY

IF   NO,   SPECIFY   RESTRICTIO

Two

HOW TO BE A RECORD PRODUCER

WHAT IS A RECORD PRODUCER

Being a record producer these days isn't what it used to be. Record company budgets have been slashed, revenues are in decline, and the proliferation of affordable digital audio workstation software has enabled all but the tone–deaf to call themselves producers.

But for those with a little sonic vision and a great pair of monitors, it's not all bad news. In times of turmoil and rapid technological change, fresh opportunities arise, allowing those with the right skills the opportunity to make their mark.

Producers today do a whole lot more than mere knob–twiddling. Studio time has to be booked, budgets managed, session players and equipment hired not to mention the visionary, technical and interpersonal skills required to deliver an album on time to expectant A&R. What's more, if the producer doesn't have a manager to share the load, they'll need to do all these things for themselves — in addition to handling the legal and financial side of their day–to–day business!

Most producers these days work on a freelance basis, recording artists and bands for various labels in project studios, high–end facilities, or even specially built studios at home and abroad. Independent producers of major label artists have all experienced huge mainstream success working on a range of artist projects, in different musical genres.

More and more record labels outsource the artist development process to trusted producers and smaller independent labels, or simply rely on them to deliver finished product, which can then be marketed and distributed. Consequently, the role of producer as creative and business person has expanded. Whether you produce dance tunes in your bedroom, work with a chart–topping act on a major label, or produce bands in a local studio, you'll need to be familiar with the legal and contractual side of your business, if you're to stay in the game and get paid for your efforts.

PRODUCER AGREEMENTS VS PRODUCTION AGREEMENTS

There are two contracts of particular note for the producer:
- Producer Agreements are entered into by the producer and the record label for the production of an artist's record.
- Production Agreements are increasingly common, yet distinct. By signing a production agreement, an artist enters into a form of recording contract with a production company to make a record, which, if successful, will be sold or licensed to a third–party label for release.

THE PRODUCER AGREEMENT

Prior to starting work on a record, the producer should try to finalize a producer agreement. This contract provides the only real means of protection should the record label decide to switch producers halfway through a project, rework your demos, or simply not pay you. In this situation, you'll need written evidence of the parties' agreement.

It is typically the record label that funds the upfront recording costs, with the producer providing a written assignment of ownership in the sound recording copyright(s) to the record label. For the sake of clarity, the artist is also called upon to do the same in their recording contract.

In addition to the creative and technical side of the job, the producer normally takes on a number of administrative duties, to support the smooth running of the studio sessions. Often, producers will be asked to obtain signed consent and release forms from session musicians — allowing the record label to exploit all performances on the album or single. It's not uncommon for the producer to be required to obtain permission for the use of any uncleared samples as well. The record label should assume responsibility for that, plus any associated cost, and this needs to be clarified at the outset, as sample clearance can greatly increase the total album budget. Nor will the record label accept contractual delivery of any master recording until all samples have been cleared, which in turn will delay payment to the producer!

The producer agreement with the label will state that the producer has to deliver the master recordings to a technically and commercially acceptable standard. This condition, too, might have the effect of delaying payment of fees, or a final tranche of an advance, until the label are satisfied they have a commercial / hit record on their hands. What may amount to an artistic difference shouldn't prevent the producer from getting paid for their work, and in practice the label A&R person will ask the producer to tweak the album until it satisfies label expectations.

Producers are paid by a combination of fees, advances and royalties, and will usually charge a rate per 'master' recording' (usually a song on an album), depending on the status of the producer and artist in question.

HOW MUCH

Dollar payments to superstar producer's aside, at the higher end of the market, producers can earn $4000 to $12,000 per master, and at the lower end, somewhere in the range of $500 to $1,200 per track. Top producers will earn considerably more: $40,000 to $160,000 per master is not unheard of, especially where the song is intended for release as a single. Any fee, however, depends greatly on negotiation and individual bargaining power. Some producers are willing to forgo fees and advances altogether, preferring to work instead for a bigger royalty payment further down the line — 20 percent of five million album sales is better than $60k up front!

Alternatively, producers may opt for an 'all–in' budget' for an album project, paying themselves, after recording costs, out of the total fund. Where the producer has his own studio, this may well prove more cost–effective. The record label can either make a lump sum payment to the producer, or pay separate payments with a final payment on delivery of the master. In this situation, since the producer is responsible for recording costs, he or she will need to know how to manage the budget prudently.

The producer, or their lawyer, must also negotiate the all–important royalty rate, providing for an interest in the future success of the record. Producers are, in fact, paid a percentage of the artists' royalty. So, for instance, an artist earning a 17 percent royalty (under their recording contract) might agree to pay the producer a 4 percent royalty. This leaves the artist with only 13 percent. This is more acceptable in the case of a solo artist, but where, for instance, the producer works with a five–piece band, each band member will only earn a 2.6 percent royalty, compared with the producer's 4 percent. Let's not forget that the artist will also be expected to repay the recording costs! When such financial disparities become apparent, it can cause real friction. Where several producers contribute tracks independently to an album, as is common in the pop/urban market, each producer will pocket a pro–rata share of the total allocated royalty. For example, were you to produce three tracks on an 11–track album, you'd be entitled to 0.27 (3/11) x 4 = 1.08 percent royalty.

A successful producer might object to being paid in this way, especially if the artist has secured a lower than normal royalty rate in their record deal. In this case, the lawyer acting for the producer should attempt to secure a higher royalty rate independently, with any shortfall made up by the record label.

PROTECT YOURSELF

HOW TO BE A RECORD PRODUCER

Record companies pay producers their royalties after recoupment of any advances paid to the producer. However, the producer should strongly resist provisions calling on him to repay recording costs, or any portion thereof, prior to receiving any royalties. The usual practice is to delay payment of producer royalties until the label has recouped the recording costs from the artist's royalty account. At this point the record label will pay producer royalties 'retroactively'.

Aside from production and programming, many producers collaborate with artists on songwriting and on song arrangement. If this is the case, the producer will be a co-writer on the project, and entitled to a share of copyright in any co-written song(s), as well as a share of all publishing revenues. It's important, therefore, that producers agree publishing splits in writing, before the sessions come to an end. Recollections about one another's contributions can become a little hazy after the event!

The record label will expect the producer's interest in all mechanical and synchronization rights to be assigned to the record company also. This will enable the record company to manufacture and sell the finished record, and to benefit from any secondary exploitation of the recordings such as sync agreements for film, TV or advertising. The producer's agreement, if drafted by the label, might allow the producer a royalty only on record sales. This should be resisted, with the producer arguing for payment on all other secondary exploitation. A sought-after producer should be able to secure a share of anything the artist receives. So, for example, where an artist is paid $30,000 on a sync fee for a car commercial, the producer will be entitled (on the figures above) to 0.24 (4/17) x $30,000 = $36,000.

The producer should also seek to include what's known as 'A-side protection' in a producer agreement. This means that where the producer has contributed the A-side, but another producer is responsible for 'B-side' cuts or mixes on a single or EP, the A-side producer will suffer no reduction in their royalty. This, again, depends on the bargaining power of the producers in question, and whether the producer of the B-side is willing to forgo his royalty. Likewise, the producer's royalty should not be reduced where the record label brings in additional producers to mix the record. Mixing and mastering costs, if undertaken separately at the label's request, should be borne by the label.

After all the hard work, it's nice to get paid. So an equally important contract clause to obtain is one entitling the producer to receive regular royalty statements, and to audit the record label's books. In practice audits can be costly, and should only be undertaken where the producer has reason to believe there's been a significant underpayment during an accounting period, but it's an important weapon to keep in your armory.

PRODUCTION AGREEMENTS

As mentioned earlier, many producers today take on the role of talent scout, discovering new artists and developing their sound, long before any record company gets involved. Often the producer will work with the artist on songs, assemble a group of musicians around the project, and invest their own time and money to produce demos or even master–quality recordings. In addition to nurturing the artist, often over several years, the producer may organize industry showcases and pitch the artist to record labels, all with the aim of securing a recording contract. The record label benefits, of course, since where a producer's done all the groundwork, all they need do is market the album.

In this scenario, the best way for the producer to protect him– or herself is to set up a production company, and require that the development artist enter into a Production Agreement with the company. The production agreement provides the producer with a greater degree of security than an informal verbal agreement, and can help safeguard the producer's right to future income from his work.

Under a production agreement, the producer actually stands to gain significantly more than the traditional 3–4 percent royalty typical of the producer agreement. The Production Company will own, take an assignment of, the master recordings and exclusive rights to the artist's recording services. The production company is now in a position to 'shop the artist' to a major or independent label, or alternatively sign a physical or digital distribution deal.

The problem, where the artist is concerned, is that unless they've already got some sort of track record, unlikely in this scenario, the production agreement will most likely be drafted in favor of the production company. The production company is ostensibly a middle man between artist and label, providing songs, the sound and a producer, as well as industry contacts, and hence can dictate the commercial terms entered into. Unfortunately, artists often fail to take proper legal advice before signing production agreements (although, ironically, this may render the deal unenforceable against the artist in a court of law, over–zealous producers should take note of this latter point, should they attempt to 'fleece' the artist at the outset!). The artist will have to decide whether they can get a record deal under their own steam, or whether they need an arrangement of this type to get them in the door.

HOW TO BE A RECORD PRODUCER

On the up side, as far as the artist is concerned, is the fact that the production company normally pays recording, mixing and mastering costs, which, should the artist not play an instrument, could include session musicians and paying for engineers.

The production agreement will encompass either master–quality recordings, or demos. The advantage of finished masters is that they can be licensed to record companies on a territory, by, territory basis, or the artist project sold outright. The producer could turn up at an international trade fair, album in hand, and walk away with a bunch of licensing deals for key international markets.

PRODUCERS PROFIT

Under the production agreement, recording costs are usually subject to recoupment against artist royalties (as they would be in a traditional recording contract), only the royalty tends to work out lower than under a recording agreement. The production company normally splits net profits 50-50 with the artist. So where, for instance, a major record label pays down a 20 percent royalty to the production company, this will entitle both company and artist to a 10 percent royalty. Under a standard recording agreement, by contrast, the 20 percent artist royalty might incur a 4 percent producer royalty reduction, leaving the artist with a more respectable 16 percent. A production agreement thus permits the producer to raise his pay by 6 percent, and also to apply this royalty clause to more revenue streams than would be the case in a standard producer agreement. For example, a production agreement will often cover a share of secondary exploitation rights (sync, audio–visual, interactive, compilation albums and so on), as well as publishing rights, where the production company is associated with a publisher.

If the artist didn't receive an advance on signing, then they'll need sufficient resources to cover their living expenses while the record's being made and a deal pursued. Even where a deal is signed, it may be many months before the artist sees any income. In some situations, production companies accept advances from major record labels, pocket the money, and then recoup it from the artist's account! If you're an artist, or you act for one, pay close attention to the wording of the contract.

Furthermore, any recording costs should only be recouped from an artist's share of earnings if there are sufficient funds generated from sales. Understandably, the production company will try to pass on as much of the financial risk to the artist as possible, whereas the artist and their lawyer will need to resist all unreasonable demands.

One significant advantage of the production company arrangement, as far as the producer is concerned, is that more than one artist can be signed to a production deal with the same company. The artist, however, is tied to an exclusive contract, and takes a huge gamble on the reputation and talents of one producer. If the production company strings the artist along or fails to secure the promised record deal, the artist's only comeback will be where they've retained a right of termination on failure to meet any agreed targets.

MONEY AND INDUCEMENTS

After all the hard work and patience, the producer will want some money in his pocket. He should reserve the right to receive payment from, and be directly accounted to by the record label his artist signs to. Accordingly, the production company should pay their artist within 30 days of receiving royalties from the record label, provided any agreed recording costs and advances have been recouped. Record labels usually account twice a year, and in the same way that the producer will reserve a right to audit the record label's books, so the artist will seek a corresponding right to challenge royalty statements against the production company in the case of underpayment.

Last but not least, where the artist has signed a production agreement, and the production company has entered into a recording contract with a label, the label will expect the artist to sign an 'inducement letter'. This has the effect of cementing a direct contractual relationship between artist and record label, whereby the artist promises to adhere to the terms of the agreement between the production company and the label. It also ties the artist into an exclusive contract with the record company, regardless of the production company's future involvement.

In this article we've only been able to cover some of the issues arising out of producer and production agreements. Music business contracts are long and complex, and it's essential that both producer and artist seek independent legal advice prior to signing any such agreement.

Who Owns The Copyright?

The copyright in a sound recording belongs to "the person who undertook the arrangements necessary" for making that sound recording. This somewhat ambiguous definition can give rise to problems. Artists paying producers to record demos for them often assume they own their recordings. This may, or may not be the case. The question is whether 'arrangements' refers to a purely monetary contribution, or an organizational one, or both. Where the producer is providing his time and expertise speculatively, without charging the artist, the artist probably won't be the lawful owner of the master recording. A well–

drafted contract can remedy any confusion, instead of leaving it to the vagaries of the courtroom to decide.

HOW LONG SHOULD A PRODUCTION AGREEMENT LAST

Where an artist is signed to a production company, the term of the agreement can be measured in relation to time, or by reference to delivery of a minimum number of recordings, or both (for example, a five–album deal lasting no longer than eight years). The production company is not actually obliged to release all five albums. Normally they'll commit to one album proper, with the option to continue the deal, dependent on the success of any prior release.

It's advisable to agree an initial period, perhaps 12-18 months, to allow the production company sufficient time to develop the artist, record masters, and try to secure a record deal. Of course a production agreement cannot guarantee the ultimate record deal. If the artist is unhappy and a record deal isn't procured, the artist should be free to terminate the arrangement. But if a record deal is signed, and success should follow, the production company will be able to exercise its option to continue the deal; it might take until the second or third album before an artist starts selling records in any significant quantity.

A key protection the producer should aim for is a provision allowing him to continue producing the artist in situations where a major or independent label tries to cut the producer out by signing the artist directly. The artist would, of course, be in breach of their production agreement, allowing the producer to sue him or her, but he can't compel the artist to continue recording for him. One alternative is for a record label to lawfully buy out the artist from the production agreement. Sometimes even where the artist sticks with the production company, there may be downward pressure from a label to ditch the recordings and bring in another 'name' producer.

This is where an override royalty provision in favor of the original producer is essential. An override provision allows for ongoing royalty payment on future albums, sometimes including those not produced by the original producer. This will ensure our man (or woman) gets at least something for his troubles. The producer might obtain anywhere between 0.5 and 2.5 percent royalty override, and if the producer is tenacious in his negotiations the override might include a share of the advances paid by the record label to the artist. Of course, the artist will try to limit such override payments, particularly where they're paying their new producer a likely 3–5 percent royalty as well.

FIVE YEAR MUSIC PRODUCTION AND DISTRIBUTION DEAL AGREEMENT. LABEL DISTRIBUTION CONTRACT (P&D)

This AGREEMENT (hereinafter referred to as the "Agreement") is made effective this _____ day of _____, 201__ by and between _____ _____, located at _____ (hereinafter referred to as the "Label") and _____, located at _____ (hereinafter referred to as the "Distributor") with respect to exclusive manufacturing and distribution worldwide ("Territory") of all the records in all configurations now known or hereafter devised owned and exploited by Label and/or any successor or affiliated companies of Label.

WITNESSETH:

In consideration of the respective covenants contained herein, the parties hereto, intending to legally bound hereby, agree as follows:

1. Period. The initial term of the agreement (the "Term") shall commence on the date of the first Master's release hereunder and continue for a period of Five (5) years. Notwithstanding the above however, each new Master released during the contract Term shall be retained by Distributor as an exclusive title for no less than two (2) months from the date of release of the applicable Master by Distributor. Thereafter, Distributor shall have a non-exclusive sell-off period of six (6) months. In lieu of the sell-off period, Label shall have the option to buy back all current stock at Distributor's cost, plus a 15% mark-up, by giving notice to Distributor at least sixty days prior to end of term.

2. Manufacture. Distributor will regularly consult and advise Label on manufacturing, inventory, stock issues and any costs likely to be incurred by Distributor for which Label will be responsible for payment. All moneys paid to/or on behalf of Label by Distributor during the Term, including but not limited to manufacturing advances, mastering, marketing, promotion and all other expenses otherwise incurred by Distributor only with consent of Label, not to be unreasonably withheld, shall constitute Advances recoupable by the cross-collateralization of any and all moneys owed by Distributor under this agreement. Any advances not reasonably expected to be recouped from Label's earnings hereunder may be invoiced to Label for prompt payment at such intervals determined by Distributor in its sole and sole and reasonable discretion; however, no earlier than two (2) months from commencement of the term hereunder and no more often than four (4) times annually.

3. Label's Obligations. Label shall actively function as a record label during the Term and shall be solely responsible for all activities and shall pay all costs, expenses, and charges in connection with the following:

A. Acquiring or recording the Masters (including all tracking, mixing, and other studio costs), and all steps required to utilize the Masters in the manufacture of Records.

B. The procurement, in writing, of all necessary rights, licenses, consents, authorizations and clearances to record, manufacture, use, sell, advertise, promote and distribute Records.

C. Deliver records to Distributor. Label shall supply Distributor with all components necessary and suitable to manufacture Records therefrom.

D. The payment of all royalties, fees, costs, and other sums payable to any third party in connection with the Masters or Distributor's distribution of Records, including without limitation all royalties and fees payable to artists, producers, musicians, publishers, writers, composers, and other persons and all mechanical license fees.

4. Returns. Label shall remain solely liable for one hundred percent (100%) of all returns of records from Distributor of from Distributor's customers to Distributor, and Distributor shall have the right to deduct from Label's account (and the reserve) the full amount of all returns.

5. Payment. As full compensation for rights granted herein, Distributor shall pay Label in connection with Distributor's focused distribution, consultancy, and marketing direction and efforts for records released hereunder on the basis of One Hundred (100%) percent of "net" sales of the following:

HOW TO BE A RECORD PRODUCER

A. Seventy percent (70%) of "Net Receipts" (hereinafter defined).

B. No moneys shall be payable to Label in respect of Records sold or distributed for advertising purposes which shall be deemed as "free," "no charge," or "bonus" Records. Notwithstanding the foregoing, Records distributed as "free," "no charge," or "bonus" shall not exceed fifteen (15) per one hundred (sold).

C. No moneys will be payable for any Records which Distributor does not receive payment for after using customary reasonable efforts to collect. Distributor will receive no fee for Distribution of said product. Label will be responsible for payment of all costs exclusive of manufacturing and one-way shipping costs on such Records. In the case of Distributor being unable to obtain payment by Customer for Label's Records, Label may, upon notification to Distributor, take whatever actions necessary to collect its monies owing from Customer. If Label is able to collect 50% or greater of such outstanding monies Distributor shall be due its fees hereunder.

D. "Net Receipts" is defined as gross billings less actual returns, credits, and any other discounts and approved charges, however, Distributor's fee is calculated after such returns, credits, discounts and charges. Label will determine all applicable discounts on product sold hereunder apart from that which is contained elsewhere herein.

6. Sell-off Period. Label grants to Distributor the right during the Term and sell-off period to use Label's trademark and logo as well as the recording Artists whose performances are embodied in the Masters (an "Artist" herein) name, approved likeness, and approved biographical material to the extent contractually conferred to Label in connection with records manufactured and distributed hereunder. Label must notify Distributor in writing of any restrictions pertaining to use of such materials in advance of manufacturing and in no event later than upon the delivery of parts for manufacture.

7. Distributor's Obligations.
A. The manufacture of Records (and all packaging components comprising Records) from Masters, artwork, and other elements supplied by Label. In connection with its manufacturing activities,

Distributor shall:

(i) Assign a catalog number to each Record,

(ii) Use the Manufacturer's Identification Number assigned to Distributor by the Uniform Code Council, Inc. and place appropriate bar codes on all Records,

(iii) Determine the quantities of Records to be manufactured, in consultation with and subject to the approval of Label, in an amount sufficient to meet Distributor's product flow requirements, and in such configurations as Label determines.

B. The marketing and promotion of records. As used herein, the term "marketing" shall mean and refer to attempting to induce consumers to purchase records, and the term "promotion" shall mean and refer to attempting to secure radio airplay for Records in appropriate format. Distributor shall distribute promotional records, advertise and merchandise Records in a professional manner, including without limitation, the preparation of artwork and design layouts of all types, the furnishing of merchandising posters, sales sheets, displays, and "point of purchase" materials for distribution by Distributor, and the furnishing of all similar materials and services; and advertise Records. Distributor will not spend money for marketing or promotion unless Label has previously approved funds for such purpose. Distributor will deduct marketing or promotion credits from Net Receipts otherwise payable by Distributor to Label (or the reserve) for that accounting period. Label will comply with all of the Distributor's other trade policies, practices, and procedures.

C. Distributor shall be responsible for and shall pay Label any moneys due hereunder after recouping any advances. Distributor will send Label statements and payment covering these moneys within (30) days following the end of each calendar month, for all Net Receipts credited to Distributor's account during the applicable quarterly calendar period.

D. Label shall have the right at Label's sole cost and expense to appoint an independent certified public accountant, to whom Distributor has no reasonable objection, to examine Distributor's relevant books and records of account during Distributor's normal business hours upon sixty (60) days written advance notice, not more than once each calendar year, and not more than once with any respect to any particular accounting period, at Distributor's offices in the United States to determine whether appropriate accounting and payment have been made by Distributor hereunder during the preceding accounting periods. Such independent certified public accountant shall treat all information as confidential and shall not disclose to Label any information other than information specifically pertinent to Distributor's accounts for the releases hereunder in light of the mutual covenants hereunder. Any statement not objected to within 12 months of its rendering shall be deemed accurate and not subject to objection by Label.

8. Copyrights. With respect to records containing copyrighted musical material, Label warrants that it shall obtain all necessary licenses and furnish copies of same to Distributor. Label shall promptly pay to the copyright proprietors all mechanical royalties which may become due to accordance with these licenses. In connection herewith Label hereby grants Distributor an irrevocable license under copyright for the term of this agreement to distribute each composition embodied on the Masters hereunder. Label shall be responsible for any and all royalties and other sums which may become due Artist, Publishers, Producers, Unions (including without limitation per record payments) and any other party entitled to receive royalties or other payments in connection with the Masters.

9. Samples. Label warrants that is solely owns all rights granted to distributor herein and that it has the rights to enter into this agreement and all its provisions. Label warrants they will clear all "samples" contained in any product addressed under this agreement prior to the delivery of the parts for manufacture of the Masters hereunder. Label indemnifies Distributor for any and all claims arising from samples contained in such product prior to delivery of the parts for manufacture of any Masters hereunder.

10. Notification. All notices to either party shall be in writing and delivered by registered or certified mail, return receipt requested, at the addresses shown above or at such other addresses as may be designated in writing.

11. Waivers. This agreement contains the entire understanding of the parties hereto and cannot be modified except by an instrument signed by the parties hereto. A waiver by either party of any term of condition herein shall not be deemed a future waiver thereof with respect to subsequent breaches and does not affect the enforceability of the other terms herein.

12. Breach. Neither party shall be entitled to recover damages or to terminate this agreement by reason of any material breach hereof unless said material breach has not been remedied within sixty (60) days, or such cure has not been commenced in such 60-day period where the remedy of the breach cannot occur within the 60 days, of receipt of written notice of said material breach to the breaching party.

13. Governing Law. This agreement has been entered into in the State of New York and the validity, interpretation, and effect of this agreement shall be governed by its laws applicable to Contracts wholly entered into and performed entirely herein and any other actions shall be brought in the Courts of the State of New York. Any controversy arising under this agreement, if litigated, shall be adjudicated in a court of competent jurisdiction within the county of New York, City of New York, in the State of New York.

14. Indemnification. Both parties mutually agree to and do hereby indemnify, save and hold the other party harmless for any and all claims, losses, and damages (including court costs and reasonable attorney's fees) arising out of, connected with or as a result of any inconsistency with, failure of, or breach by the other party of any warranty, representation, agreement, undertaking, or covenant contained in this agreement including, without limitation, any claim by any third party in connection with the foregoing. In addition to any other rights or remedies Distributor may have by reason of such inconsistency, failure, breach, threatened breach of claim, Label shall promptly reimburse Distributor, in demand, for any reasonable payment made by Distributor at any time after the date hereof with respect to any loss, damage, or liability resulting directly therefrom, and in addition thereto, Distributor shall have the right to withhold from any and all moneys otherwise payable to Label under this agreement, a sum(s) equal to such loss, damage, and liability (included anticipated and actual court costs and reasonable attorney's fees). Distributor shall give Label notice of any third party claim to which the foregoing indemnity applies and Label shall have the right to participate in the defense of any such claim, provided that if litigation has not been commenced within one (1) year of such claim first being made, Distributor will promptly pay such moneys to Label, provided that such payment to Label shall not limit Distributor's right to withhold sums at a later date if litigation based upon such claim is thereafter commenced.

IN WITNESS WHEREOF, the parties hereto have executed this Agreement on the day and year first above written.

AGREED TO AND ACCEPTED:

BY:
"ARTIST"

_____
(an authorized signatory)

BY:
"COMPANY"

_____
(an authorized signatory)

TONY ROSE

RECORD COMPANY AND PRODUCER CONTRACT

Date _____

This letter will serve as the agreement with_____
_____ (hereinafter designated as "Producer"), with respect to Producers services in connection with the production of the master recordings of performances with the recording artist known professionally as _____ (hereinafter individually, jointly, and/or severally designated as "Artist").

1. The term of this agreement shall commence as of the date hereof and shall continue until the completion of your services.

2. During the term of this Agreement Producer agrees to produce _____ ( ) master recordings embodying the performance of said Artist (hereinafter designated the "Masters")and to perform all other obligations required under this Agreement.

3. Recording sessions for the Masters shall be conducted by Producer under the _____ (hereinafter designated as "Record Company"), recording agreement between Artist and Record Company at such times and places as shall be designated by Record Company. All individuals rendering services in connection with the recording of Masters shall be subject to Record Companies approval. Record Company shall have the right and opportunity to have Record Companies representatives attend each such recording session. Each Master shall embody the performance by the Artist of a single musical composition designated by the Artist (subject to Record Companies approval, not to be unreasonably withheld) and shall be subject to Record Companies approval as technically satisfactory for the manufacture, broadcast and sale of phono records, and, upon Record Companies request, you shall re-record any musical composition or other selection until a Master technically satisfactory to us shall have been obtained. You agree to begin pre-production, rehearsals, and recording on _____, 20_____. The Masters shall be, at Record Companies election, maintained at a recording studio or other location designated by Record Company, in Record Companies name and subject to our control.

4. All Masters produced hereunder, from the inception of the recording thereof, and all phono records and other reproductions made therefrom, together with the performances embodied therein are solely Record

HOW TO BE A RECORD PRODUCER

Companies property, free of any claims whatsoever except as provided herein.

5. For Producers services Producer will be paid a deposit of _____($) _____ ( ) working days before the start of rehearsals. Upon completion of all recording, re-recording, mixing and mastering along with received delivery of technically satisfactory masters, you will be paid a balance of _____ ($). The payment of the deposit and balance is Producers total compensation for the service provided herein. The initial deposit is not refundable to Record Company.

I, hereby agree to and am bound by these terms.
I set my name to this Agreement the _____ day of_____, 20___.

_____
Producer

_____
Record Company

TONY ROSE

PRODUCER LETTER OF AGREEMENT FOR ARTIST

Date: _____

Dear Mr./Ms._____,
address_____

This letter shall serve as our agreement in respect to _____ (hereinafter referred to as the "Producer") services in producing Master Recordings (hereinafter referred to as the "Masters") of the recording artist(s) professionally known as _____ (hereinafter referred to as the "Artist").

1. TERM.

The term of this agreement shall commence as of the date hereof and shall continue until the completion of Producer's services.

2. PRODUCTION.

(a) Recording sessions for the Masters shall be conducted by Producer under this Agreement at such times and places as shall be mutually designated by you and Producer. All individuals rendering services in connection with the recording of Masters shall be subject to your approval. You shall have the right and opportunity to have your representatives attend each such recording session. Each Master shall embody the performance by the Artist of a single musical composition designated by the Artist (subject to your approval, not to be unreasonably withheld) and shall be subject to your approval as technically satisfactory for the manufacture, broadcast and sale of phono records, and, upon your request, Producer shall re-record any musical composition or other selection until a Master technically satisfactory to you shall have been obtained, provided additional production costs will be paid by you. Producer agrees to begin pre- production, rehearsals, and recording on _____, 199_.

(b) Producer shall deliver to you a two-track stereo tape suitable for duplication and manufacture of phono records for each Master. All original session tapes, rough mixes and any derivatives or reproductions thereof shall also be delivered to you, or, at your election, maintained at a recording studio or other location designated by you, in your name and subject to your control.

3. MASTERS.

All Masters produced hereunder, from the inception of the recording thereof, and all phono records and other reproductions made therefrom, together with the performances embodied therein and all copyrights therein and thereto, and all renewals and extensions thereof, shall be entirely your property, free of any claims whatsoever by Producer or any other person or person engaged in the production of the Masters. (It being understood that for copyright purposes Producer and all persons rendering services in connection with such Masters shall be Contractors for hire).

4. COMPENSATION.

(a) Conditioned upon Producer's full and faithful performance of all the terms and provisions hereof, you shall pay Producer, as an advance recoupable by us from any and all royalties payable by you to Producer hereunder, the sum of $ _____ DOLLARS payable upon commencement of recording, and the balance upon the delivery to you of the Masters.

(b) Notwithstanding anything contained in (a) above to the contrary:

(i) in the event the Masters are released on any label other than _____ or its subsidiary or affiliate label or labels, Producer shall not receive a royalty in connection with the sale of such records;

(ii) in the event the Masters are released on the _____ label or a subsidiary or affiliate label, Producer shall be paid in respect to the sale of such phono records a royalty rate of three percent (3%) of the suggested retail price of each phono record sold and paid for in the United States. Payments of royalties from foreign sources shall be ONE HALF of the United States royalty rate. All fees paid to Producer hereunder shall constitute recoupable advances which shall be recouped prior to further payment of royalties.

5. ASSISTANCE.

Producer has agreed to assist you in presenting the Masters to major record companies in pursuit of a record production agreement with a major label. Producer understands that you will also be presenting the Masters to major labels and that Producer will not be your exclusive representative. Therefore, Producer agrees to notify you prior to making any formal contact with representatives of any major record company on your behalf in order to coordinate our respective efforts and agrees to contact on your behalf only those companies we mutually agreed upon. In the event you enter into a record production agreement with a major label for the Masters recorded hereunder and the further services of "Artist" as a result of substantial efforts and negotiations by Producer with such company within the period of ONE YEAR following the completion of the Masters we agree to pay you a commission of six percent (6%) of the actual cash advances (exclusive of recording budgets) received by you upon execution of said agreement. A major record company as defined herein shall be a company or corporation with gross sales of one million (1,000,000) units in the calendar year 1998.

6. WARRANTIES.

Producer hereby warrants, represents, and agrees that he is under no disability, restriction, or other incumbency with respect to his right to execute and perform the services described in this Agreement.

7. TRANSFERABLE.

You shall have the right, at your election, to designate other producers for recording sessions with the Artist, in which event Producer shall have no rights hereunder with respect to the Masters produced at such other recording sessions.

8. ASSIGNMENT.

We shall have the right, at our election, to assign any of our rights hereunder, in whole or part, to any subsidiary, affiliated, or related company, or to any person, firm or corporation acquiring rights in the Masters produced hereunder.

9. THIS AGREEMENT.

(a) This contract sets forth the entire understanding of the parties hereto relating to the subject matter hereof. No amendment or modification of this contract shall be binding unless confirmed in writing by both parties.

(b) We shall not be deemed to be in breach of any of our obligations hereunder unless and until you have given us specific written notice of the nature of such breach and we have failed to cure such breach within thirty (30) days after our receipt of such notice.

(c) Nothing herein contained shall constitute a partnership or joint venture between you and us.

(d) This contract has been entered into in the State of _____, and its validity, construction, interpretation, and legal effect shall be governed by the laws of the State of _____.

(e) This contract shall not become binding and effective until signed by you and countersigned by a duly authorized agent of ___(Company)____. If the foregoing correctly reflects your understanding and agreement with us, please indicate by signing below.

Sincerely,

_____
PRODUCER

Agreed and Accepted:

ARTIST
PRODUCER AND ARTIST "WORK MADE FOR HIRE" AGREEMENT

1. GRANT OF RIGHTS

Producer and Artist agree that each Master, and all derivatives thereof (but not including the underlying compositions), (collectively "Works") shall constitute "works made for hire" as that term is defined under 17 U.S.C. sec. 101, and the author and owner of the Works is deemed to be Artist (or its authorized designee).

In any event, Producer does hereby assign, transfer and set over to Artist, its successors and assigns, one hundred percent (100%) of Artist's entire right, title and interest, including without limitation any and all so-called "moral rights," in and to the Works, together with all copyrights therein and thereto throughout the world and any and all renewals and extensions of copyright therein now known or hereafter existing under any law, rule, statute and/or regulation now known or hereafter enacted or promulgated, and including without limitation the exclusive right to administer such copyrights.

The Works shall be the sole and exclusive property of Artist in perpetuity, free from any claim whatsoever by Producer. Producer will execute and deliver to Artist such instruments of transfer and other documents regarding the rights of Artist in the Works as Artist may reasonably request to carry out the purposes of this agreement and Producer will sign any and all necessary documents to effectuate the disposition of same.

Artist shall have the unlimited, perpetual right to exploit the Works for all purposes by any means or media now or hereafter devised, and in any form whatsoever, under any trademarks, trade names and labels with no additional compensation payable to Producer other than as stated herein, it being understood that Producer shall have the right to grant and negotiate and grant all licenses sought and obtained for derivative works.

Neither the expiration nor termination of the agreement pursuant to which the Works were produced shall affect the ownership by Artist of the Works it being understood, however, that the Recordings shall remain the sole and exclusive property of Producer until all monies, as mentioned below in paragraph 3(a), due Producer by Artist are received by Producer."

2. RECORDING SESSIONS

Recording sessions for the Masters shall be conducted by Producer under this Agreement at such times and places as shall be mutually designated by Artist and Producer. Recording sessions for the Master will be conducted by Artist at Artist's sole cost and expense. Artist shall pay all Recording Costs ("Costs") of the Masters recorded hereunder as and when due. Producer shall deliver to Artist upon completion, a final two-track equalized tape copy, CDR or digital audio tape (DAT)) commercially satisfactory to Artist for use on a record ("Record"). Each Master shall embody the performance by Artist of a single musical composition designated by the Artist, and shall be subject to Producers final approval as to selection of Artist, technical satisfaction for the manufacture, broadcast and sale of phono records.

3. COMPENSATION

(a) In consideration for Producer's services hereunder, Artist agrees to pay Producer a minimum of One Thousand Dollars ($1000.00) as recording fee per song or track to be created, produced and recorded by Producer hereunder, Half of which, Five-Hundred Dollars (500.00), to be paid before execution hereof and the remaining Five-Hundred Dollars (500.00) to be paid to Producer at the time of completion of project, or, the full amount to be paid before execution hereof, whichever method the Artist chooses.

(b) In addition to the fee set forth in paragraph 3a. above, Producer shall also receive an amount equal to Three percent (3%) of the Suggested Retail List Price (SRLP) of any Record in which the Master(s) is/are embodied on divided by a fraction, the numerator of which shall be the number of Masters produced by Producer appearing on any Record embodying the Masters and the denominator of which shall be the total the number of all royalty bearing masters appearing on the Record.

(c) Notwithstanding the foregoing, Producer's royalties payable hereunder shall be calculated in the same manner as Artist's royalties are calculated under Artist's recording agreement ("Recording Agreement") with Artist's record Artist ("Record Artist") with respect to the Master(s) recorded hereunder and released by Record Artist. Producer's royalties shall be subject to the same reductions, deductions, exclusions and category variations as is Artist's royalties under Artist's Recording Agreement with Record Artist; and shall be paid at the same time as Artist is paid by Record Artist pursuant to the Recording Agreement. Producer shall not be paid any monies in respect of any exploitation of the Master for which Artist is not paid royalties, accordingly, no royalties shall be payable to Producer hereunder unless and until all Advances under this Agreement or Artist's Recording Agreement or third party recording or distribution agreement, shall have been recouped. As used herein, the term "Advances" shall refer to the following sums but only to the extent such sums are recoupable by me or a royalty paying third party: (a) all recording and mastering costs incurred with respect to the Master, (b) all costs incurred with respect to production of the audio-visual recordings with respect to the master, (c) all artwork costs associated with the Master; (d) all costs for so-called tour support and (e) payments to Producer, and (f) any other costs incurred under this Agreement for recording and manufacturing, promoting, creating and selling the Master.

(d) Whenever the Master(s) produced hereunder are coupled with other master recordings on phonograph records or other devices, Producer's royalty rate under this Agreement shall be computed by multiplying our otherwise applicable royalty rate by a fraction, the numerator of which is the sum of selections contained on the Master(s) and a denominator of which is the total number of master including the Master(s) embodied in the record or other device."

4. OVERRIDE ROYALTY

(a) In the event Producer is not engaged to produce the Artist's Masters for Record Artist, and one (1) or more of the Recordings (even though edited or re-mixed) is commercially released by Record Artist, Producer shall be entitled to a three (3%) percent royalty override of the suggested retail list price ("SRLP") of records embodying any Artist Recording hereunder and sold through normal retail channels throughout the United States ("USNRC") and not returned. Such royalty shall be paid on all singles and for LP's shall be computed on a pro-rated basis, with the numerator to be the number of Artist Recordings and the denominator to be the total number of masters on the record. Producer shall also be entitled to receive applicable credit for the Recording(s) embodied in said record.

(b) Artist agrees to use its best efforts to cause Record Artist to pay all royalties due to Producer hereunder directly to Producer and Artist agrees to execute letters of direction and any and all other instruments necessary to effectuate same.

5. NO ADDITIONAL COMPENSATION; ACCREDITATION

a) The compensation set forth herein is full and complete payment to Producer for all services and rights in respect of the Work. No additional sums will be due to Producer or any other entity as a result of the exploitation of the Works.

(b) As additional consideration, Artist shall use its best efforts to have Producer credited as a "producer" and shall give Producer appropriate production and songwriting credit on all compact discs, record and cassette labels or any other record configuration manufactured which is now known or created in the future that embodies the Masters created hereunder and on all cover liner notes. Any records containing the Masters and on the front and/or back cover of any Album listing the Masters and other musician credits. Such credit shall be in substantial form: "Produced by_____.". Artist shall use its best efforts to ensure that Record Artist properly credits Producer and Artist shall check all proofs for accuracy of credits, and shall use its best efforts to cause Record Artist releasing the record to cure any mistakes regarding Producer's credit on the next print run of such materials. If Artist fails to comply with this clause in any instances or sole obligation to Producer by reason of such failure Producer's sole remedy is to have Artist add the appropriate credit. Artist shall provide Producer with five (5) copies of the completed Records within thirty (30) days after manufacture of the Record to review for accuracy.

6. SONGWRITING; CONTROLLED COMPOSITIONS

(a) Producer shall be considered the author of the music recorded on the Masters recorded hereunder which are written or composed by Producer, in whole or in part, alone or in collaboration with Artist or with others. Such ownership percentage shall be accorded to Producer in accordance with Producer's percentage of authorship based on the copyright laws of the United States and as set forth on Schedule "A" attached hereto. Appropriate credit as a song writer and author of the music showing author's performance right society affiliation shall be given to Producer based on the songs produced and created under this Agreement. If Producer is the sole writer of the music produced under this Agreement, then Producer shall have the right to prepare and file copyright registration forms for the music produced under this Agreement. Producer shall provide Artist with a copy of the filed registration form upon receipt by Producer of the filed form from the Copyright Office. Artist shall have the right to incorporate lyrics with the music created hereunder to create a new song ("New Song") and Artist shall have the right to give the New Song a new title and register the New Song for copyright, providing Producer the copyright credit in the music in the New Song as set forth in this Agreement. If Producer contributes original lyrics to the compositions recorded, he shall receive a pro-rata share of the songwriter credit, and associated publishing, with any other original lyricist, and it shall receive a pro-rata share of the songwriter credit, and associated publishing, with any other original composer, unless all songwriters agree in writing to another division of writer credit. Claimed percentages of authorship for each title are set forth in Schedule A hereto. Any compositions to which Producer contributes songwriting are referred to herein as "Controlled Compositions".

(b) Subject to the terms of this agreement, Producer member hereby retains his publishing rights in connection with his share of all compositions and Artist further grants to producer the right to participate and be present during all negotiations with Record Artist and/or any other person or entity with whom Artist may enter into negotiations regarding the sale, license or distribution of the Masters to be produced hereunder.

7. WARRANTIES AND REPRESENTATIONS

Producer and Artist hereby make the following representations and warranties:

(a) Producer has the full right and ability to enter into this Agreement, and is not under any disability, restriction, or prohibition with respect to the grant of rights hereunder.

(b) Producer warrants that the manufacture, sale, distribution, or other exploitation of the Masters hereunder will not infringe upon or violate any common law or statutory right of any person, firm, or corporation; including, without limitation, contractual rights, copyrights, and right(s) of privacy and publicity and will not constitute libel and/or slander. The foregoing notwithstanding, Producer undertakes no responsibility whatsoever as to any elements added to the Masters by Artist and/or Artist, and Artist indemnifies and holds Producer harmless for any such elements.

(c) Producer warrants that he shall not "sample" (as that term is commonly understood in the recording industry) any copyrighted material or sound recordings belonging to any other person, firm, or corporation (hereinafter referred to as "Owner") without first having notified Artist and obtaining Artist's consent. Artist shall have no obligation to approve the use thereof; however, if approved, any payment in connection therewith, including any associated legal clearance costs, shall constitute an additional recording cost and expense and shall be borne by Artist, recoupable from royalties hereunder. Knowledge by Artist that "samples" were used by Producer which were not affirmatively disclosed by Producer to Artist shall shift, in whole or in part, the liability for infringement or violation of the rights of any third party arising from the use of any such "sample" from Producer to Artist. At Artist's request, Producer shall cooperate with respect to any matters concerning "sampling" which may arise hereunder.

8. INDEMNIFICATION

Parties hereto shall indemnify and hold each other harmless from any and all third party claims, liabilities, costs, losses, damages or expenses as are actually incurred by the non-defaulting party and shall hold the non-defaulting party, free, safe, and harmless against and from any and all claims, suits, demands, costs, liabilities, loss, damages, judgments, recoveries, costs, and expenses; (including, without limitation, reasonable attorneys' fees), which may be made or brought, paid, or incurred by reason of any breach or claim of breach of the warranties and representations hereunder by the defaulting party, their agents, heirs, successors, assigns and employees, which have been reduced to final judgment; provided that prior to final judgment, arising out of any breach of any representations or warranties of the defaulting party contained in this agreement or any failure by defaulting party to perform any obligations on its part to be performed hereunder the Non-defaulting party has given the defaulting party prompt written notice of all claims and the right to participate in the defense with counsel of its choice at its sole expense. In no event shall Artist be entitled to seek injunctive or any other equitable relief for any breach or non-compliance with any provision of this   Agreement.

9. ACCOUNTING AND AUDIT

Payments and royalties earned and payable, if any, shall be accounted for and paid to Producer (or Producer's designee, as applicable) within thirty (30) days after the end of each respective calendar quarter ending March 31, June 30, September 30 and December 31, or in accordance with such accounting period as designated pursuant to Recording and/or Distribution Agreement, and royalties shall be paid and accounted for within thirty (30) days after the end of each respective calendar quarter in accordance with the terms as set forth therein. Artist shall have the right to retain, as a reserve against subsequent charges (said reserve not to exceed thirty (30%) percent), credits or returns (collectively "returns"), a reasonable percentage of royalties otherwise payable hereunder; provided that said reserved amount shall be liquidated fully by the fourth accounting period following the period for which the reserve was first established. Producer, or a certified public accountant on Producer's behalf, may at Producer's cost and expense examine Artist's books relating to the sale or other distribution of Records hereunder solely for the purpose of verifying the accuracy of any statement rendered, only during Artist's normal business hours and upon reasonable written notice. Artist's books relating to any particular royalty statement may be examined within two (2) years after the date a statement is rendered by Artist to Producer. Artist shall immediately pay the balance due of any understatement of royalties paid or payable as revealed by such examination.

10. WITHOLDING ROYALTIES

Parties hereto agree to save, defend, indemnify and hold each other and any of their Artist's, agents, heirs, successors, assigns and employees free, safe, and harmless against and from any and all claims, suits, demands, costs, liabilities, loss, damages, judgments, recoveries, costs, and expenses; (including, without limitation, reasonable attorneys' fees), which may be made or brought, paid, or incurred by reason of any breach or claim of breach of defaulting Artist's warranties and representations hereunder which have been reduced to final judgment; provided that prior to final judgment, Artist shall be entitled to withhold royalties otherwise payable in an amount equal to Artist's reasonably estimated exposure in connection with such claimed breach by Producer, and provided further that if no legal action is commenced in connection with such claim of breach within one (1) year after notification to Artist of such claim, then Artist shall release all royalties so withheld. As an alternative to the withholding of royalties, Producer shall be entitled to post a bond for the benefit of Artist in an amount equal to Artist's reasonably estimated exposure. Parties shall be entitled to designate any defense attorneys engaged in connection with any such claim or action.

11. SEVERABILITY

If any provision of this Agreement shall, for any reason be illegal or unenforceable, then and in such event, the same shall not affect the validity of remaining portions and provisions of the Agreement.

12. RELATIONSHIP OF PARTIES

Nothing contained herein shall be construed to constitute a partnership or joint venture between the parties hereto, and neither Artist shall become bound by any representation, act, or omission of the other.

13. CONSTRUCTION

This Agreement shall be deemed entered into within the State of _____ and shall be construed in accordance with and governed by the laws of that State and/or by U.S. federal law.

14. NOTICES

All notices which either party may desire or be required to give hereunder, shall be in writing and sent by certified mail postage prepaid. Notice shall be deemed effective five (5) days after posting. (A simultaneous transmission of all notices and statements via facsimile is recommended.) The address of the parties for all notices, statements, and payments shall be as first set forth above.

15. ATTORNEY'S FEES

In the event of any controversy, claim, or dispute as to the terms of this Agreement, or the subject matter thereof, or breach, thereof, and/or litigation resulting there from, the prevailing party shall be entitled to recover from the other party reasonable attorney's fees and costs resulting there from.

16. ENTIRE UNDERSTANDING

This Agreement sets forth the entire understanding between the parties regarding the subject matter hereof, and cannot be modified except by written instrument signed by the parties hereto. This agreement may be executed in counterpart and shall have the same validity, force and effect as if executed in whole.

17. HEADINGS

The headings set forth herein are for convenience only and shall not be construed as defining the terms and conditions contained hereunder or utilized to assist in the interpretation of any ambiguity or ambiguities contained in any of the provisions of this Agreement.

18. FUTURE DOCUMENTS

The parties hereto agree to execute any and all further documents, which are necessary, required or desired to make this Agreement effective and binding upon the parties hereto and which are necessary, required or desired for the performance of any of the terms or conditions hereof.

19. NOTICE AND CURE

a) If Artist fails to account for and make payments hereunder and such failure is not cured within thirty (30) days after written notice thereof to Artist, or if Artist fails to perform any other obligations required of it hereunder and such failure is not cured within thirty (30) days after written notice thereof to Artist, or in the event that Artist shall go into liquidation, or shall go into bankruptcy or make an assignment for the benefit of creditors, or any insolvency or composition proceeding shall be commenced against or by Artist, then and in any one or all of such events, this agreement shall automatically terminate, and the Artist shall have no further rights of any kind whatsoever in and to the Masters and/or records hereunder. In any such event the Artist shall continue to account to Producer for royalties and/or other sums earned in respect of records embodying the Masters manufactured by or for the Artist prior to the date of such termination.

(b) If Artist fails to perform any obligations required of it hereunder and such failure is not cured within thirty (30) days after written notice thereof to Artist, then Producer shall have the right to terminate this agreement and suspend its performance thereof. In any such event the Artist shall continue to account to Producer for royalties and/or other sums earned in respect of records embodying the Masters manufactured by or for the Artist prior to the date of such termination.

20. ASSIGNMENT

Producer may freely assign all or any portion of Producer's rights, duties, and obligations under this Agreement to any other business entity established by Producer, provided, however, that no such assignment shall result in an increase of Producer's fee payable by ARTIST under this Agreement, nor otherwise result in the modification of any other material or substantive provisions of this Agreement, absent written agreement to the contrary.

21. LEGAL REPRESENTATION

Artist and producer hereto acknowledge that each has read and fully understand the contents of this agreement and/or have had the contents fully explained to them. Each has further been advised that it is their right to have this agreement reviewed and explained by an attorney of their own choosing and at their own expense before executing same; however, any individual's failure to do so will not affect the validity of this agreement.

IN WITNESS WHEREOF, the parties hereto have accepted this Agreement on the date first set forth above.

PRODUCER: _____

ARTIST:_____

PROMOTER AND ARTIST AGREEMENT

AGREEMENT, made this day of April, 201 by and between NAME with a principal office at _____ (**"Promoter"**) and **NAMES** with a principal office at NAME _____ (**"Artist"**). This Agreement in its entirety shall constitute a binding Agreement between the parties referenced above.

1. Name of Event:

2. Address of Event:

3. Name of Artist:

4. Date of Event:

5. Time of Event:

6. Promoter shall be responsible for providing the following:

   a. Three (3) roundtrip first-class airline tickets between Los Angeles, California and Louisville, Kentucky
   b. Up to three (3) roundtrip economy class airline tickets between Los Angeles, California and Louisville, Kentucky
   c. Three (3) suites and up to three (3) singles rooms in a 4-star hotel for Friday and Saturday, April 30th and May 1st
   d. Security for Artist
   e. Up to six (6) complimentary passes to the Kentucky Derby for May 1, 201__

7. Artist agrees to perform the following:

   a. Red Carpet photos and media interviews
   b. Artist has the option to provide a photograph for the press announcement prior to the Event
   c. Artist has the option to provide a quote or statement for the press release to be used to promote the Event

d. Artist agrees to make a welcome announcement from the stage and to acknowledge the NAME (comments to be limited to five minutes).

8. Compensation: Promoter agrees to pay to Artist the total sum of Thirty-Six Thousand ($36,000) Dollars ($12,000 per member of Artist), which shall be paid fifty (50%) percent upon the full execution of this Agreement via wire transfer. The balance of said sum ($18,000) shall be due and payable to Artist, in cash, no less than two (2) hours prior to Artist's arrival at Event. In the event less than all three (3) of the above referenced members of the NAME should appear at the Event, then Promoter shall be entitled to reduce the Compensation by Twelve Thousand ($12,000) Dollars for each such member who has not appeared and in the event only one (1) member appears, then Artist agrees to promptly refund to Promoter the sum of Six Thousand ($6,000) Dollars.

9. Artist acknowledges that Promoter customarily does not compensate her celebrity guests for appearing at and participating in this annual Event. Accordingly, Artist agrees to preserve as confidential and not disclose the financial arrangements between themselves and Promoter to any third parties, other than their management representatives, attorneys and accountants.

10. Breach of Contract – Arbitration of Claims:

(a) All claims and disputes which may arise between the Promoter and the Artist regarding the interpretation and performance of any of the terms and conditions of this contract, including any disputes between the parties as to their obligations and responsibilities hereunder, shall be referred exclusively to binding arbitration.

(b) Should a court of competent jurisdiction confirm or enter judgment upon an award of the Arbitrator, then the parties expressly agree that the prevailing party in the arbitration shall be additionally entitled to judgment for reasonable attorneys' fees and costs incurred in enforcing the Agreement. A judgment confirming an arbitration award, for attorneys' fees, and for costs may be enforced in the courts of any jurisdiction in which a party to this contract either resides of maintains an office or place of business.

11. Miscellaneous:

HOW TO BE A RECORD PRODUCER

(a) This Agreement shall be construed in accordance with the laws of the State of Kentucky.

(b) All notices to be given hereunder shall be in writing and sent to the recipient by overnight courier i.e. Federal Express.

IN WITNESS WHEREOF, the parties hereto have hereunto set their names and seals on the day and year first above written.

PROMOTER							ARTIST(S)

_____					_____
NAME								NAME(S)

BOOKING MUSICIANS CONTRACT

THIS CONTRACT, entered into on this _____ day of _____, 201_____, is for the personal services of the Musician(s) for the performance described below. The undersigned employer and the undersigned musician(s) agree and contract as follows:

1. NAME OF MUSICIAN(S):
2. NUMBER OF MUSICIAN(S):
3. NAME AND ADDRESS OF PLACE OF PERFORMANCE
4. DATE(S) OF PERFORMANCE:
5. TIME(S) OF PERFORMANCE:
6. WAGE AGREED UPON:
7. DEPOSIT:
8. PAYMENT OF BALANCE TO _____ MADE IN U.S. CURRENCY OR CERTIFIED CHECK AT THE END OF PERFORMANCE.
9. ADDITIONAL TERMS:

10. This contract constitutes a complete and binding agreement between the employer and the musician(s). AGENT acts only as agent and assumes no responsibility as between the employer and the musician(s).

11. In case of breach of this contract by Employer, the Employer agrees to pay the amount stated in Section 6 as mitigated damages, plus reasonable attorney's fees, court costs, and legal interest.

12. The Employer agrees to be responsible for harm, loss, or damage of any kind to musician(s) person or property while located at the place of performance (Section 3 herein).

13. The persons signing for Employer and the Musician(s) agree to be personally, jointly and severally liable for the terms of this contract.

_____

for Employer for Musician(s)

MUSIC / DANCE REMIX RECORDING CONTRACT
WORK FOR HIRE - (FLAT FEE)

This AGREEMENT (hereinafter referred to as the "Agreement") is made effective this _____ day of _____, 201__ by and between _____, located at _____(hereinafter referred to as the "Remixer") and _____, Located at_____
_____
(hereinafter referred to as the "Company").

WITNESSETH:

In consideration of the respective covenants contained herein, the parties hereto, intending to legally bound hereby, agree as follows:

1. Work-For-Hire. Whereas the Remixer, an employee for hire of the Company, has at its request and under its direction, made the following musical contributions:

Dance remix for the Master recording: _____ (SONG TITLE) by _____(ARTIST)

2. Ownership of Masters. All Masters recorded by Remixer hereunder, from the inception of the recording thereof and all reproductions derived therefrom, together with the performances embodied thereon, shall be the property of Company for the world free from any claims whatsoever by the Remixer or any person deriving any rights or interest from the Remixer. The Masters (referring only to the sound recordings as opposed to the underlying musical works) shall be considered a "work made for hire" for Company.

A. Without limiting the generality of the foregoing, Company and its designee(s) shall have the exclusive, perpetual, and unlimited right to all the results and proceeds of the uninhibited exploitation of the Masters throughout the Universe (the "Territory"), including, but not limited to:

(i) The right to manufacture, advertise, sell, lease, license, distribute or otherwise use or dispose of, in any or all fields of use by any method now or hereafter known, records embodying the Masters delivered hereunder, upon such terms and conditions as Company may elect, or at its discretion to refrain therefrom;

(ii) The right to use, reproduce, print, publish or disseminate in any medium, and to permit others to do the same, Remixer's name (including any professional name now or hereafter adopted by Remixer), photos, likeness, and biographical material concerning Remixer in all connections which relate in any manner to the Masters or Company, including, without limitation, in the marketing, sale or other exploitation of records, and as news or other information, in connection with Company's business;

(iii) The right to perform the records publicly and to permit public performances thereof by means of radio broadcast, television or any other method now or hereafter known, and to synchronize such performances with visual images.

(iv) The right to license the Masters to third parties for use on a flat-fee and/or royalty basis.

(v) To include the Masters on compilations with masters by other artists, producers, and/or remixers.

B. All the rights herein granted to Company hereunder shall be for the Universe (the "Territory").

C. Remixer acknowledges that the sale of records is speculative and agrees that the judgment of Company with regard to any matter affecting the sale, distribution and exploitation of such records shall be binding and conclusive upon Remixer. Nothing contained in this Agreement shall obligate Company to make, sell, license, or distribute recordings manufactured from masters recorded hereunder.

3. Publishing. Remixer does hereby relinquish all claims to any publishing rights in regards to the Masters, and the Remixer further acknowledges that the publishing copyright belongs to the original writers of the musical composition that formed the basis the for the Masters.

4. Payment. The enticement and consideration for this Agreement is the promise by the Company to pay the Remixer the amount of $_____. This is a one-time compensation for the Remixer's and Remixer understands that this will comprise Remixer's complete and sole payment.

5. Governing Law. This Agreement is entered into in the City of _____ and State of _____ and is guided by and governed by the laws of that State.

IN WITNESS WHEREOF, the parties hereto have executed this Agreement on the day and year first above written.

AGREED TO AND ACCEPTED:

BY:
"REMIXER"

_____
(an authorized signatory)

BY:
"COMPANY"

_____
(an authorized signatory)

TONY ROSE

ARTIST RELEASE FORM

ASSIGNMENT OF INTEREST AND RELEASE

This AGREEMENT (hereinafter referred to as the "Agreement") is made effective this _____ day of _____, 201__ by and between _____, located at _____ (hereinafter referred to as the "Artist") and _____, located at _____ _____ and its parents, subsidiaries, affiliates, principals, members, managers, employees, former employees, representatives, counsel and/or agents (hereinafter referred to as the "Company").

WITNESSETH:

Reference is hereby made to the Recording Contract, dated _____, 200__, between Artist and Company.

The claims of all of the parties with respect to the Company have been resolved, and the parties hereby enter into this Release Agreement in full settlement and full satisfaction of all such issues. Upon execution hereof, Artist shall be released from his responsibilities as an exclusive recording artist for the Company. Accordingly, Artist and the Company agree as follows:

1. Upon the date hereof, Artist shall have no further obligation to perform any services of whatever nature for the Company, and the Company shall have no further obligation compensate Artist in any form of whatever nature, except as specifically provided herein.

2. The Company hereby forever releases and discharges Artist from any and all claims, demands, actions, causes of action, suits, sums of money, accounts, covenants, agreements, contracts, and promises in law or in equity, which the Company now has, has had, or at any time may have, against Artist, whether or not they have been subject to dispute or otherwise and whether known or unknown to the Company, by reason or any matter, cause or thing whatsoever from the beginning of the world to the date hereof, except as otherwise provided for herein.

3. Artist hereby forever releases and discharges the Company and all of its principals, agents, officers and directors, members and managers from any and all claims, demands, actions, causes of action, suits, sums of money, accounts, covenants, agreements, contracts, and promises in law or in equity, which Artist now has, has had, or at any time may have, against the Company, its principals, agents, officers, directors, members, managers, successors and assigns, whether or not they have been subject to dispute or otherwise and whether known or unknown to Artist, by reason or any matter, cause or thing whatsoever from the beginning of the world to the date hereof, except as otherwise provided for herein.

4. Artist agrees to and do hereby indemnify, save and hold the Company harmless of and from any and all loss and damage (including court costs and reasonable attorneys' fees) arising out of or connected with any claim by Artist or any one or more third parties or any act by Artist which is inconsistent with any of the warranties, representations and/or agreements made by Artist herein.

5. The Company agrees to and does hereby indemnify, save and hold Artist harmless of and from any and all loss and damage (including court costs and reasonable attorneys' fees) arising out of or connected with any claim by the Company or any one or more third parties or any act by the Company which is inconsistent with any of the warranties, representations and/or agreements made by the Company herein.

6. The Company, or its officers, agents, and designees, shall have full and sole authority on behalf of the Company to file all papers and official documents in Artist's name to effect any changes which the Company, in its sole discretion, deems necessary or advisable to carry out the covenants, directives, intent and spirit of this Agreement, including without limitation, the filing of any certificates of change with any department, agency or bureau of the State and/or Federal governments.

7. It is the Company's and Artist's intention in entering into this agreement that this agreement shall be effective as a full and final accord and satisfaction and release of each other with respect to every matter between the Company and Artist herein referred to, with the exception of any matters specifically dealt with herein. The Company and Artist acknowledge that no party hereto has executed this agreement in reliance on any promise, representation or warranty not contained herein.

TONY ROSE

8. This is the entire Agreement of the parties. This Agreement shall be construed in accordance with the laws of the State of California and may not be modified except by an instrument in writing signed by all of the parties hereto.

IN WITNESS WHEREOF, the parties hereto have executed this Agreement on the day and year first above written.

AGREED TO AND ACCEPTED:

BY:
"ARTIST"

_____
(an authorized signatory)

BY:
"COMPANY"

_____
(an authorized signatory)

Three

HOW TO BE A MUSIC PUBLISHER

WHAT IS A MUSIC PUBLISHER?

This section is about music publishing. Music publishing is about the ownership of songs. Music publishing is about the rights of songwriters and song owners. And perhaps most importantly, music publishing is about money.

Music publishing can be complex and confusing. The aim here is to simplify the most basic concepts of music publishing as they relate to "covers." Covers are normally songs written by established artists like, for instance, "Life on Mars" by David Bowie. But covers don't have to be popular songs. A cover can be a song that has been recorded by an unknown artist. The important thing to remember is that any song which you record that was written and previously recorded by someone else is a "cover."

SOUND RECORDING OR A COMPOSITION

The first thing we have to understand is that a song and a recording of a song are two different things. They are two distinct properties. These two properties are called the "sound recording," (sometimes called the "master") and the "composition," (sometimes called the "work"). Music contracts of all types use these terms to designate one or the other.

Here we are mainly interested in the "composition." The common everyday word we use for "composition" is the word song. In the following, whenever you see the word song, you can think composition and when- ever you see the word composition, you can think song. These two words are synonymous and are used here interchangeably.

Like all property, these two properties, the "sound recording" and the "composition," come with rights. Just as you have a right to determine who uses your personal property, owners of the "sound recording" and owners of the "composition" (song) have the right to determine who uses their property. Who owns what? Let's see by way of the following examples. Let's say you record David Bowie's song "Life on Mars," Since you have made the recording, you own the property called the "sound recording," that is, your particular recording of the song. But the recording is a cover of a song. You did not write the song. You do not own the song. The song is owned by David Bowie, (or more likely a music publishing company, but more on that later). The song or "composition" is also property.

Another example. Let's say three separate bands record the song "Life on Mars." We still have only two properties, three of one kind, the "sound recordings," and one of the other, "the "composition." To sum up, we have the "composition" and we have the "sound recording" of the "composition." Two separate properties.

INTELLECTUAL PROPERTY

These kinds of properties are called "intellectual property." Other kinds of intellectual property are books, movies, paintings and so on. And, as mentioned earlier, these properties come with rights. The particular right you have to your "sound recording" and the particular right David Bowie has to the "composition" is called a Copyright. A copyright is the right to reproduce or make copies. This right is granted by the United States Copyright Law and similar laws in other countries. If you would like to learn more about the United States Copyright Law, please go to: http://www.copyright.gov/circs/circ1.html#wci

Only the owner of the song has the right to reproduce or make copies of his or her song. The owner also has the right to grant permission to others to reproduce or make copies of his or her song. So, before you can record and make copies of someone else's song, you need to get permission from the owner. You get that permission by getting a license, just like you get permission to drive by obtaining a driver's license.

This license is called a mechanical license. By getting this mechanical license from the songwriter or from a music publishing company acting on behalf of the songwriter, you will then have permission to record, reproduce or make copies of the song.

MUSIC PUBLISHING COMPANIES

Music publishing companies and the ownership of songs - The songwriter is the owner of the song. But most songwriters do not look after the rights to their songs. Issuing licenses for the use of a song, collecting the royalties, accounting, etc. is a lot of work. This kind of work is called administration. In most cases, songwriters have music publishing companies do this administration for them. But in many cases, the songwriter sells the song to the music publisher. In this case, of course, the music publisher is the owner of the song and the rights that go with it. But whether the music publishing company owns the song or administers the rights to the song on behalf of the songwriter, the music publishing company will issue the mechanical license.

To sum up. Getting a mechanical license gives you permission to reproduce (copy) the song. Of course, in using Tune Core, the song is being reproduced digitally, but it's the same principle, every time someone downloads the song, a copy is made.

WHO GETS PAID

For every copy sold, the songwriter or publisher must be paid. The amount required to be paid for the sale of each copy of a "composition" is called the mechanical royalty. The royalty rate is established by the Copyright Royalty Board of the Library of Congress; a government agency empowered by Congress to determine the royalty rate. The royalty rate set by the Copyright Royalty Board is called the "statutory rate." Statutory is a fancy legal word meaning required by law. So, the rate set by the Copyright Royalty Board is the statutory mechanical royalty rate.

The current statutory mechanical royalty rate that must be paid to the song owner or publisher is 9.1 cents ($.091) per copy. When you record a cover song, every time that recording sells, you owe the songwriter or publisher 9.1 cents. All mechanical licenses will specify this rate. Sometimes the rate is specified in pennies; otherwise the license will specify the "statutory rate." In some cases, you can negotiate with the songwriter or publisher for a lower rate, but unless you can demonstrate that you will have enormous sales, the likelihood of getting a lower rate is slim. Finally, the rate does not remain static or permanent.

COMPULSORY LICENSES

A word about the "Compulsory License." You may have heard of something called a "compulsory license." The U. S. Copyright Law allows you to get a "compulsory license" in lieu of getting a mechanical license directly from the publisher or songwriter. But this method is a lot more work. Using this method entails specific requirements for notifying the song owner and stringent requirements for accounting. And you will still pay the full statutory mechanical royalty rate. It is not recommended that you try this method. The best and easiest way to get a mechanical license is from the songwriter or the publisher directly.

SYNCHRONIZATION LICENSES

Now, let's say you want to make a video of your recording of "Life on Mars." You'll need another license. This license is called a "synchronization license." This "sync license" gives you the right to synchronize the "composition" (song) with visual images. The sync license also contains the same right as a mechanical license; the right to make copies. But the sync license is not a substitute for a mechanical license. The only reproductions or copies you can make with a sync license are copies of your video containing the "composition." And, depending on how you want to use the video, you may be restricted as to how many copies you can make. For instance, if you want only to have your video broadcast on TV, the Internet, cell phones, etc., you may be restricted to making copies for just that purpose. But if you also want to sell your video over iTunes or anywhere else, you must have that right specified in the license. A synchronization license is a lot more fluid and flexible than a mechanical license, so when you get one, be sure you know what you want to do with the video and make sure you ask for those rights to be included in the license.

You get a sync license the same way you get a mechanical license. You must contact the publisher or songwriter. There is no set royalty rate for a sync license. It is all negotiable between you and the songwriter or publisher. You can negotiate to pay a one-time up-front fee or pay a royalty. The royalty rate will be the amount agreed upon between you and the publisher for the sale of each copy. In some cases, you may have to pay both an up-front fee and a royalty, or an advance against future royal- ties and subsequent royalties once the advance is paid off. It all depends on your negotiations with the publisher. The mechanical right, the synchronization right; these, along with others, like the reprinting of lyrics, are called publishing rights. This is what music publishing is all about.

THE HARRY FOX AGENCY

The Harry Fox Agency is a giant agency that also administers music publishing rights, though they do not issue sync licenses nor do they grant permission to reprint lyrics. Just like music publishers act on behalf of songwriters, The Harry Fox Agency acts on behalf of songwriters and publishers too. In many cases, they will be the source you will go to for a mechanical license.

WHO OWNS THE SONGS

At this point you are probably asking yourself, how do I find the owner or publisher of a song. Just about every song in existence is registered with either ASCAP, BMI or SESAC. ASCAP, BMI and SESAC all have web sites that you can search to find the owner or publisher of a song. Remember, there are many songs with the same title, so be sure you are identifying the right song. If you know who wrote the song, it will make your search a lot easier. Once you have found the right song title and writer, the information regarding the owner or publisher will be there alongside it. Another good site that will help you track down the administrator of a song is the Harry Fox Agency web site called Song File. By visiting these web sites and doing a little detective work, you will, in most every case, find out who you must contact in order to get a license. The license will be very specific about who to pay, how often you must pay and, of course, the amount to be paid.

WHAT DOES A MUSIC PUBLISHER DO?

You may be wondering: why should songwriters and their heirs deal with music publishers at all? What does a music publisher do, exactly?

In a nutshell, a music publisher owns or administers copyrights in songs, and licenses them to companies and other entities that use music, such as record labels, radio stations, filmmakers, and advertisers. The publisher then collects the license fee, keeps a cut, and pays the rest to the songwriters or their heirs. Note that a music publisher controls the *song* -- the words and music -- as opposed to any particular recording of the song. Recordings are generally owned by recording artists and record labels.

The most important function of a music publisher is to promote songs to licensees, thus getting the songs used in ways that earn money. Today, many large music publishers control so many thousands of songs that the employees of the company can't be familiar with all of them, and wind up promoting only their newest or best-known songs.

But other companies, especially smaller ones, still actively promote a larger percentage of their catalogs: talking to record label executives to get new versions recorded; talking to music supervisors to get the songs into films, TV shows, and advertisements; and licensing newer uses like ringtones, videogames, and digital downloads. Printed sheet music, once the largest source of income for songwriters and publishers, is now generally the smallest, but it can still be an important source of revenue for some works, such as those written specifically for use in music classes.

A good music publisher will have contacts and experiences allowing him or her to promote songs to the maximum number of potential licensees and negotiate good terms for their use. Most subscribe to specialized industry publications and services that give them an early "heads up" if someone is looking for music for a particular recording artist or film, for example. A good publisher will also stay on top of industry developments and actively seek out new sources of income. Without access to industry contacts, publications, and experience, an independent songwriter may be unable to place music with licensees at favorable terms.

All these different kinds of licenses and royalties require that the publisher create, receive and review a lot of paperwork consisting of various contracts, forms, and royalty statements. Some are simple and some are complex. Forgetting about or making an error on a form or contract can mean a loss of royalties.

For example, if the publisher and a filmmaker agree that a particular song can be used in a film, the rights are granted in a synchronization license (or "synch" license for short). The terms of these can vary widely. If the contract is written by a lawyer at a large film production company, the first draft may be very biased in favor of the film company. Conversely, a new, independent filmmaker may not know how to write a synch license and may leave out important points, which could cause problems or even lawsuits down the road. A music publisher can help negotiate a better agreement in both of these situations. The music publisher will also ensure that a cue sheet, listing every song used in the film, has been provided to the performing rights societies, allowing the writers and publishers to receive additional royalties each time the film is broadcast on television or cable channels.

After the music publisher negotiates a license, he collects the fee from the licensee, keeps the publisher's share (usually 50%), and forwards the rest to the songwriter or heir at the end of each royalty period (usually every six months). The task of collecting royalties from a large number of licensees, and forwarding the correct percentages to the correct writers and heirs, can be labor and paperwork intensive. Many publishers use specialized royalty-processing software to do the calculations. If a particular licensee doesn't pay the agreed upon fee, a publisher may have an attorney or specialized collections person on staff to go after them.

A music publisher also has foreign affiliates to collect royalties on foreign uses. For example, a TV show or film produced in one country may eventually be shown on cable channels in many different countries. Foreign affiliates are better equipped than the songwriter or original publisher to become aware of such uses and ensure that the proper royalties are paid. The foreign affiliate can also negotiate and promote uses originating in the affiliate's territory, such as translations of lyrics into the local language or advertisements for local products. The foreign affiliates collect royalties in their territories, keep their cuts, then forward the royalties to the U.S. publisher, who keeps a cut and pays the songwriter.

Another reason to have a publisher is that many potential licensees don't want to deal with individual songwriters. For example, if you called up a cell

HOW TO BE A MUSIC PUBLISHER

phone service provider and said "I just wrote a song and I'd like to make it available as a ringtone," I doubt they'd be interested. Generally, cell phone companies license catalogs of songs in order to provide ringtone choices for their customers.

The above is just a brief summary of some of the benefits of having your songs represented by a music publisher. Every songwriter and every song has unique attributes, so if you are a songwriter or songwriter's heir and have questions about your own situation, you should consult an attorney with experience in this area.

TONY ROSE

HOW TO START A MUSIC PUBLISHING COMPANY

THE FIRST THING TO DO

Before you do anything, and I mean before you do anything, you must take this first step: Affiliate your company with ASCAP or BMI. The reason you have to do this first is that these societies won't let you use a name that's the same (or similar to) the name of an existing company. They don't want to accidentally pay the wrong party, and so they're tough about the name you can use. And you don't want to have label copy, printed music, copyright registrations, and everything else in the name of a company that can't collect performance royalties.

You can affiliate and secure your name by completing an application and giving the society three name choices, ranked in order. That way, at least one of the names should be clear. If you're also a songwriter and haven't yet affiliated, you should affiliate as a writer with one of the two societies at the same time (they won't let you affiliate with both.) You'll have to affiliate as a publisher with the same society that you affiliate as a songwriter. This is because the societies insist on having a song's publisher affiliated with the same society as the song's writer. And for this same reason, if you're going to be a "real" music publisher (meaning you're going to publish other people's songs, as opposed to only your own), you'll need to have two companies, one for ASCAP and one for BMI.

The publishing company affiliation forms are pretty straightforward; they ask you who owns the company, the address, and similar questions. You also need to give them information about all songs in your catalog (writers, publisher, foreign deals, recordings, etc.), so they can put the info in their system and make sure you're properly credited and paid.

HOW TO BE A MUSIC PUBLISHER

You can get affiliation applications by contacting ASCAP or BMI at the following address and telephone number:

ASCAP
www.ascap.com
One Lincoln Plaza
New York, NY 10023
212-621-6000
FAX 212-724-9064

2 Music Square West
Nashville, TN 37203
615-742-5000
FAX 615-742-5020

7920 Sunset Blvd.
Suite 300
Los Angeles, CA 90046
323-883-1000
FAX 323-883-1049

BMI
www.bmi.com
320 West 57th St.
New York, NY 10019
212-586-2000
FAX 212-489-2368

10 Music Square East
Nashville, TN 37203
615-401-2000
FAX 615-401-2702

8730 Sunset Blvd.
3rd Floor West
Hollywood, CA 90069
310-659-9109
FAX 310-657-6947

It can take about five weeks to get an approval. Here's a tip in picking a name. The more common your name, the less likely you're going to get it. So steer clear of name like "Hit Music" and similar choices that won't clear. Names using just initials, such as "J.B. Music" and the like, also seem to have a hard time clearing. For some reason, many people enjoy naming their publishing companies after their children or their streets, and those seem to clear routinely.

SETTING UP YOUR MUSIC PUBLISHING BUSINESS

If you're not a corporation using the corporate name, the next step is to file what, in California, is known as a "fictitious business-name statement." This is a document filed with a county recorder and published in a newspaper, and it has its counterpart in most states. It tells the world you're doing business under a name that isn't your own and makes it legal to do so. At least in California, you need this statement to open a bank account and, even more importantly, to cash checks made out to that name.

COPYRIGHT REGISTRATION

Next, register the songs with the Copyright Office in the name of your publishing entity. If the songs were previously copyrighted in your name, you need to file an assignment transferring them to the publisher's name. www.loc.gov

PERFORMING RIGHTS SOCIETY REGISTRATION

To the extent you didn't do so when you originally affiliated, you must register all your songs with the performing rights society. The societies will send you the forms, which are self-explanatory. You only have to register the songs as either the writer or the publisher, not both.

After that, you're in business. You can begin to issue licenses to record companies and other users, as well as make foreign sub-publishing agreements, print deals, and so forth. However, there's no particular need to rush into these deals, nor will anybody be interested in making them, until you have a cd released. In fact, unless you've got a cd coming out (or some other exploitation, like a film or TV show using your songs), the societies won't even let you affiliate, and frankly there's not much point in doing any of this. You'll just be all dressed up with no place to go.

EXCLUSIVE SONGWRITER AGREEMENT

Agreement made as of the _____ day of _____ , by and between _____ with a principal place of business at _____ (hereinafter referred to as "Publisher") and _____ (hereinafter referred to as "Writer").

WITNESETH:

In consideration of the mutual promises herein contained and payment to Writer of the sums set forth below and other good and valuable consideration in hand paid by Publisher to Writer, receipt of which is hereby acknowledged, Writer and Publisher agree as follows:

SECTION I

SCOPE AND TERM

1.(a) Publisher hereby employs Writer and the Writer undertakes and agrees to render their exclusive services to the Publisher in the writing and composing of original musical compositions for an initial period of two (2) years from the date hereof, both alone and in collaboration with others as designated, directed and required by the Publisher. For the purpose of this Agreement the term Writer shall be deemed to include each of the above-mentioned persons, both individually as well as jointly. With respect to the calculation of royalties and advances, payments shall be shared equally unless otherwise stipulated.

(b) Publisher shall have the exclusive right to renew and extend the Term of this Agreement for an additional period of one (1) year, commencing upon the expiration of the initial period and subject to the same terms and conditions as set forth below. Said option shall be exercised, if at all, in writing with notice given to Writer no less than fifteen (15) days prior to the expiration of the initial period. Writer shall have the right to revoke the above-described option, in writing, in the event Publisher shall not have (i) secured the commercial exploitation of at least five (5) compositions delivered hereunder; or (ii) paid Writer a recoupable option renewal advance in the amount of ($) Dollars, payable one half (½) upon the exercise of the option and the balance upon the fulfillment of the "minimum delivery commitment" for the option period.

(c) In the event Publisher should enter into a co-publishing or administration agreement with a major U.S. music publisher, during the Term of this Agreement, then: (i) the Term of this Agreement shall be deemed co-terminus with the term of the major publisher agreement, provided however, the Term hereof shall not extend beyond an aggregate period of four (4) years from the date of commencement; and (ii) Publisher shall pay to Writer the following recoupable advances:
  (x) $50,000 for the initial period
  (y) $60,000 for the first option period
  (z) $70,000 for the second option period

Each payment shall be made one half (½) upon the commencement of the applicable period and the balance upon the delivery of the "minimum delivery commitment".

(d) For the purpose of this Agreement, the "minimum delivery commitment" for the option period(s) shall be deemed to be six (6) fully (100%) owned and controlled Compositions which have been released by a major U.S. record company or a record label which is owned or distributed by a major U.S. record company.

SECTION II

GRANTS OF RIGHTS

2. (a) Writer hereby irrevocably sells, assigns, transfers and delivers to Publisher, its successors and assigns fifty (50%) percent of all musical works, all musical compositions and all arrangements of musical works and compositions in the public domain in and for a territory consisting of the entire world (herein referred to as the "Territory") which: (i) have been written, composed, created or conceived by Writer in whole or in part prior to the date hereof (except that Publisher's rights herein shall be subject to any encumbrances specifically set forth in Schedule "A" below, with respect to those works, compositions and arrangements listed therein, if any); (ii) are now owned or controlled directly or indirectly by Writer as an employer or

otherwise; and (iii) may hereafter, during the term of this Agreement and any extensions thereof, be written, composed, created or conceived by Writer in whole or in part, including the title, words and music, and all copyrights within the Territory thereof, whether statutory or common law, and all rights, claims and demands in any way relating thereto, including, but not limited to, the exclusive right to secure copyrights therein, and to have and to hold the said copyrights and all rights of whatsoever nature now and hereafter thereunder existing and/or existing under any agreements or licenses relating thereto, for and during the full terms of all said copyrights. In consideration of the agreement to pay royalties herein contained and other good and valuable consideration in hand paid by Publisher to Writer, Writer hereby irrevocably sell and assign, all renewals and extensions of the copyrights of said musical compositions and all registrations thereof, and all rights of any and every nature now and hereafter thereunder existing, for the full terms of all such renewals and extensions of said copyrights. The works, compositions and arrangements referred to in this Paragraph 2(a) and in Paragraph 5, below, are collectively called the "Compositions" and individually called a "Composition". Publisher shall have the absolute right to assign, license and/or transfer any of the rights conveyed hereunder, in whole or in part, in order to exploit the Compositions (including without limitation, the right to issue mechanical licenses) in exchange for rates, fees or amounts determined by Publisher in its sole discretion. Upon the completion or acquisition of any Composition, Writer shall deliver to Publisher a complete and lyric copy thereof. Writer agrees, as a material obligation hereof to deliver to Publisher a minimum of five (5) wholly (100%) owned or controlled compositions during each year of the initial period of the Term of this Agreement. "Complete Compositions" is defined to mean a Composition, written entirely by Writer for which a completed leadsheet embodying such Composition has been delivered to Publisher. For purposes of computing the number of Complete Compositions delivered to Publisher a Composition co-written by Writer with one (1) additional writer shall count as 1/2 of a Complete Composition, a Composition written by Writer with two (2) other writers shall count as 1/3 of a Complete Composition and so on unless a different copyright allocation is agreed to in writing amongst the co-writers.

(b) Writer hereby grants to Publisher, its successors and assigns:

(i) one (1) irrevocable and exclusive options to renew and extend the term of this Agreement for successive periods of one (1) year on all the same terms and conditions applicable to the initial period, except as otherwise provided herein, each period to commence automatically upon the expiration of the preceding initial or option period, and the related option shall be deemed exercised by Publisher, unless, not later than the 10th day before the end of the preceding period, Publisher shall sends Writer a written notice terminating this Agreement at the end of said period.

(ii) The sole and exclusive right and privilege in all media in the Territory to issue and authorize publicity concerning Writer and to use and grant others the right to use Writer' name (including any professional name heretofore or hereafter adopted by Writer), (or facsimile thereof), likeness and biographical material concerning Writer for the purpose of exploiting all rights granted to or derived by Publisher hereunder and with respect to publicity and advertising concerning Publisher, its successors and assigns and licensees. It is agreed that after the expiration of the term of this agreement and any extensions thereof, Publisher shall have the non-exclusive right and privilege to continue to use and to grant to use Writer's approved name and likeness, and biographical material concerning Writer on all sheet music, song folios, composite works and other printed uses and Publisher shall have the right to continue to print and vend such song folios, composite works and other printed uses on the same terms and conditions as provided herein.

(iii) The right to make changes, adaptations, dramatizations, new versions, translations, transpositions, editing and arrangements of the Compositions, and the setting of words (or other words) to the music and of music (or other music) to the words (all of which are hereinafter referred to as "New Versions" as Publisher in its reasonable discretion deems desirable from time to time, and with respect to New Versions of a Composition, the right to allocate to the writer and/or composer of New Versions such a share of Writer's royalties as Publisher may deem proper and the right to treat such New Version as a joint work or corporate work as Publisher may in its sole discretion determine. Publisher shall not make any material alterations to the title, music or lyrics of a Composition without Writer's prior consent, not to be unreasonably withheld. Writer hereby waives any claim which they may have under any doctrine of moral right or any similar doctrine existing under the laws of any country or hereafter recognized.

(iv) The sole and exclusive right within the Territory during the terms of this Agreement and any extensions thereof to use as descriptive of Writer the phrase "Exclusive Writer" or other appropriate appellation. Writer will not consent to or permit the use of Writer's name (or any professional name heretofore or hereafter adopted by Writer) in connection with the advertising of any other music publisher, or as the author and/or composer of any musical composition of which Writer is not the actual author or co-author, or composer or co-composer, unless said composition is published or owned by Publisher. Writer agrees that Writer will not write or compose any musical composition under any name other than Writer's own name, which is the name set forth at the beginning of this Agreement without the prior consent of Publisher. These undertakings are of the essence of this Agreement.

SECTION III

ROYALTIES

3. (a) In consideration of the execution of this Agreement, Publisher shall pay Writer, during the original, renewal and extended terms of copyrights in the Compositions, the following royalties in connection with the exploitation of the Compositions in the Territory:

(i) A royalty of six cents ($.06) per copy of regular piano copies sold and paid for (and not returned) in the U.S.A. and fifty percent (50%) of all net sums paid to and received by Publisher for regular piano copies for the rest of the Territory.

(ii) A royalty of five percent (5%) percent of the wholesale selling price per copy of dance orchestrations or other group arrangements in any form, paid for (and not returned) in the U.S.A. and fifty (50%) percent of all net sums paid to and received by Publisher for dance orchestrations or other group arrangements sold and paid for in the rest of the Territory.

(iii) A royalty of five (5%) percent of the net wholesale selling price received by Publisher within the Territory on (i) any and all folios and composite works containing words and music and consisting entirely of the Compositions, and (ii) any printed uses of Compositions (or any part thereof) for which a royalty is not otherwise specifically designated in this Agreement (hereinafter referred to as "other printed uses"). If any such folio, composite work or other printed use contains Compositions together with compositions written by other writers and composers, then and in that event the royalty payable to Writer hereunder with respect to such folio, composite work or other printed use shall be prorated in direct ratio as the number of

TONY ROSE

Compositions published therein bears to the total number of all compositions published therein; provided that Publisher shall have the discretion as to whether or not to allocate a pro-rata share of such royalty with respect to arrangements of compositions in the public domain of the Territory (and as to whether or not to include such arrangements for the purpose of computing the pro-rata share of such royalty applicable to Compositions).

(iv) If and when a Composition is published in lyric form only as part of a folio, composite work, or lyric magazine, Writer shall be entitled to a single payment of fifty (50%) percent of any monies actually credited to or paid to Publisher but not less than ten dollars ($10.00) in respect to such publication in the U.S.A. and five dollars ($5.00) in respect to such publication in the rest of the Territory with the understanding that the aforementioned payments shall be made only if Publisher is paid or credited therefore.

(v) A royalty of fifty (50%) percent of all net sums received and actually retained by or credited to Publisher under any license issued by Publisher authorizing (i) seventy-five (75%) percent with respect to the manufacture of phonograph records and other parts of instruments serving to reproduce the Compositions mechanically and (ii) seventy (70%) percent with respect to the use of the Compositions in synchronization with sound motion pictures and television tapes and films.

(vi) A royalty of fifty (50%) percent of all net sums paid to and received by Publisher on account of any presently known or future devised use of any Composition that is not specifically stated in this Paragraph 3(a).

(vii) In the event that Publisher, in its sole and absolute discretion, from time to time, permits, licenses or authorizes others in the Territory to exercise all or any part of Publisher's rights in the Compositions, Publisher shall pay Writer the royalties specified in this Paragraph 3, as applicable, or, at Publisher's election, Publisher shall pay Writer fifty (50%) percent of Publisher's net receipts with respect to such usages of the Compositions. If Publisher authorizes the exercise of such rights by sub-publisher, either directly or indirectly (whether or not Publisher has an ownership interest in such sub-Publisher), Publisher shall in any event be obligated to pay Writer no more than fifty (50%) percent of the net sums actually received by Publisher from any such sub-Publisher with respect to usage of the Composition, less any collection fees retained by organizations or societies not controlled by such sub-publisher. Sub publisher's administration fees shall not exceed twenty (20%) percent.

(b) Publisher shall retain any and all sums received by Publisher from any performing rights organization and Writer shall retain any sums which Writer receives from any performing rights organization, and neither party shall be obligated to the other for such receipts. Writer hereby acknowledges that they are affiliated with _NAME_____.

(c) Publisher shall not be required to pay any royalties with respect to professional or complimentary material or any copies or mechanical derivatives which are distributed gratuitously to performing artists, orchestra leaders, record producers, disc jockeys or for promotional or advertising purposes or sold at less than fifty (50%) percent of normal wholesale prices (or sold and/or disposed of as remainders).

(d) In all cases the royalties payable pursuant to Paragraph 3(a) shall be computed and paid by Publisher to Writer with respect to uses of Compositions for which Publisher has previously been paid, in each applicable royalty category, after deducting returns, rebates, collection commissions and credits (when applicable), and Publisher shall be entitled to withhold from such payments a reserve for such returns, rebates collection commissions and credits on a pass through basis as withheld from any record companies or other licensees. No separate reserves shall be withheld. Publisher shall have the right to offset any sums which may become payable hereunder against any sums, including advances which have been previously paid to Writer, which may at any time be owed by Writer to Publisher or to any parent, subsidiary or affiliate of Publisher, or to any corporation, joint venture, partnership, association, or sole proprietorship in which a person owning or controlling a substantial proprietary or beneficial interest in such corporation, joint venture, partnership, association or sole proprietorship also owns or controls a substantial proprietary or beneficial interest in Publisher.

(e) Publisher shall not be obligated at any time to maintain a separate account or otherwise to segregate any sums as royalties payable to Writer hereunder. Writer shall have no interest in any specific fund but shall be entitled solely to compensation measured as herein specified.

(f) Publisher makes no representation that there will be any royalties payable to Writer hereunder, and except as expressly provided for otherwise herein and in Paragraph 3(a) above, no royalties or any other sums shall be paid with respect to the Compositions.

(g) Writer shall not be entitled to receive any portion of any amounts received by Publisher as advances in connection with any license or other agreement relating to the exploitation of the Compositions, it being understood that royalties shall be payable to Writer hereunder as actually earned and received by Publisher from the exploitation of the Compositions.

SECTION IV

ACCOUNTING

4. Publisher agrees to render to Writer on or about each October 1st, covering the six (6) months ending the preceding June 30th and each April 1st, covering the six (6) months ending the preceding December 31st, royalty statements showing the amount of royalties due Writer hereunder, accompanied by remittance for any royalties shown to be due Writer by said statement. Any such statement shall be binding upon Writer, unless Writer shall object to it in writing within twenty-four (24) months after it is transmitted to Writer. Writer may select an independent certified public accountant on writer's behalf who may, at Writer's expense, at reasonable intervals, examine Publisher's books pertaining to royalties' payable hereunder, during Publisher's normal business hours and upon reasonable written notice. Publisher's books relating to such activities during any accounting period may only be examined as aforesaid during the twenty-four (24) month period following service by Publisher of the statement for said accounting period, and only once for each accounting rendered hereunder. Publisher shall have the right, in its sole discretion, by giving Writer written notice, to change Publisher's accounting periods from time to time during the term of this Agreement, and in the event of any such changes, Publisher will provide Writer with at least two (2) semi-annual statements per year for the changed accounting periods. Any suit by Writer or on writer's behalf with respect to a particular accounting statement shall be forever barred if not commenced within two (2) years from the date such statement is rendered.

SECTION V

COLLABORATION

5. Prior to collaborating with any other author(s) and/or composer(s) (herein called "Collaborator(s)"), Writer agrees to obtain Publisher's written permission which shall not be unreasonably withheld. If Publisher grants such permission, prior to any collaboration (i) Writer must agree to advise Collaborator(s) that Writer are under exclusive agreement to Publisher, and (ii) Writer and Collaborator(s) must agree to share their interest in the Composition in the same proportion which Writer and Writer's Collaborator(s) notify Publisher. However, in the event of any dispute, Publisher shall have the right to hold said royalties until Publisher has received a full written release, reasonably satisfactory to Publisher, from Writer and Collaborator(s) as to the allocation of such royalties.

SECTION VI

DEMONSTRATION RECORDS

6. With respect to any demonstration records which Publisher elects to make of the Compositions, Publisher shall advance the costs thereof, but one-half (1/2) of such costs shall be deemed a general advance to be recouped by Publisher from any royalties theretofore or thereafter payable to Writer by Publisher.

SECTION VII

POWER OF ATTORNEY

7. Writer hereby irrevocably constitutes and appoints the Publisher, or any its officers, directors, general manager or licensees, Writer's attorney and representative, in the names of the Writer and/or in the name of Publisher, its successors and assigns to make, sign, execute, acknowledge and deliver any and all instruments which Publisher may at any time deem desirable or necessary to vest in Publisher any or all of the rights granted hereunder, Writer shall promptly cause to be executed and delivered to Publisher such documents as Publisher may reasonably require to effectuate the purposes of this Agreement.

SECTION VIII

ADVANCES

8. See Schedule annexed hereto

SECTION IX

WARRANTIES AND REPRESENTATIONS

9. (a) Writer hereby acknowledge the representation and warranty set forth in Schedule "A" and Writer further represents and warrants that: Writer have the full right and power to make this Agreement; that the Compositions are and shall be Writer's sole, exclusive and original works; that the Compositions are not taken from any other source (except the public domain of the Territory); that the Compositions have not been previously published and do not infringe on any other works; that there does not exist and shall not exist any adverse claim in or to the Compositions; that the exercise by Publisher of any or all rights acquired by it hereunder will not infringe or invade the personal and/or property rights of any person, firm or corporation; and that Writer have not made and will not make or enter into any undertaking or agreement which will interfere with Writer's full performance of his obligations hereunder or with Publisher's full enjoyment of the rights granted or agreed to be granted to it hereunder.

(b) Publisher will use its reasonable efforts to assist the Writer in soliciting and securing an exclusive recording agreement for Writers' recording and performing services with a major U.S. record company or a substantial U.S. independent record company.

SECTION X

INDEMNITY

10. Each party hereto hereby agrees to indemnify, save, defend and hold harmless the other party, its officers, stockholders, directors, agents, employees, licensees, assignees and transferees from any and all loss, claims, actions, suits and demands (including all costs, fees, attorney's fees and expenses relating to the defense, settlement or other disposition thereof) arising out of or connected with any matter or thing which if true could constitute a breach of any of such party's warranties or representations made in any part of this Agreement.

HOW TO BE A MUSIC PUBLISHER

SECTION XI

CLAIMS BY AND AGAINST PUBLISHER

11. (a) If Publisher shall elect to bring any legal action against any alleged infringer of any Composition, such action shall be initiated and prosecuted at Publisher's sole expense. Any such action may be discontinued at any time at Publisher's election. If there is any recovery in such action, Publisher shall deduct therefrom and retain all costs and expenses (including reasonable attorney's fees) of such litigation and pay Writer (or, if applicable, Writer and Writer's Collaborators jointly) a sum equal to fifty (50%) percent of the balance of such recovery, if any, when and if received by Publisher.

(b) If a claim or action is presented against Publisher with respect to any Composition (including but not limited to claims and/or actions brought by Writer's Collaborator(s) and/or persons claiming to be Writer's Collaborator(s)), it shall thereupon serve notice upon Writer, containing the full details of such claim or action known to Publisher, and thereafter until such claim or action has been adjudicated or settled, Publisher shall hold all monies becoming due to Writer under this Agreement, or any other agreement between Writer and Publisher or any parent, subsidiary or affiliate or Publisher, or any sole proprietorship in which a person owning or controlling a substantial proprietary or beneficial interest in Publisher owns or controls a substantial proprietary or beneficial interest, in an amount reasonably related to the amount of any such claims, pending the outcome of such claim or action, provided in the event a formal legal action is not commenced within 12 months after the date of the initial claim, any withheld sums shall be released. Publisher shall have the right to settle or otherwise dispose of such claim or action in any manner it may determine in its sole discretion. If there is a recovery against Publisher, either by way of judgment or settlement, all of the costs, expenses, charges, disbursements, attorneys' fees and the amount of the judgment or settlement may be deducted by Publisher from the amount so held or from any and all royalties or other sums theretofore and thereafter payable to Writer by Publisher or by any of its parent, associated, affiliated or subsidiary corporations, whether under this or any other past, current or future agreement. If at any time after an action is instituted against Publisher, Writer shall elect to file a bond, the terms of which are acceptable to Publisher, then the amounts held by Publisher and all sums thereafter becoming due to Writer from Publisher or any parent, subsidiary or affiliate of Publisher, or any corporation, joint venture, partnership, association, or sole proprietorship] in which a person owing or controlling a substantial proprietary or beneficial interest in Publisher owns or controls a substantial proprietary or beneficial interest, shall be paid to be in an amount which exceeds a reasonable estimate of the amount of the possible recovery, plus costs, expenses, charges, disbursements and attorneys' fees.

SECTION XII

REMEDIES

12. Writer expressly acknowledges that Writer's services and all rights assigned by Writer hereunder are of a special, unique, extraordinary and intellectual character which gives them a peculiar value, which value cannot be calculated or money compensation for their loss determined, and that in the event of a breach by Writer of any term, condition, or covenant hereof Publisher may be caused irreparable injury. Writer expressly agrees that in the event Writer shall breach any provision of this Agreement, Publisher shall be entitled to seek injunctive and other equitable relief and/or damages, in addition to any other rights or remedies available to Publisher, and Publisher shall have the right to recoup any damages as determined by a final non-appealable judgment of a court of competent jurisdiction from any sums which may thereafter become due and payable to Writer after the expiration or termination of this Agreement.

13. No failure by Publisher to perform any of its obligations under this Agreement shall be deemed a breach of this Agreement until Writer has given Publisher written notice of Publisher's failure to perform and such failure has not been corrected within forty-five (45) days from and after the giving of such notice. In the event such failure is a material breach and has not been corrected within said forty-five (45) days, Writer may, terminate this Agreement by notice in writing given to Publisher only within forty-five (45) days from the date of service of Writer's original notice. Any termination of this Agreement shall not diminish or impair any rights granted by Writer to Publisher hereunder, or the ownership by Publisher of the results, proceeds and benefits of all services rendered by Writer hereunder prior to such termination. In the event this Agreement is terminated by Writer for Publisher's failure to pay royalties hereunder, Writer's sole remedy shall be an action at law for the sum of royalties due Writer, if any.

14. (a) Publisher reserves the right at its election to suspend the operation of this Agreement if Writer refuses or is unavailable to perform hereunder. Upon written notice to Writer such suspension shall last for the duration of any such refusal or unavailability. At Publisher's election, a period of time equal to the duration of such suspension shall be added to the end of the then current term or option period. Such term or option period shall be accordingly extended and specific dates, periods and time requirements referred to herein shall be postponed or extended. However, in no event shall the term of this Agreement, including any suspensions, be greater than seven (7) years.

(b) Publisher shall be relieved of the obligation to make payments or accountings hereunder if a court of law determines that Writer commits a breach of any material provision of this Agreement. All Publisher's rights and remedies pursuant to this Agreement shall be cumulative and Publisher's exercise of its rights of any one provision, or its rights at law shall not be deemed an election of remedies. The waiver of or Publisher's failure to exercise the same right or remedy shall not be deemed to be a waiver of Publisher's right to exercise any other right or remedy hereunder or to exercise the same right or remedy at a subsequent date.

(c) If Writer becomes mentally or physically incapacitated, or if he should fail, refuse or neglect to perform services required of them hereunder, Publisher shall be relieved of any obligation to make further advance payments pursuant to this Agreement.

MISCELLANEOUS

15. Nothing contained in this Agreement shall obligate Publisher to print or publish copies of the Compositions or to take any particular steps to exploit its rights. Publisher shall have the right in its sole and absolute discretion, from time to time, to permit, license or authorize others inside the Territory to exercise all or any part of Publisher's rights in the Compositions in which event Publisher shall elect to pay Writer the royalties specified in Section III herein.

16. Publisher may assign this Agreement or any part thereof, or Publisher's rights in any Composition, in whole or in part, to any person, firm, or corporation, and this Agreement shall inure to the benefit of Publisher, its successors and assigns provided NAME shall remain actively involved in the

discharge of the Publisher's obligations hereunder. Writer's performance under this Agreement is personal and Writer agree not assign, hypothecate or transfer any of Writer's rights under this Agreement and any attempted assignment hypothecation or transfer shall be void however, Writer shall have the right to assign this agreement to a wholly-owned furnishing company subject to a personal guaranty to be executed by each member of Writer. Publisher shall not be obligated to recognize any assignment of any sums due or to become due from Publisher to Writer; however, this agreement shall inure to the benefit of Writer's heirs.

17. All notices which Publisher shall desire to give to Writer hereunder shall be addressed to Writer at the address set forth on Page 1 hereof, until Writer shall give Publisher written notice of a new address. All statements, royalties and other payments which are due to Writer hereunder shall either (i) be addressed to Writer at the address set forth on Page 1 hereof until Writer shall give Publisher written notice of a new address, (ii) be delivered personally by Publisher to Writer, or (iii) be available at company's offices for Writer. All notices which Writer shall desire to give to Publisher hereunder shall be addressed to Publisher at the address set forth above to the attention of NAME until Publisher shall give Writer written notice of a new address. A copy of all notices sent to Publisher shall be sent simultaneously to NAME. A copy of all notices to Writer shall be sent to NAME. All notices shall be in writing and shall either be delivered personally (to an officer if the party is a company), or by registered or certified mail or telegraph, all charges prepaid. The date of making personal service, or mailing, or deposit in a telegraph office, whichever shall be first, shall be deemed the date of the service except for change of address which shall only be deemed effective when notice of such is actually received by an officer of the other party.

18. This Agreement sets forth the entire agreement between Publisher and Writer with respect to the subject matter hereof. Writer acknowledges that Writer has not executed this Agreement in reliance on any representation or warranty made by Publisher or any of Publisher's representatives, agents, or employees other than those expressly contained in this Agreement. No warranty by either party other than those expressly set forth in this Agreement shall be implied in the construction of this Agreement. No modification, amendment, waiver, termination or discharge of this Agreement or any provisions hereof shall be binding upon Publisher, unless confirmed by a written instrument signed by a duly authorized officer of Publisher as well as by all members of Writers group. No waiver by Publisher of any provision of

this Agreement or of any default hereunder shall affect Publisher's rights thereafter to enforce such provision or to exercise any right or remedy in the event of any other default, whether or not similar.

19. This Agreement shall not become effective until signed by Writer and Publisher's duly authorized officer. This Agreement shall be deemed to have been made in the State of Arizona and its validity, construction, and effect shall be governed by the laws of the State of Arizona applicable to agreements wholly to be performed therein, and it is agreed that all disputes between Writer and Publisher shall be litigated in the appropriate courts situated in and all process in any action or suit arising under or in connection with this Agreement may be served upon Writer by mail with the same force and effect as if served personally in that place. If any part of this Agreement shall be unenforceable or invalid, it shall not effect the enforceability or validity of the remaining portions of this Agreement. Nothing contained herein shall be construed as placing the parties hereto in the relationships of joint venturers, partners, or in a fiduciary relationship.

20. By the execution of this Agreement, Writer acknowledges, confirms and agrees that nothing contained herein shall be deemed to create a relationship between Publisher and Writer of employer-employee. Writer and Publisher acknowledge that all activities on Writer's part rendered to Publisher pursuant to the terms of this Agreement shall be rendered by Writer solely as an independent contractor and Writer specifically waives any and all rights, claims or interests that Writer might have had or has with respect to unemployment compensation, workman's compensation, or any other claim, right or interest whatsoever that Writer might have been entitled to if Writer were deemed to be an employee of Publisher.

21. Writer acknowledges, confirms and agrees that Writer's execution of this Agreement shall constitute only an offer by Writer to enter into an agreement, which offer shall not become a binding agreement unless and until this Agreement has been fully executed by Publisher and delivered to Writer. Writer further acknowledges and agrees that Writer shall bring no claim whatsoever against Publisher based on the existence of a contract or other matters arising out of the negotiations thereof in the event that Publisher does not for any reason whatsoever execute this Agreement and deliver same to Writer.

IN WITNESS WHEREOF, the parties hereto have caused this Agreement to be signed as of the day and year first above set forth.

MUSIC PUBLISHING

By: _____
        President

ACCEPTED AND AGREED TO:

_____
Soc. Sec. #   Soc. Sec. #

_____
Soc. Sec. #

TONY ROSE

SCHEDULE "A" OF THE EXCLUSIVE SONGWRITER AGREEMENT DATED _____, BY AND BETWEEN _____ MUSIC PUBLISHING and _____ ("WRITER").

Writer hereby represents and warrants that all Compositions written, composed created or conceived by Writer in whole or in part prior to the date hereof, which have previously been acquired or contracted by any other person, firm or corporation (or in any other way encumbered) in whole or in part, are listed below, if any, together with all such encumbrances:

Title of Composition Writer(s) Writer's Share RIDER ATTACHED HERETO AND MADE A PART OF EXCLUSIVE SONGWRITER AGREEMENT DATED _____, BY AND BETWEEN _____ MUSIC PUBLISHING ("PUBLISHER") and _____ ("WRITER").

1. As additional consideration for the execution of this Agreement, the following shall be paid to Writer as advances:

(a) The sum of One Thousand ($1,000) Dollars for each fifty (50%) percent share of the musical composition which is written by Writer hereunder and which is recorded and commercially released in the United States by a major U.S. record company or a substantial established independent record company. Said advance shall be reduced pro rata in the event Writer's share of any particular composition is less than fifty (50%) percent. Payment of each such advance shall be made upon the official commercial "street date" of the recording embodying the subject musical composition.

(b) Promptly following the execution of this Agreement, Publisher shall pay an advance to Writer (collectively) in the amount of Ten Thousand ($10,000) Dollars, payable as follows:

(i) Six Thousand ($6,000) Dollars, payable Two Thousand ($2,000) Dollars to each individual Writer; and

(ii) A "demonstration records" production fund of up to Four Thousand ($4,000) Dollars to be made available for the recording of demos during the initial period. Publisher shall administer the "demo production fund" and shall satisfy production costs upon the presentation of invoices or paid bills.

(c) Publisher shall pay to Writer a bonus advance in the amount of Five Thousand ($5,000) Dollars upon the certification of each Composition as achieving a Top 5 position on Billboard Magazine's R&B singles chart. In the event Writer should own or control less than one hundred (100%) percent of the copyright in and to such Composition, then the bonus advance shall be reduced pro rata in proportion to the share of ownership.

(d) A counsel fee of upon the full execution of this agreement. The Counsel Fee shall be deemed to be a recoupable advance made on behalf of the Writer(s) hereunder.

2. The amounts set forth above shall be deemed to be advances which are recoupable from any sums payable to Writer pursuant to this Agreement or any other agreement between Publisher and Writer or any parent, subsidiary or affiliate or Publisher, or any corporation, joint venture, partnership, association or sole proprietorship in which a person owning or controlling a substantial proprietary or beneficial interest in Publisher also owns or controls a substantial proprietary or beneficial interest in such joint venture partnership, association or sole proprietorship.

ACCEPTED AND AGREED:

MUSIC PUBLISHING

By:_____
Publisher

_____
Writer

TONY ROSE

SHORT FORM COPYRIGHT ASSIGNMENT

IN CONSIDERATION of the sum of one dollar ($1.00) and other good and valuable consideration, receipt of which is hereby acknowledged, the undersigned does hereby sell, assign, transfer and set over unto MUSIC PUBLISHER, its successors and assigns, all of its right, title and interest in and to the copyrights in the following musical compositions which were written by the following indicated persons.

Copyright Office

Title
Writer
Identification No

See Schedule Attached

And all of the right, title and interest of the undersigned, vested and contingent, in and to the full term of copyright therein and thereto.

    IN WITNESS WHEREOF, the undersigned has hereunto set his hand and seal this day of _____, 20____.

_____
Writer

FOUR

HOW TO BE A PERSONAL MANAGER

WHAT IS A PERSONAL MANAGER

In the life and career of any entertainer, the personal manager is the most important member of the artist's machine. The lines between personal manager, business manager, and talent agent can be vague and blurry, but this person has the greatest impact on every professional decision made within the client's career.

Duties

To better understand what a personal manager does, it is important to understand the structure of the mechanism that runs a celebrity's career. Of course, the client is the talent in the operation and earns the income that supports the entourage. The talent agent is hired to book jobs for the artist; the business manager advises the client on financial matters and contract negotiations; the publicist hustles the press to keep the good news flowing to the public, while running damage control against the bad news. Finally, there is the personal manager, which is the least defined role. In many cases, he or she will take on tasks of all of the abovementioned roles by booking gigs with event promoters, making contacts with entertainment journalists, and playing hardball with a brand manager over endorsement deals.

The personal manager is an adviser that guides the client's professional choices. When confronted with multiple offers for competing film projects, the personal manager points the client to the production that is most likely to benefit the actor's career. If a singer is clamoring to work with a particular producer, the personal manager goes to the record label A&R rep and lobbies to make that collaboration happen. When working with a client that has yet to hit celebrity status, the personal manager may front money to the client for necessities like headshots, press kits, instruments, or touring capital. Under such circumstances, this person is investing in the longevity of the artist and will be highly involved in future deals signing with a record label or multi-picture agreement with a production studio.

Skills & Education

A specific college degree is not required for this career, though extensive experience and education in entertainment business is beneficial. Those representing clients within the music industry must be familiar with the process of record labels, recording and producing albums, music publishers, and performing rights organizations. Similarly, representing clients in film and television production or live entertainment requires specific knowledge of production processes and negotiating experience with studios, networks, and event producers. A legal background is not mandatory, but even undergraduate courses in communications law, copyright, and licensing will save you a great deal of grief; the entertainment business is fraught with legal snares.

What to Expect

There tend to be two types of personal managers in the entertainment industry: professionals and friends/relatives. An amateur performer that gets a big break after a chance cattle call audition usually hires a parent or close friend to manage his or her fledgling career, as the artist is certain that a friend or family member has his or her best interest at heart. For some, this wise choice benefits them well into their careers. However, there are countless tales of child stars that have turned on their once-trusted loved ones with court battles ensuing over embezzled funds and broken promises.

Professional personal managers, like agents, scout for talent. These managers visit clubs and musician showcases to find talented artists or attend local plays and festivals for tomorrow's silver screen star. Professionals tend to be less emotionally invested in the client but have a significant economic interest in seeing the client succeed. Just as with an agent, the personal manager usually receives a percentage of the artist's earnings as compensation. Under some circumstances, the manager may negotiate a salary. All agreements require binding contracts.

PERSONAL MANAGEMENT AGREEMENT (1)

The following having been signed by _____ NAME (Artist), and by NAME _____(Manager(s), shall constitute a complete and binding agreement (the "Agreement") between you and Manager(s) with respect to your engagement of Manager(s) as your exclusive personal manager(s). In consideration of the mutual covenants herein the parties agree to the following:

1. Territory

The World

2. Manager's Activities:

(a) Manager(s) shall be your exclusive personal manager(s) throughout the territory and shall confer with you in all matters pertaining to your entertainment career, including, without limitation, recording activities, music publishing, personal appearance, motion pictures and commercial purposes.

(b) You shall immediately advise Manager of all offers of employment, and of all inquiries concerning your career, so that Manager(s) may determine and advise you whether same are compatible with your career.

3. Term:

(a) The terms of this Agreement (the "Term") shall consist of an initial period of three (3) years commencing on the date hereof (the "First Contract Period") plus additional Contract Periods, if any, by which they may be extended by the Manager's exercise of the option granted to Manager(s) in 3 (b) below.

(b) Manager(s) shall have the option to extend the term for a period of Two (2) years. This option shall be agreeable between Artist and Manager(s).

4. Manager's Commission

(a) Manager(s) shall be entitled to receive from you twenty percent (20%) of your Gross Income from your activities in all phases of the entertainment industry, including, without limitation, all recording activities, personal appearances, songwriting, music publishing, television, motion pictures, Internet and commercial uses of your name and likeness, Notwithstanding the foregoing sentence, Gross Income shall not include, and there shall be deducted from notes, the following

(i) all music publishing income actually retained by or payable to third parties including, without limitation, manager-less royalties payable to third party co-writers and publishing company administration fees.

(i) actual recording, production and other recoupable costs of master recordings and audiovisual tracks other than payments maintained by you (e.g., producer fees and animation fees) as a portion of those recordings (provided, however, not more than sixty (60%) percent of any "all-in" proceeding or productions fund payable to you shall be deemed to be non-commissioned costs for purposes of this paragraph 4(a)(b) and fund shall be deemed Gross Income hereunder);

(iii) advances and royalties paid to (A) third party record producers and (B) third party producers and directors of audio-visual works;

(i) invoices derived by any entity in which Manager(s) have a proprietary or income interest (but only to the extent of Manager's interest therein);

(b) Notwithstanding the expiration of the Term, Manager's commission on your Gross Income after the Term which is derived from agreements entered into or services performed during the Term shall continue for an additional period (the "Post Term Period") equal to twice the actual duration of the Term. For illustration purposes only, if the term extends for two (2) years, the Manager's participation in such Gross Income earned by, paid or payable to you after the term shall extend for a Post Term Period equal to six (6) years.

(c) Subject to paragraph 4 (d) of this Agreement, all Gross Income shall be paid directly to and collected by Manager(s) and Manager's Commission shall be payable immediately upon receipt of the Gross Income upon which such Manager's commission is based. In this connection, you shall notify authorities and irrevocably direct any and all Gross Income directly to Manager(s), and Manager(s) are hereby authorized by you to deduct and retain for its own account Manager's Commission (and all reimbursable expenses pursuant to paragraph 6 of this Agreement) directly from your Gross Income prior to remitting the balance to you. Manager(s) will render quarterly accountings and payment hereunder (if any) to you of the remaining balance of your Gross Income. Any and all Gross Income received directly by you shall be delivered by you to Manager(s) within five (5) days following your receipt thereof.

(d) At your own cost and expense, you shall be entitled to retain a business manager provided that (i) such business manager is acceptable to manager(s);

5. Manager's Power of Attorney:

In order to effectuate the purpose and provisions of this Agreement, you hereby irrevocably authorize and appoint Manager(s) during the Term, as your true and lawful agent and attorney-in-fact to do for you on your behalf the matters listed in this paragraph 5. You agree that you shall execute any documents as Manager(s) deems necessary to carry out the intent of this Agreement, including without limitation, the power of attorney granted in this paragraph 5. This power of attorney is limited to the right, power and privilege:

(a) to execute for you, in your name, and on your behalf, any and all agreements, documents and contracts for your services, talents, artistic and literary creations; provided, Manager(s) shall obtain your approval beforehand concerning actions taken under paragraph 8(a) of this agreement, except in situations in which (i) decisions must be made and actions taken immediately in order and not to jeopardize a career or business interest of yours; and (ii) you are unavailable for at least forty-eight (48) hours to approve or disapprove the action beforehand, despite Manager's attempts to contact you, with respect to such action. In such situations, Manager(s) shall promptly inform you in writing of actions Management has taken under this paragraph 5;

(b) to approve and permit the use of your names (actual and professional), photographs, likenesses, sound effects, caricatures, and the like for purposes of advertising of any and all products and services and for any other purposes whatsoever; and

(c) To collect and receive all Gross Income payable to you and (with your written approval in each instance) to endorse your name and to deposit all checks payable to you, and to retain all sums owing to Manager hereunder.

6. Management Expenses:

(a) You will reimburse Manager(s) for any and all expenses incurred by Manager(s) on your behalf in connection with activities referred to in paragraph 2 hereof, provided that: (i) you will not be responsible for any portion of manager's overhead expenses; (ii) subject to paragraph 6 (a)(iii) of this Agreement, if Manager(s) incurs travel expenses on behalf of both you and other of Manager's clients, you shall be responsible only for your pro rata share of such expenses; and (iii) Manager(s) shall not incur without your prior consent (A) any single expense in excess of five Hundred ($500.00) Dollars or (B) aggregate monthly expenses in excess of Three Thousand ($3,000.00) Dollars.

(b) Manager(s) shall furnish you (or Business Manager) with appropriate documentation of Manager's expenses and reimbursement of such expenses shall be made in connection with the monthly accountings referred to in paragraph 4(c) of this Agreement.

7. Accounting and Audit Rights:

Upon written notice from you, we shall furnish an accounting to you of all transactions between us since the last such accounting, within thirty (30) days of such request. You shall have the right to reasonable inspection of our books and records in order to verify the accuracy of such accountings.

8. Warranties and Representation:

(a) You warrant, represent and agree that:

i. You are not under any disability, restriction or probation, either contractual or otherwise, with respect to your right to execute this agreement or to fully perform its terms and conditions; and

ii. You have the full right, power and authority to use the NAME and to do business there under, and Manager's activities on your behalf under this agreement will not infringe upon, violate or interfere with the rights, whether statutory, or otherwise, of any one or more third parties.

(b) Manager(s) warrant, represent and agree that Manager(s) are not under any disability, restriction or prohibition, either contractual or otherwise, with respect to Manager's right to execute this agreement or to fully perform its terms and conditions.

9. Indemnities:

You and Manager(s) agree to and do hereby indemnify, save and hold the other harmless from all loss, damage and expenses (including reasonable attorneys' fees) arising out of or connected with any claim by any third party which shall be inconsistent with any agreement, warranty or representation made by you or Manager in this Agreement; provided same is reduced to final adverse judgement or settled with the prior written consent of the indemnifying party. You and Manager(s) agree to reimburse the other, on demand, for any payment made at any time after the date hereof with respect to any liability to which the foregoing indemnity applies.

10. Cure:

In order to make specific and definite and/or eliminate, if possible, any controversy which may arise between us hereunder, you and Manager(s) agree that if at any time you or Manager(s), as applicable, believes that the terms of this Agreement are not being fully performed hereunder, you or manager, as applicable, will so advise the other in writing by registered or certified mail, return receipt requested, of the specific nature of any claim, non-performance or miscellaneous, and the party receiving such notice shall have a period of thirty (30) days after receipt thereof within which to cure such claimed breach.

11. Notions:

All notions pursuant to this Agreement shall be in writing and shall be given by registered or certified mail; return receipt requested or telegraph (prepaid) at the respective address herein above set forth or such other address or addresses as may be designed by either party. Such notice shall be deemed given when mailed or delivered to a telegraph office, except that a notice of change of address shall be effective only from the date of the receipt.

12. Artist's Escape Clause:

(a) Notwithstanding anything to this Agreement to the contrary, you shall have the right to terminate this Agreement. If, within two (2) years following the date of this Agreement (as first written above), you (Artist) have not received a binding commitment for the recording of a new photograph record album or single embodying your recorded and/or written performances and/or lyrics as the featured artist and/or songwriter.

(b) If upon the aspiration of the foregoing two (2) year period substantial negotiations for a recording agreement as contemplated hereunder have commenced, then the Term shall be extended for an additional period of six months.

13. Independent Consent

(a) You expressly acknowledge that you have independently evaluated the terms and conditions contained herein and have been advised by Manager(s) to seek independent legal counsel to connection herewith.

(b) You hereby waive any claim against Manager(s) based upon failure to be represented by legal counsel.

14. Miscellaneous:

(a) This Agreement contains the entire understanding of the parties relating to the subject matter hereof, and cannot be terminated except by a written instrument signed by Company and You,

(b) No breach of this Agreement on the part of company or Artist shall be deemed material, unless the party alleging such breach shall have given the other party notice of such breach, and the other party receiving such notice shall have failed to cure such breach within thirty (30) days following receipt of such notice.

(c) The validity, interpretation and legal effects of this Agreement shall be governed by the laws of the State (STATE) applicable to omissions to be fully performed therein with support to any claims, dispute or disagreement which may arise out of the interpretation, performance or breach of this agreement.

(d) If any part of this Agreement shall be determined to be invalid or unforeseeable by a court of competent jurisdiction, the remainder of this Agreement shall be in full force and effect.

(e) In reading into this Agreement and in providing services pursuant hereto, you have the status of an independent contractor, and nothing herein contained shall contemplate or constitute you as Manager's agent or employee.

BY_____
         (Manager)

CONSENTED and AGREED TO THIS ____DAY OF _____ IN 20_____.

_____
(Artist)

_____
SS#

TONY ROSE

PERSONAL MANAGEMENT CONTRACT (2)

I desire to obtain your advice, counsel and direction in the development and enhancement of my artistic and theatrical career. The nature and extent of the success or failure of my career cannot be predetermined and it is therefore my desire that your compensation be determined in such manner as will permit you to accept the risk of failure and likewise benefit to the extent of my success.

In view of the foregoing we have agreed as follows:

I do hereby engage you as my personal manager for a period of _____ years from date. As and when requested by me during and throughout the term hereof you agree to perform for me one or more of the services as follows: advice and counsel in the selection of literary, artistic and musical material; advice and counsel in any and all matters pertaining to publicity, public relations and advertising; advice and counsel with relation to the adoption of proper format for presentation of my artistic talents and in the determination of proper style, mood, setting, business and characterization in keeping with my talents; advice, counsel and direction in the selection of artistic talent to assist, accompany or embellish my artistic presentation; advice and counsel with regard to general practices in the entertainment and amusement industries and with respect to such matters of which you may have knowledge concerning compensation and privileges extended for similar artistic values; advice and counsel concerning the selection of theatrical agencies and persons, firms and corporations to counsel, advise, seek and procure employment and engagements for me.

You are authorized and empowered for me and in my behalf and your discretion to do the following: approve and permit any and all publicity and advertising; approve and permit the use of my name, photograph, likeness, voice, sound effects, caricatures, literary artistic and musical materials for purposes of advertising and publicity and in the promotion and advertising of any and all products and services; execute for me in my name and/or in my behalf any and all agreements, documents and contracts for my services, talents and/or artistic literary and musical materials, collect and receive sums as well as endorse my name upon and cash any and all checks payable to me for my services, talents and literary and artistic materials and retain therefrom all sums owing to you; engage, as well as discharge and/or direct for me, and in my name theatrical agents and employment agencies as well as other persons, firms and corporations who may be retained to obtain contracts, engagements or employment for me. The authority herein granted to you is coupled with an interest and shall be irrevocable during the term hereof.

    I agree to at all times devote myself to my career and to do all things necessary and desirable to promote my career and earnings therefrom. I shall at all times engage proper theatrical agencies to obtain engagements and employment for me and I agree that I shall not engage any theatrical or employment agency of which you may disapprove. It is clearly understood that you are not an employment agent or theatrical agent, that you have not offered or attempted or promised to obtain employment or engagements for me that you are not obligated, authorized or expected to do so.

    This Agreement shall not be construed to create a partnership between us. It is specifically understood that you are acting hereunder as an independent contractor and you may appoint or engage any and all other persons, firms and corporations throughout the world in your discretion to perform any or all of the services which you have agreed to perform hereunder. Your services hereunder are not exclusive and you shall at all times be free to perform the same or similar services for others as well as engage in any and all other business activities. You shall only be required to render reasonable services as and when reasonably requested by me. Due to the difficulty which we may have in determining the amount of services to which I may be entitled, it is agreed that you shall not be deemed to be in default hereunder until and unless I shall first deliver to you a written notice describing the exact service which I require on your part and then only in the event that you shall thereafter fail for a period of fifteen consecutive days to commence the rendition of the particular service required. You shall not be required to travel or to meet with me at any particular place or places except in your discretion and following arrangements for costs and expenses of such travel.

    In compensation for your services I agree to pay to you, as and when received by me, and during and throughout the term hereof, a sum equal to percent of any and all compensation, sums and other things of value which I may receive as a result of my activities in and throughout the entertainment, amusement, musical recording and publishing industries, including any and all sums resulting from the use of my artistic talents and the results and proceeds thereof and, without in any manner limiting the foregoing, the matters upon which your compensation shall be computed shall include any and all of my activities in connection with matters as follows: motion pictures, television, radio, music, literary, theatrical engagements, personal appearances, public appearances, in places of amusement and entertainment, records and recordings, publications, and the use of my name, likeness and talents for purposes of advertising and trade. I likewise agree to pay you a similar sum following the expiration of the term hereof upon and with respect to any and all engagements, contracts and agreements entered into during the term hereof relating to any of the foregoing, and upon any and all extensions, renewals and substitutions thereof.

In the event of any dispute under or relating to the terms of this agreement it is agreed that the same shall be submitted to arbitration to the American Arbitration Association in (Insert New York City or Los Angeles) and in accordance with the rules promulgated by the said association. In the event of litigation or arbitration the prevailing party shall be entitled to recover any and all reasonable attorney's fees and other costs incurred in the enforcement of the terms of this agreement.

This agreement shall be deemed to be executed in the State of _____ and shall be construed in accordance with the laws of said State. In the event any provision hereof shall for any reason be illegal or unenforceable then, and in any such event, the same shall not affect the validity of the remaining portions and provisions hereof.

This agreement is the only agreement of the parties and there is no other or collateral agreement (oral or written) between the parties in any manner relating to the subject matter hereof.

If the foregoing meets with your approval, please indicate your acceptance and agreement by signing in the space herein below provided.

Very truly yours, (Artist)_____

I DO HEREBY AGREE TO THE FOREGOING

Manager

HOW TO BE A PERSONAL MANAGER

NON-DISCLOSURE / NON-COMPETE AGREEMENT

This Agreement is made as of the DATE day of MONTH AND YEAR by and between NAME, COMPANY, LOCATION and NAME, COMPANY, LOCATION.

This Agreement shall govern the conditions of disclosure by NAME to NAME or their assigns, of certain Confidential Information including but not limited to the Manuscript tentatively titled (NAME) and any prototypes, drawings, data, photos, text, trade, trade secrets and intellectual property relating to their development, production or prospective or actual commercial exploitation ("Confidential Information").

1. NAME hereby agree not to use the Confidential Information in any form and in any way except for evaluating his own interest. Further, NAME, agrees to safeguard the Confidential Information against disclosure to others with at least the same degree of extreme care as exercised with his own clients when acting in a fiduciary capacity.

2. NAME agree not to disclose the Confidential information to others without the express written permission of NAME, and to use the Confidential Information only for the purpose for which it was disclosed and not use or exploit the Confidential Information for his own benefit or the benefit of another without the prior written consent of NAME.

3. NAME agree that neither he nor his employees, agents, assigns, partnerships, corporations, assigns or heirs shall directly or indirectly acquire any interest in, or design, create, produce or manufacture, sell or otherwise deal with any book, magazine, newspaper, script, screenplay, television, film, video, Internet, or other creative property, foreign or domestic, containing, based upon, or derived from the Confidential Information in any form or in any way, except as may be expressly agreed to in writing by NAME .

4. That the confidentiality obligations of NAME, their employees, agents, assigns, partnerships, corporations, assigns and heirs with respect to the Confidential Information shall continue for a period ending no less than 20 years from the date hereof.

TONY ROSE

IN WITNESS WHEREOF, The parties have hereunto executed the Agreement as of the day and year first above written.

_____
NAME   Date

_____
NAME   Date

CONFIDENTIALITY AGREEMENT

This AGREEMENT (hereinafter referred to as the "Agreement") is made effective this _____ day of _____, 200__ by and between _____ (hereinafter referred to as the "Owner") and _____, located at _____ (hereinafter referred to as the "Recipient").

WITNESSETH:

In consideration of the respective covenants contained herein, the parties hereto, intending to legally bound hereby, agree as follows:

1. Confidential Information. Owner proposes to disclose certain of its confidential and proprietary information (the "Confidential Information") to Recipient. Confidential Information shall include all data, materials, products, technology, computer programs, specifications, manuals, business plans, software, marketing plans, business plans, financial information, and other information disclosed or submitted, orally, in writing, or by any other media, to Recipient by Owner. Confidential Information disclosed orally shall be identified as such within five (5) days of disclosure. Nothing herein shall require Owner to disclose any of its information.

2. Recipient's Obligations.
A. Recipient agrees that the Confidential Information is to be considered confidential and proprietary to Owner and Recipient shall hold the same in confidence, shall not use the Confidential Information other than for the purposes of its business with Owner, and shall disclose it only to its officers, directors, or employees with a specific need to know. Recipient will not disclose, publish or otherwise reveal any of the Confidential Information received from Owner to any other party whatsoever except with the specific prior written authorization of Owner.

B. Confidential Information furnished in tangible form shall not be duplicated by Recipient except for purposes of this Agreement. Upon the request of Owner, Recipient shall return all Confidential Information received in written or tangible form, including copies, or reproductions or other media containing such Confidential Information, within ten (10) days of such request. At Recipient's option, any documents or other media developed by the Recipient containing Confidential Information may be destroyed by Recipient. Recipient shall provide a written certificate to Owner regarding destruction within ten (10) days thereafter.

3. Term. The obligations of Recipient herein shall be effective [Non-Disclosure Period] from the date Owner last discloses any Confidential Information to Recipient pursuant to this Agreement. Further, the obligation not to disclose shall not be affected by bankruptcy, receivership, assignment, attachment or seizure procedures, whether initiated by or against Recipient, nor by the rejection of any agreement between Owner and Recipient, by a trustee of Recipient in bankruptcy, or by the Recipient as a debtor-in-possession or the equivalent of any of the foregoing under local law.

4. Other Information. Recipient shall have no obligation under this Agreement with respect to Confidential Information which is or becomes publicly available without breach of this Agreement by Recipient; is rightfully received by Recipient without obligations of confidentiality; or is developed by Recipient without breach of this Agreement; provided, however, such Confidential Information shall not be disclosed until thirty (30) days after written notice of intent to disclose is given to Owner along with the asserted grounds for disclosure.

5. No License. Nothing contained herein shall be construed as granting or conferring any rights by license or otherwise in any Confidential Information. It is understood and agreed that neither party solicits any change in the organization, business practice, service or products of the other party, and that the disclosure of Confidential Information shall not be construed as evidencing any intent by a party to purchase any products or services of the other party nor as an encouragement to expend funds in development or research efforts. Confidential Information may pertain to prospective or unannounced products. Recipient agrees not to use any Confidential Information as a basis upon which to develop or have a third party develop a competing or similar product.

6. No Publicity. Recipient agrees not to disclose its participation in this undertaking, the existence or terms and conditions of the Agreement, or the fact that discussions are being held with Owner.

7. Governing Law and Equitable Relief. This Agreement shall be governed and construed in accordance with the laws of the United States and the State of [State of Governing Law] and Recipient consents to the exclusive jurisdiction of the state courts and U.S. federal courts located there for any dispute arising out of this Agreement. Recipient agrees that in the event of any breach or threatened breach by Recipient, Owner may obtain, in addition to any other legal remedies which may be available, such equitable relief as may be necessary to protect Owner against any such breach or threatened breach.

8. Final Agreement. This Agreement terminates and supersedes all prior understandings or agreements on the subject matter hereof. This Agreement may be modified only by a further writing that is duly executed by both parties.

9. No Assignment. Recipient may not assign this Agreement or any interest herein without Owner's express prior written consent.

10. Severability. If any term of this Agreement is held by a court of competent jurisdiction to be invalid or unenforceable, then this Agreement, including all of the remaining terms, will remain in full force and effect as if such invalid or unenforceable term had never been included.

11. Notices. Any notice required by this Agreement or given in connection with it, shall be in writing and shall be given to the appropriate party by personal delivery or by certified mail, postage prepaid, or recognized overnight delivery services.

12. No Implied Waiver. Either party's failure to insist in any one or more instances upon strict performance by the other party of any of the terms of this Agreement shall not be construed as a waiver of any continuing or subsequent failure to perform or delay in performance of any term hereof.

13. Headings. Headings used in this Agreement are provided for convenience only and shall not be used to construe meaning or intent.

TONY ROSE

IN WITNESS WHEREOF, the parties hereto have executed this Agreement on the day and year first above written.

AGREED TO AND ACCEPTED:

BY:
"OWNER"

_____
(an authorized signatory)

BY:
"RECIPIENT"

_____
(an authorized signatory)

LIFE STORY RIGHTS ACQUISITION AGREEMENT

This Agreement (the "Agreement") April 1, 201 memorializes the acquisition by   , located at   ("Producer"), of the life story rights of   , an individual residing at   ("Grantor").

WHEREAS, Producer wishes to produce and distribute a feature-film and related productions, which recount actual events and/or fictionalize material regarding   ; and

WHEREAS, Grantor wishes to grant exclusively to Producer all rights, title, authority and permission to produce and distribute a film based on the life of............ and related productions;

NOW THEREFORE, in consideration of the promises, representations, warranties, covenants, conditions and other obligations herein, the receipt and sufficiency of which consideration is hereby acknowledged, the parties hereto agree as follows:

I ACQUISITION OF RIGHTS

A. Irrevocable Grant and Acquisition; the Acquired Rights. Grantor hereby irrevocably grants, assigns, conveys and transfers to Producer, and Producer hereby acquires the Grantor's Life Story Rights as defined in paragraph C of this Part I, for Producer's use in the Productions, as defined in paragraph B of this Part I. The grant of Life Story Rights made hereby shall include the full and exclusive rights, title, property, privileges, covenants, authority and permission to use such rights in and in connection with the Productions and the Distribution and Exploitation Rights, as defined in paragraph B of this Part I (the Life Story Rights and the Distribution and Exploitation Rights, collectively, identified herein as the "Acquired Rights").

B. The Productions; Distribution and Exploitation Rights. The Life Story Rights may be used perpetually and exclusively in and in connection with: (1) motion pictures (whether intended for theatrical exhibition, videogram distribution, television broadcast or otherwise, and including without limitation, all prequels, sequels and remakes), television productions (including without limitation series, MOW's, and miniseries, and whether live, taped or filmed), videogram (DVD, videocassette, video disc, laser disc or other home video format), live dramatic or stage productions, all forms of broadcast (including without limitation radio, cable, internet and satellite), publication (including without limitation, novelizations, transcripts, screenplays, scripts, and teleplays), theme and amusement parks, soundtracks and sound recordings, merchandising, commercial tie-ups and tie-ins, and any and all ancillary and allied media, formats, products, productions and programs of any and every kind, whether now in existence or hereafter devised, and the advertising, marketing, promotion, and publicity in connection with any and all of the foregoing (collectively, the "Productions"); and (2) the transmission, distribution, exhibition, broadcast, and commercial exploitation of any and every kind, now in existence or hereafter devised, including without limitation theatrical distribution and exhibition, television (commercially sponsored, in whole or in part, sustaining and subscription, satellite, cable or cable modem, PPV, VOD, NVOD, or other), videogram (DVD, videocassette, video disc, laser disc or other home video format), all forms of broadcast (radio, cable, internet, satellite and other), all merchandising (including commercial tie-ups and tie-ins), and any other form of commercial exploitation in any medium (the content in this subparagraph (2), collectively, identified herein as the "Distribution and Exploitation Rights" or "DER").

C. Life Story Rights. The Life Story Rights shall include without limitation:

1. the right to use, depict, portray, impersonate and represent, in whole or in part, Grantor's name or any variant, substitute or alternative therefor or thereof, and Grantor's picture, likeness, voice, characterization, personality, personal identification, photograph, portrait or representation or any simulation of any of the foregoing in and in connection with the Productions;

2. the right to use, depict, portray and represent, in whole or in part, Grantor's life and all episodes, exploits, events, incidents, personal experiences, incidents, situations and events which heretofore occurred or hereafter occur, or any simulation of any of the foregoing in and in connection with the Productions;

3. the property and/or personal rights in Grantor's right of publicity and right of privacy insofar as such rights appertain to the any of the rights expressly granted herein, the Productions, and/or the DER; and

4. the right to institute and prosecute, in Producer's sole discretion, any and all actions or proceedings at law or in equity for: the violation of, or impairing or impeding of any of the Acquired Rights, including without limitation, actions for defamation of Grantor and violation of Grantor's rights of publicity or privacy; and the protection of any other of the rights, property, covenants, and privileges herein acquired by Producer.

D. Unconditional, Irrevocable, Exclusive, Perpetual and Universal. The Acquired Rights shall be unconditional, irrevocable, exclusive, and perpetual, and shall subsist worldwide and throughout the universe, as now understood or hereafter discovered.

E. No Reservation of Rights. The grant of the Acquired Rights hereunder shall be complete and without exception, and Grantor reserves none of his Life Story Rights and reserves none of the Distribution and Exploitation Rights.

F. No Representations Regarding Portrayal; Unrestricted Right to Fictionalize; Use of Alternative Name. The Life Story Rights shall include: (a) the right to portray Grantor by live actors, animation, sound recording or any other feasible means by actors, performers, or present or future technology, which actors, animation, sound recording, or feasible means may or may not resemble Grantor; and (b) the right to use historical, factual or fictional scenes, action and dialogue, or any combination of the foregoing. Grantor acknowledges and agrees that Producer: has not made and shall not make any representation or promise regarding the genre, tone, nature, or thematic or narrative content of the Productions, or the manner or light in which Grantor may be portrayed in the Productions; and may add to, subtract from, dramatize, change, interpolate, and adapt Grantor's life story or any part thereof, and may use any actual events or scenarios in conjunction with any other material, or property of any kind in the Productions and in connection with the DER. Grantor acknowledges and agrees that Producer may in its sole discretion refrain from using Grantor's real name, and may use a pseudonym which will be similar or dissimilar to Grantor's real name.

G. No Obligation. Producer shall have no obligation whatsoever: (1) to use any of the Life Story Rights in or in connection with the Productions or the DER; (2) to use Grantor's actual name, voice, likeness or picture. (3) to produce any of the Productions; and/or (4) to distribute, transmit, exhibit, perform or exploit any of the Productions.

H. Public Domain; No Diminishment of Rights. Producer and it successors, assigns and licensees shall retain the same rights, licenses, liberties and privileges as any member of the general public with respect to Grantor's life story and the production, distribution or exploitation of any productions based thereon or related thereto, and neither Producer's entering into this Agreement, nor anything contained herein, nor any consultations or interviews with Grantor or any others in connection with this Agreement shall be construed to be prejudicial to, operate in derogation of, or diminish such rights, licenses, liberties and privileges.

II CONDITIONS PRECEDENT

All of Producer's promises, covenants and other obligations hereunder, are expressly conditioned upon and subject to occurrence of Producer's receipt of fully executed originals or original counterparts of:

A. An agreement between Producer and   regarding Producer's acquisition of   life story rights to the extent such rights relate to Grantor's Life Story Rights.

III REPRESENTATIONS AND WARRANTIES

Grantor represents, warrants and agrees that:

A. Grantor has not previously granted, assigned, licensed, encumbered, sold, transferred or otherwise disposed of any of the Acquired Rights, and in particular and without limiting the generality of the foregoing, Grantor has not written an autobiography and has not authorized any party to write a biography of Grantor;

B. Grantor has the right to grant the Acquired Rights, and possesses the Acquired Rights free and clear of any encumbrance, lien or claim of any third party;

C. Grantor shall not hereafter grant, assign, license, encumber, sell, transfer or otherwise dispose of any or all of the Acquired Rights, and shall not grant, assign, license, encumber, sell, transfer or otherwise dispose of any rights, property, privileges or covenants similar to, competing with, or diminishing the value of any of or any part of the Acquired Rights;

D. Grantor shall neither publicize nor authorize the publicity of the preparation, negotiation, or execution of this Agreement, without the written consent of Producer. Nor shall Grantor publicize or authorize the publicity of the fact that Producer is producing, distributing, or exploiting a film or any of the Productions, without the written consent of Producer.

E. The Interview Content, as defined in this Agreement, to the extent it is characterized as factual, shall be true; and the Interview Content, to the extent it is subject to copyright protection, shall not infringe the copyright of any other person, firm or corporation.

F. Grantor shall abide by and comply full with its indemnification obligations outlined in this Agreement.

IV INDEMNITIES

Grantor shall defend, indemnify, save and hold harmless Producer and its successors, assigns, principals, agents, attorneys, directors, managers, officers and employees from and against any and all damages, charges, costs, expenses (including reasonable attorney's fees), losses, actions, judgments, penalties, recoveries, awards and other losses of any and every kind which may be obtained against, imposed on, or incurred, sustained, or paid by Producer or its successors, assigns, principals, agents, attorneys, directors, managers, officers and employees, which damages, charges, costs, expenses, losses, actions, judgments, penalties, recoveries, awards or other losses arise or result from or in conjunction with, or by reason of, or relate to the breach of any warranty, representation, covenant, agreement, obligation or undertaking of or made by Grantor in this Agreement.

V GRANTOR'S INTERVIEW AND CONSULTATIONS;

A. Interviews. At Producer's request, Grantor agrees to be interviewed by, and consult with Producer and Producer's designated agents or representatives with respect to the Productions at reasonable times and places, subject to Grantor's availability. Grantor shall not give interviews relating to Grantor's life story or the Acquired Rights to any person, firm or corporation, excluding only Producer and its designated agents or representatives. Grantor hereby grants to Producer the sole, exclusive, irrevocable and unconditional right to use any information, episodes, exploits, events, incidents, personal experiences, incidents, situations and events (the "Interview Content") conveyed or disclosed in such interviews in and in connection with the Productions.

B. Consultation Rights. Provided Grantor is not in breach or otherwise in default of this Agreement, and provided Grantor is available to exercise the rights granted under this paragraph at the times and places reasonably required by Producer, Grantor shall have the right to consult with Producer.

VI RELEASE, WAIVERS, AND FURTHER COVENANTS

A. Release. Grantor, for himself and his agents, successors and assigns, and each of them, acting on their behalf, hereby unconditionally releases and forever discharges Producer and its successors, assigns, officers, directors, principals, managers, members, agents, representatives, attorneys, and insurers, and all of their respective predecessors, successors, and assigns, from any and all past, present and future claims, causes of action, suits, demands, debts, losses or damages of any kind, whether based in contract, tort, statutory or other legal or equitable theory of recovery, whether now known or unknown, suspected or unsuspected, existing, claimed to exist or which can hereinafter exist, including without limitation any claims that arise or which could be claimed to arise out of or in connection with, or related in any way to, the Productions and/or Producer's use of the Acquired Rights, or any of them. Without limiting the foregoing, this release is intended to include any and all past, present and future claims, causes of action, suits or demands, based upon any civil rights statute, libel, defamation, invasion of privacy or right of publicity, infringement of copyright or violation of any other right arising out of or relating to any utilization of the Acquired Rights, or based upon any failure of or omission by Producer to make use of any or all of the Acquired Rights.

B. Release of Unknown and Unsuspected Claims; This Agreement also constitutes a complete release of unknown claims. Having read the above with full understanding of its meaning, Grantor makes the following statement and places his initials adjacent to same:

"In full understanding of the above language regarding my complete and absolute release of claims relating to my life story, I have placed my initials here: [GRANTOR'S INITIALS]

C. Further Covenants; Strict Compliance. Grantor further covenants not to sue or bring or join in any type of claim, action, proceeding or investigation against Producer, person or business entity released herein based upon or related to in any way to any matters covered by this

Agreement. Grantor expressly acknowledges that any and all attorneys' fees and other costs and expenses incurred in defending any suit, claim, action, investigation or proceeding brought in breach of this covenant shall constitute part of the measure of damages, pursuant to California Civil Code Section 3300, recoverable for any such breach. The Parties acknowledge and agree that the terms are of the essence of this Agreement, and agree that strict compliance with its terms shall be required.

VII GENERAL PROVISIONS

A. Assignment. The Agreement and all rights herein shall inure to the benefit of Producer's successors, assigns, licensees and grantees and associated, affiliated and subsidiary companies and Producer shall have the right to freely assign the Agreement and/or any of Producer's rights hereunder to any person, firm, corporation, or other entity. Producer shall have the right at any time to sell, transfer or assign all or any of its rights in any or all of the Productions, the physical materials and copyright thereof, and the agreements with Producer's licensees, assignees, sales agents, distributors and sub distributors. Any assignment shall be subject to Grantor's rights hereunder, provided Producer shall only be released and discharged of and from any further liability or obligation hereunder if such Assignee is a major or mini-major studio-distributor. The Agreement is non-assignable by the Grantor.

B. Notices. Notices to Producer must be given in writing, and all written notices to Grantor or to Producer shall be given as set forth in this paragraph. Either Grantor or Producer may hereafter designate a substitute address by written notice to the other. Written notices shall be delivered by registered mail to the address set out below, or transmitted by facsimile (provided there is written confirmation of receipt of such transmission). The date of mailing or transmission of any such notice shall be deemed the date of service thereof.

To Grantor:

To Producer:

C. Action and Settlement of Claims; Appointment of Attorney-in-Fact. Producer's right to institute and prosecute actions or proceedings for the violation or impairment of the Acquired Rights, shall include actions or proceedings at law or in equity for: the violation of, or impairing or impeding any of the Life Story Rights granted and acquired hereunder, including without limitation, actions for defamation of Grantor and violation of Grantor's rights of publicity or privacy; and the protection of any of the rights, property, covenants, and privileges herein acquired. Producer's rights under this paragraph shall be exercised in Producer's sole discretion and under Producer's sole and absolute control, and any such action or proceeding may be asserted, brought, maintained and settled by Producer either in Producer's name or in Grantor's name, in Producer's sole discretion. Grantor agrees to execute any documents and do any acts reasonably required by Producer for the prosecution and enforcement of such actions, proceedings, and resulting judgments, recoveries and awards. Grantor hereby irrevocably appoints Producer his attorney-in-fact to do all acts and to execute all documents which Grantor could lawfully do and execute in prosecuting and enforcing such actions, proceedings, and resulting judgments, recoveries and awards, this power being coupled with an interest and therefore irrevocable. The proceeds of all such judgments, recoveries and awards shall be Producer's sole, absolute and exclusive property, and Grantor shall have no interest therein.

D. Default; Remedies.

1. Grantor's Default. If Grantor breaches any representation, warranty or agreement contained herein, or fails in any material way to perform his obligations hereunder, then Producer may, in addition to any other rights or remedies which it may have at law or in equity, under this Agreement or otherwise, terminate this Agreement in its entirety and thereafter Producer shall be relieved of any obligations to Grantor hereunder.

E. Further Instruments and Documents. Grantor agrees to execute such documents and do such other acts and deeds as may be reasonably required by Producer, its successors, assignees, or licensees to further evidence or effectuate Producer's rights, title, properties or interest hereunder, and hereby irrevocably appoints Producer Grantor's attorney-in-fact for the purposes of execution, acknowledgement, delivery, and recordation of documents evidencing or effecting such rights, this power being coupled with an interest and therefore irrevocable.

F. Relationship of the Parties; No Third-Party Beneficiaries. As between Grantor and Producer, Grantor shall be an independent contractor. Nothing herein creates between Producer and Grantor an employer-employee relationship, joint venture, partnership, agency, or lease agreement, and neither party shall hold itself out contrary to the terms of this paragraph and neither party shall become liable by any representation, act or omission of the other contrary to the terms herein. Producer will not make available to Grantor any employment benefits, and will not withhold any sums for income or other taxes, unemployment insurance, social security or any other withholding relating to the Services, pursuant to any law or requirement of any governmental entity, and Grantor agrees that all such payments, withholdings, and benefits, if any, are the sole responsibility of Grantor.

G. Arbitration. Producer and Grantor agree to have any dispute that arises from or relates to this Agreement, including any and all disputes that relate to the scope and effect of the release, waiver and further covenants, the Productions, the DER, the Acquired Rights, and including but not limited to claims relating to any civil rights statute, libel, defamation, invasion of privacy or right of publicity, or infringement of copyright, decided only by binding arbitration in accordance with the rules of the American Arbitration Association and not by court, commission or administrative action, except as provided by Arizona law for judicial review of arbitration proceedings. Judgment upon an award rendered by the arbitrator(s) may be entered in any court having jurisdiction thereof. Neither party shall have the right of discovery in such arbitration action. Provided, however, that nothing in this paragraph shall require Producer to arbitrate claims against any person, firm, corporation or other entity, excluding only Grantor.

H. Miscellaneous. The Agreement constitutes the entire agreement between the parties with respect to the subject matter hereof, and supersedes any prior oral or written representations with respect thereto, any such representations having been merged herein. Any amendment to the Agreement must be in writing and signed by both parties. No provision of the Agreement may be waived except in writing signed by the party against whom enforcement of the waiver is sought. If any provision contained in this Agreement is found in a court having jurisdiction or any dispute resolution proceeding, including arbitration, to be unenforceable or invalid, such provision shall be unenforceable or invalid only to the extent necessary to bring it within the legal requirements, and all other provisions contained herein shall remain in full force and effect and enforceable according to their terms. Nothing herein shall be construed so as to require the commission of any act contrary to applicable law, and wherever there is any conflict between any provision of this Agreement and applicable law, contrary to which the parties hereto have no legal right to contract, the latter shall prevail, but then any provision of this Agreement so affected shall be limited only to the extent necessary to bring it within the legal requirements, and all other provisions of this Agreement not so contrary shall remain in full force and effect. The Agreement shall be construed and interpreted pursuant to the laws of the State of Arizona applicable to contracts made and fully performed entirely therein, and the parties consent to the jurisdiction of the courts of the State of Arizona, including the federal courts located in Arizona should federal jurisdictional requirements exist, in any action brought to enforce or otherwise relating to this Agreement.

IN WITNESS WHEREOF, THE PARTIES HEREOT HAVE EXECUTED AND DELIVERED THIS AGREEMENT AS OF THE DAY AND YEAR FIRST WRITTEN ABOVE.

PRODUCER　　　　　　**GRANTOR**

By _____　　_____

[Grantor's address]

_____

_____

HOW TO BE A PERSONAL MANAGER

HOW TO BE A FILM PRODUCER

WHAT IS A FILM PRODUCER

Film producers prepare and then supervise the making of a film before presenting the product to a financing entity or a film distributor. Either employed by a production company or independent, they help the creative people as well as the accounting personnel. The average Hollywood film made in 2016 had just over 10 producer credits (3.2 producers, 4.4 executive producers, 1.2 co-producers, 0.8 associate producers and 0.5 other types of producer). During the "discovery stage" the producer has to find and acknowledge promising material. Then, unless the film is supposed to be based on an original script, the producer has to find an appropriate screenwriter. For various reasons, producers cannot always personally supervise all of the production. As such, the main producer will appoint executive producers, line producers or unit production managers who represent the main producer's interests. Among other things, the producer has the last word on whether sounds or music have to be changed or scenes have to be cut and they are in charge of selling the film or arranging distribution rights.

CLARIFICATION OF TERM

Whereas historically in television, the primary role of the producer was to oversee all aspects of video production, in film and often in television today, this role is filled by the Line Producer. The line producer may manage a film's budget and maintain a schedule. The Executive Producer oversees the filmmaking with regard to film financing. They liaise with the line producer and report to production companies and distributors. Whether the person credited as "producer" or a person credited as "executive producer" has more input on a production is not always clear, and is subject to change as the film is substantiated. Since filmmaking is a dynamic process, responsibilities can grow or shift in the process and credits for producers can get adjusted retroactively. For example, somebody hired as "line producer" might later be credited as "executive producer".

HOW TO BE A FILM PRODUCER

Because of these dynamics, all involved producers must agree on production standards from the start. Negligence in that matter can lead to a domino effect. Other producers are more involved with the day-to-day workings, participating in activities such as screenwriting, set design, casting, and even directing. Currently, because of the restrictions the Writers Guild of America screenwriting credit system places on writing credits, many scriptwriters are credited as "producers" instead, even though they may not engage in the responsibilities generally associated with that title. In this limited sense, the producer and the screenwriter may be the same person. Producers differ from Production Management (Production and Unit Managers and Production Coordinators) in part because the responsibilities of Production Management are more logistical than creative.

TYPES OF PRODUCERS

Different types of producers in the industry today include (in order of seniority):

Executive producer
The Executive Producer addresses the finances in that they pitch films to the studios, but upon acceptance they may focus on business matters, such as budgets and contracts.

Co-executive producer
Second in seniority to executive producer.

Line producer
Manages the staff and day-to-day operations. Finds staff to hire for the production. Most line producers are given the title of "produced by".

Supervising producer
Supervises the creative process of screenplay development, and often aids in script re-writes. They usually supervise less experienced story editors and staff writers on the writing team.

Producer
Traditional producers, who are responsible for physical facilities, are given the credit of "produced by". A producer can also be a writer who has

not written enough of the screenplay to receive approval from the Writers Guild of America to be listed as a screenwriter.

Co-producer
A writer who may not have written the script, but contributed significantly through table reads or revisions. Co-producer credits also often require approval from the Writers Guild of America.

Coordinating producer or production coordinator
This producer manages the schedule and arranges the staff into teams.

Consulting producer
These producers are former executive or possibly co-executive producers, or in rare cases directors. They are called upon to assist the writers.

Associate producer
Runs day-to-day operations.

Segment producer
Writes or produces one segment of a film.

Field producer
Selects areas to film (outside of a set) and coordinates production in the field. They also form a trusting relationship with the cast/participants in order to get interviews while in the field. They may fill a number of different roles, including production manager/coordinator, videographer and also Production assistant.

Edit producer
Helps co-ordinate the edit by working with the editor and relaying information from other producers. Involved in creating stories and writing script if necessary.

Post producer
Supervises the overall post-production process, including editing, dubbing and grading. Post-producers are typically employed by facilities houses rather than by production companies directly.

HOW TO BE A FILM PRODUCER

In film or video productions, the executive producer is almost always given an opportunity to comment on a rough cut but the amount of attention paid to his/her comments is highly dependent on the overall personnel structure of the production.

RESPONSIBILITIES
Development (film rights)
During the "discovery stage" the producer has to find and acknowledge promising material. Often a producer must then retrieve the film rights or an option. If the rights owner is worried about preserving the integrity, voice and vision of their work, the producer might have to comply with a variety of demands concerning the screenplay, the film director, casting, or other topics. Thus it occasionally takes a lot of time and effort before the actual pre-production can begin.

Pre-production
Unless the film is supposed to be based on an original script, the producer has to find an appropriate screenwriter. If an existing script is considered flawed, they are able to order a new version or make the decision to hire a script doctor. The producer also has the final say on which film director gets hired. In some cases, they also have the last word when it comes to casting questions.

Production
For various reasons, producers cannot always personally supervise all parts of their production. For example, some producers run a company which also deals with film distribution. Also cast and film crew often work at different times and places and certain films even require a second unit. Consequently, it is normal that the main producer will appoint executive producers, line producers or unit production managers who represent the main producer's interests.

Post-production
Among other things, the producer has the last word on whether sounds or music have to be changed or scenes have to be cut. Even if the shooting has officially been finished, the producers can still demand that additional scenes be filmed. In case of a negative test screening producers may even demand and get an alternative film ending. Producers are also in charge of selling the film or arranging distribution rights.

TONY ROSE

Career Process

There are different ways to become a film producer. Some producers start as editors and writers. Other producers started as actors or directors.

Film schools offer degree courses that include film production knowledge. Some courses are especially designed for future film producers, focusing on key topics like pitching, script development, script assessment, shooting schedule design and budgeting. The students can also expect practical training regarding post-production.

The average annual salary for a producer in the U.S. is $109,860. If one examines just the 15,000+ producers in the Los Angeles metropolitan area, the average annual salary is $138,640. Producers also often have an agreement to take a percentage of the movie's sales.

WHAT ARE THE RESPONSIBILITIES OF A MOVIE PRODUCER

Movie producers can do everything from finding the idea and developing the script to working with the studio to market and distribute the film -- all to create the highest quality movie, delivered on time and within budget.

A movie producer is the person responsible for making sure an appealing, high-quality movie is produced on time and within budget. That means supervising and packaging the project from conception to distribution to theaters, while interfacing with the studio and managing the work of hundreds of individuals.

As you can see, movie producers do indeed have to wear many hats during movie production. Starting at the beginning of the process, here are some of the main producer responsibilities:

Pre-production
- Find material from a book or script.
- Get the script into good enough shape to attract a director (and studio, if this is not a studio-initiated production).
- Secure financing for the film, if it is not being made for a studio.
- Choose the director and other parts of the creative team.
- Cast the actors, working with the director.
- Determine locations and budget.
- Decide on cinematographer and special effects.
- Hire a production team including crew and producers.
- Develop a shooting schedule.
- Create a detailed plan of action for production.

HOW TO BE A FILM PRODUCER

Production
- Offer creative suggestions to the director.
- Handle problems with actors or creative staff.
- Monitor production timetable and budget.
- Review video dailies, the film shot each day.

Post-production
- Discuss order and selection of scenes with the director.
- Review the fine cut of the film after it is edited.
- In some cases, polish, revise and restructure the film to create the final cut.
- Work with a distributor to secure distribution for the film. This may include showing the distributors the final cut of the film.
- Review the distributor's advertising campaign for the film.

You may be wondering where movie producers find the material or come up with a film concept. In some cases, actors, writers or editors approach producers with a completed script. In other cases, coincidence or serendipity has led to successful movies.

The animated feature "Bee Movie" (2007), for example, started with an offhand comment by comedian Jerry Seinfeld to producer Steven Spielberg during dinner. "Wouldn't it be funny if they made a movie about Bees and called it 'Bee Movie'?" Seinfeld mused. Spielberg liked the idea, and Seinfeld found himself with a deal and the need to write a movie to go with his title. That took two and a half years.

"Rocky" (1976) started with a casual comment from an actor. Producer Robert Chartoff arranged to meet Sylvester Stallone after seeing him act in the "The Lords of Flatbush." Stallone mentioned that he had an idea for a script about a boxer and asked Chartoff if he would read it. Six weeks later, the actor brought in the first draft of the script for the film that earned him an Oscar nomination for best writing and was followed by six sequels.

THE HISTORY OF MOVIE PRODUCERS

From the beginning, movie producers have guided films from start to finish, and in doing so, they have left their mark on the motion picture industry. As casts, budgets and companies grew in the early 1900's, the role of the movie producer became more essential in bringing movies to market.

By the 1930's, movie production had grown into big business, controlled by studios that not only made and promoted the movies, but also distributed them and exhibited them in studio-owned theaters. A movie producer generally worked within the studio, taking on projects as assigned.

But in 1948, the U.S. Supreme Court ruled that the studios had established a monopoly and needed to relinquish control over the exhibition part of the industry. Independent distributors also came into being, giving independent film producers a way to bring their films to the public without going through the studios. Most movies today are made by independent producers, either for direct distribution or under contract for one of the remaining six major studios.

Throughout film history, movie producers have introduced innovations and styles that have shaped the movies we see today.

These movie producers brought their own insight and particular talents to the movie production process. Despite their individuality, a lot of movie producer responsibilities are the same.

TRAINING FOR MOVIE PRODUCERS

Technically, a movie producer doesn't need any training. But movie producers, other than Howard Hughes, rarely start at the top. As with any other business, if you're going to run it, you need to understand it. To meet producer responsibilities, you have to be familiar with all aspects of movie production and quite skilled at some of those aspects. And your contacts -- who you know -- can be important, too.

Plenty of film producers have honed their skills in acting, writing, directing or some other area of filmmaking before moving up to become a movie producer.

Here's how some famous film producers broke into the business:
- Steven Spielberg produced and directed short films in college that attracted the attention of Universal Pictures. He directed episodes for television shows and made-for-TV movies before directing movies and becoming an independent producer.
- Spike Lee directed films and met his future co-producer, Monty Ross, at Morehouse College. He won the Academy of Motion Picture Arts and Sciences' student award with the master's thesis film he completed at New York University.

If you want to become a movie producer, you may want to start small like these experts did. Get some training in writing, editing, cinematography, animation or another area of movie making. Make your own amateur films.

HOW TO BE A FILM PRODUCER

Produce something that showcases your skills, and then find a starter job in the industry.

The U.S. Bureau of Labor Statistics describes formal training as a great asset for anyone going into movie production and notes that colleges, technical schools and independent centers like the American Film Institute offer training programs for various areas of filmmaking. Some colleges and universities offer degrees with an emphasis on production management.

Here are the most important attributes for movie producers, according to the bureau:
- Talent
- Experience
- Business acumen
- Ability to deal with many different kinds of people under stress

Besides feature films, the motion picture industry produces films for specialized audiences such as documentaries and educational, business, industrial and government films. In addition, many businesses provide services to the industry, including editing, titling, computer graphics, animation and special effects. Working in any of these areas may be the start of a career as a movie producer.

Not all movie producers have exactly the same jobs. Go to the next page to learn more about some of these jobs.

TYPES OF MOVIE PRODUCERS

If you've watched all the credits roll at the end of a movie, you know that a lot of different people were involved in producing and distributing that movie. If you read closely, you may have noticed that rather than listing a single movie producer, the credits named movie producers of several different types.

Movie production is such a complicated process that usually one producer, known as the executive producers, supervises and is assisted by others who take on part of the producer responsibilities. We've already discussed the role of the main producer. Here's more about the specific jobs of producers, taken from the Producers Guild of America, a trade association for film, television and new media producers.

Executive Producer -- Supervises one or more producers as they perform their duties for one or more films. The executive producer may represent the film studio and keep watch over the producer to make sure the movie is within budget and being made the way the studio wants. Or the title may be given as a symbolic gesture or to give a movie visibility. George Clooney, for example, was listed as executive producer for "Far from Heaven" (2002) to generate publicity, but didn't spend any time on the set, according to the film's producer Christine Vachon.

Associate Producer -- Handles certain aspects of production, as assigned by the producer. Usually the associate producer has worked through all three stages of the production, from pre-production to post-production. Sometimes the associate producer title is given as a courtesy title to a key backer of the film who does not have a major role in producing the film.

Assistant Producer -- Works on tasks assigned by the associate producer.

Co-Producer -- Shares producer responsibilities as a team or group with other producers. One producer may take on creative responsibilities while another handles business functions. Or one of the producers may be a major investor who is not directly involved in the movie production. Or a co-producer may have brought the script or the film's star to the production.

Supervising Producer -- Oversees one or more producers as they perform some or all of their duties. The supervising producer may take the place of an executive producer or work for the executive producer.

Coordinating Producer -- Coordinates the work of several producers to create a unified end result. Coordinating producers are valuable when a studio produces several related films, as with "Spiderman," or particularly when two related films are being produced at the same time, as with the two sequels to "The Pirates of the Caribbean."

Line Producer -- Handles the physical aspects of a movie's production and usually is not involved in decision-making regarding creative issues. This is the person who oversees the budget and day-to-day activities during filming. In addition to making sure the movie stays on budget and on target, the line producer handles any crises that may occur.

To become a movie producer, you'll probably move up through some of these jobs. But expect stiff competition because jobs are limited at the major studios. The U.S. Bureau of Labor Statistics sees the most opportunity in filmmaking jobs related to evolving technology, such as computer specialists, multimedia animators and for job seekers skilled in digital filming, editing and computer-generated imaging.

HOW TO BE A FILM PRODUCER

But film producers will always be needed. The bureau recommends small or independent filmmakers as providing the best prospects for beginners because they are likely to grow more quickly as digital technology cuts production costs.

JOINT VENTURE FILM PRODUCTION AGREEMENT

Agreement, entered into as of the ____ day of MONTH 201___, by and between **FILM PRODUCTIONS** with a principal place of business at LOCATION (hereinafter **"FP"**) and **ENTERTAINMENT COMPANY**, with a principal place of business at LOCATION (hereinafter **"EC"**), and **XYZ ENTERTAINMENT** with a principal place of business at LOCATION (hereafter **"XE"**).

Whereas, FP is the owner of rights in and to the autobiography of the popular recording artist JZ entitled "JZ THE BOOK" (the "Book"), and a screenplay based on the Book tentatively titled "JZ SCREENPLAY" (the "Screenplay")

Whereas, FP is desirous of developing, financing, filming, producing, and securing distribution of a docudrama or miniseries based on the Screenplay through a national television network;

Whereas, EC and XE possesses considerable experience, expertise, and contacts in the film and television industries and the knowledge and acumen necessary to secure distribution of film and television projects through national television networks and motion picture studios;

Whereas, EC and XE are willing to act as FP's joint venturer in securing on behalf of EC, XE and FP a distribution deal for the Screenplay with a national television network or a motion picture studio;

Now, Therefore, for good and valuable consideration, receipt of which is hereby acknowledged, the parties agree as follows:

1. **Structure.**

(a) FP and EC and XE agree to collaborate as joint venturers for the purposes set forth above (the "Joint Venture").

(b) Reference is hereby made to the presently existing Partnership Agreement made and entered into between by NAME 1 and NAME 2 dated as of DATE/MONTH/YEAR (the "Partnership Agreement"). NAME 1 AND COMPANY and NAME 2 have assigned to EC their respective rights in and to the Book and the Screenplay.

   (i) Subject to the terms set forth below, FP agrees to assign its rights in and to the Book and the Screenplay to the Joint Venture.

(ii) Notwithstanding the foregoing, in the event that the Joint Venture has not successfully entered into a Distribution Agreement (as defined below) pursuant to which a docudrama, miniseries, or motion picture based on the Screenplay and/or the Book ("Work") is developed, filmed and financed prior to the termination or expiration of the Term hereof, any of the parties shall have the right to terminate this Agreement upon written notice to the other parties. Upon such termination, FP shall reclaim and regain, free of any claim from EC, its ownership rights to the Book and the Screenplay.

(c) It is the intent of the parties to the Joint Venture to solicit and secure a distribution agreement or production agreement with a national television network or motion picture studio that is satisfactory to FP for the purpose of distributing, financing, exhibiting, producing and otherwise exploiting the Work ("Distribution Agreement").

(d) The parties hereto shall be deemed to be independent contractors.

(e) FP shall be responsible for contributing the Book and the Screenplay to the Joint Venture for the purpose of creating, developing, and producing the Work. EC shall be responsible for using its contacts, expertise and knowledge in the film and television industries to secure a Distribution Agreement for the Joint Venture.

(f) In the event the parties should mutually decide to do a re-write of the Screenplay, then the Joint Venture shall own the rights to the Screenplay.

2. Profit Share.

The parties hereto shall each be entitled to be paid and the joint venture shall accrue to their respective accounts a share of all Capital Profits as defined below:

> FP: 33.34%
> EC: 33.33%
> XE: 33.33%

3. Copyright Ownership.

(a) FP shall own 33.34%; EC shall own 33.33% and XZ E shall own 33.33% of all worldwide right, title and interest of all copyrights, intellectual property, literary properties, scripts, treatments and other materials created or acquired by the Joint Venture. For the purpose of clarification, any ownership in the Book and Screenplay shall remain the property of MFP unless they are licensed or acquired pursuant to a Distribution Agreement that is entered into by the Joint Venture during the Term of this Agreement.

(b) The Joint Venture shall have the exclusive right to administer all copyrights owned by the Joint Venture. The Work produced pursuant to the Distribution Agreement shall be administered by and/or owned by the Joint Venture.

(c) Each party agrees to execute such further and additional documents as may be appropriate to effectuate the purposes of this Agreement.

4. Exploitation.

Each party hereto shall have mutual approval over all third party agreements to be entered into regarding the Book, Screenplay, the Work and the Distribution Agreement.

5. Accountings.

(a) Accountings as to Profit Share accruing or paid to or for the Joint Venture shall be made to the parties hereto on a quarter annual basis, within forty-five (45) days after the close of each calendar quarter (March 31, June 30, September 30 and December 31), or such other accounting periods as the parties may in the future adopt, but in no case less frequently than semi-annually, together with payment of accrued Profit Share earned from the exploitation of the Work.

(b) Amounts payable to each respective party hereunder in connection with the exploitation of the Work hereunder shall be computed in the same national currency as is paid or credited by the Joint Venture's Distributor and/or licensees and shall be paid at the same rate of exchange as is paid, and shall be subject to any taxes applicable to royalties remitted by or received from foreign sources, provided, however, that amounts payable on exploitations of the Work outside the United States shall not be due and payable until payment therefor has been received in the United States in United States Dollars.

(c) All accounting statements rendered hereunder shall be binding upon the party receiving the accounting statement and not subject to any objection for any reason unless specific objection in writing, stating the basis thereof, is given within three (3) years from the date rendered. Failure to make specific objection within said time period will be deemed approval of such statement.

(d) Each party shall have the right at their own expense to audit the other party's books and records and the Joint Venture's books and records only as the same pertain to the exploitation of the Work and calculation of Profit Share hereunder on which amounts are payable for the six (6) semi-annual accounting periods prior to the other party's receipt of written notice from the party which desires to audit such books and records. Such auditing party may make such an examination for a particular statement only once, and only within three (3) years after the date when said statement is rendered under paragraph 5(a) above. Such audit shall be conducted during usual business hours, and at the regular place of business of the party being audited in the United States where that party keeps the books and records to be examined. Such audit shall be conducted by an independent certified public accountant.

(e) The parties acknowledge that the books and records contain confidential trade information. Neither party nor its representatives shall at any time communicate to others or use on behalf of any other any facts or information obtained as a result of such examination of such books and records, unless such disclosure is required pursuant to an order of a court of competent jurisdiction. In the event such disclosure is so ordered, the party receiving said order shall notify the other party in writing promptly following receipt of such order.

(f) Neither party will have the right to bring an action against the other in connection with any accounting or payments hereunder unless it commences the suit within three and one-half (3-1/2) years from the date such statement of accounting or such payment was rendered. If the party commences suit on any controversy or claim concerning accountings rendered under this agreement, the scope of the proceeding will be limited to determination of the amount due for the accounting periods concerned, and the court will have no authority to consider any other issues or award any relief except recovery of any Profit Share found owing. Either party's recovery of any such amounts will be the sole remedy available to that party by reason of any claim related to accountings.

Without limiting the generality of the preceding sentence, neither party will have any right to seek termination of this agreement or avoid the performance of its obligations under it by reason of any such claim. Notwithstanding the foregoing, in the event any court determines fraud, gross negligence or willful misconduct on the part of either party in connection with any such claim, and such determination is not overturned or reversed, the limitations set forth in this paragraph 5(f) shall not apply.

(g) The parties hereby authorize and direct the other to withhold from any monies due the other any part thereof required by the United States Internal Revenue Service and/or any other governmental authority to be withheld, and to pay same to the United States Internal Revenue Service and/or such other authority. Each party shall provide the other with a copy of any notice received from the applicable governmental authority requiring it to withhold such monies and pay such monies to the applicable governmental authority.

(h) Capital Profits:

(i) Each party hereto shall be entitled to receive and shall be paid fifty (50%) percent of all net profits earned and paid to the Joint Venture pursuant to the Distribution Agreement. "Net Profits" shall be defined as all gross revenues (including advances, budgets, production fees, sales profits, fees and royalties) paid to the Joint Venture pursuant to the Distribution Agreement, less all actual and reasonable third party costs and expenses incurred by the Joint Venture in connection with the development, production, delivery and exploitation of the Work ("Capital Profits").

(ii) Capital Profits will be allocated to the Partners based on their ownership percentages.

(iii) The parties hereto agree to engage an independent CPA to maintain the Joint Venture's books and records, conduct authorized financial transactions and prepare and file all required tax returns. Such accountant's fees shall be paid as a Joint Venture expense.

6. Term.

The term of this Agreement shall begin as of the date hereof and continue until the expiration or termination of the Distribution Agreement; provided, however, that either party hereto shall have the right to terminate this Agreement in writing in the event the Distribution Agreement is not entered into by MONTH_____ DATE_____ YEAR_____.

7. Warranties and Representations; Indemnity.

Each partner agrees to and does hereby indemnify, save and hold the other partner harmless of and from any and all liability, loss, damage, cost or expense (including reasonable third-party attorneys' fees) arising out of any third party claim arising out of or connected with any breach of this agreement or which is inconsistent with any of the warranties or representations made by it in this agreement, provided that said claim has been settled with mutual written consent, not to be unreasonably withheld, or has been reduced to final adverse judgment by a court of competent jurisdiction, and agrees to reimburse the other partner promptly following the other partner's demand for any payment made or incurred by the other partner with respect to any liability or claim to which the foregoing indemnity applies. Notwithstanding anything to the contrary contained herein, either partner shall have the right to settle without the other partner's consent any claim involving sums of Seven Thousand Five Hundred Dollars ($7,500) or less (or involving claims of ownership or exploitation of intellectual property), and this indemnity shall apply in full to any claim so settled; if either partner does not consent to any settlement proposed for an amount in excess of Seven Thousand Five Hundred Thousand Dollars ($7,500), the other partner shall have the right to settle such claim without the other partner's consent, and this indemnity shall apply in full to any claim so settled, unless the other partner obtains a surety bond from a surety acceptable with the other partner as a beneficiary, assuring prompt payment of all expenses, losses and damages (including reasonable attorneys' fees) which the other partner may incur as a result of said claim. Pending final determination of any claim involving such alleged breach or failure, the Joint Venture may withhold sums due hereunder in an amount reasonably consistent with the amount of such claim. If no action is filed within twelve (12) months following the date on which such claim was first received by the Joint Venture, the Joint Venture shall release all sums withheld in connection with such claim, unless the Joint Venture, in its reasonable business judgment, believes an action will be filed within the reasonably foreseeable future. Notwithstanding the foregoing, if after such release of sums withheld in connection with a particular claim, such claim is reasserted, then withholding rights under this paragraph 7 will apply ab initio in full force and effect.

8. Definitions.

All capitalized terms not specifically defined herein shall have the meaning set forth in any related distribution or license agreements.

(a) "Revenues": For any period, the sum of (i) one hundred percent (100%) of the monies actually received by or credited to either party in the United States solely attributable to the exploitation of the Work including, without limitation, sales derived from the Work and other exploitations (including, without limitation, the Distribution Agreement, digital video disc sales, monies received in connection with the exploitation of the Works through ancillary distribution channels, mobile materials, promotional tie-ins, sponsorships and advertising revenue derived from the website [if any]).

(b) "Charges": For any period calculated in accordance with U.S. GAAP for such period, without duplication:

(i) all out of pocket, third-party costs paid or accrued to non-affiliated third parties by either party in connection with exploitation of the Work;

(ii) all manufacturing, artwork preparation and production costs in connection with exploitation of the Work;

(iii) all other expenses in connection with exploitation of the Work properly charged against income in accordance with U.S. GAAP;

(iv) any advances, royalties and the like paid; and

(v) all legal and accounting fees;

(c) "U.S. GAAP": Generally accepted accounting principles set forth in the opinions and pronouncements of the Accounting Principles Board of the Institute of Certified Public Accountants and statements and pronouncements of the Financial Accounting Standards Board or such other statements by such other entity as may be approved by a significant segment of the accounting profession, in each case consistent with the manner in which the same are applied to the financial statements hereunder.

(d) "Profit": Revenues less all Charges.

(e) "Person": Any individual, corporation, partnership, association, or other entity, or the legal successors or representative of any of the foregoing.

(f) "Net Sales": Gross billings less returns and credits (other than cash rebates and discounts), and less value added and similar taxes to the extent included within the price of Records concerned. Gross billings shall mean monies actually received by or credited to either party for Records shipped for sale in the United States.

9. Financial Commitments.

Neither party shall commit or bind the Joint Venture to any financial obligation in excess of Five Hundred ($500) Dollars without the prior written consent of the other party.

10. Distribution and Release.

The parties shall have mutual approval with respect to all material aspects of the distribution and sale of the Work produced by the Joint Venture. All material and substantive decisions shall be jointly made. Neither party will have the right to commit or financially bind the Joint Venture without the written approval of the other party.

11. Credit.
Subject to the terms stated in this Agreement, the parties shall use their best efforts to ensure that NAME 1, NAME 2, NAME 3, NAME 3 and NAME 4 will be afforded a shared credit as "Co-Executive Producers" in connection with the Screenplay.

12. Dispute Resolution.
In the event of a dispute by either party in connection with the performance and/or interpretation of this Agreement, then, the parties agree to initially submit such dispute to non-binding mediation to be heard by a mutually acceptable entertainment attorney based in Atlanta with the mediation/legal fees to be shared equally between the parties. In the event such mediation efforts do not result in a resolution of the dispute, then the parties agree to submit the dispute to binding arbitration in accordance with the commercial rules of arbitration promulgated by JAMS, with the proceedings to be held in Los Angeles, California, before a single mutually approved arbitrator. The prevailing party shall be entitled to have its arbitration costs and reasonable legal fees and costs incurred in connection with such proceedings to be reimbursed by the other party within thirty (30) days following the issuance of the arbitrator's award. Such award may be entered as a judgment in the local courts.

13. Miscellaneous.
(a) This writing sets forth the entire understanding between the parties hereto with respect to the subject matter hereof, and no modification, amendment or waiver of this document shall be binding upon either party hereto unless confirmed by a written instrument which is signed by an authorized signatory of each such party. No waiver of any provision of, or waiver of a default under this agreement nor any failure to exercise rights hereunder shall prejudice the rights of either party thereafter, nor shall it form precedent for the future.

(b) Notwithstanding anything expressed or implied herein to the contrary, the failure of either party to exercise any of their rights or pursue any remedies under this agreement shall not act as a waiver or an exclusion of their rights or remedies hereunder.

(c) All notices required to be sent to either party at its address first mentioned herein, and all Profit Share accounting statements and payments and any and all notices to either party shall be sent to the addresses first mentioned herein, or such other addresses as either party respectively may hereafter designate by notice in writing to the other. All notices sent under this Agreement shall be in writing and, except for Profit Share accounting statements shall be sent by overnight mail or registered or certified mail, return receipt requested, or overnight courier and the day of mailing of any such notice shall be deemed the date of the sending thereof (except notices of change of address, the date of which shall be the date of receipt by the receiving party).

(d) This agreement is entered into in the State of California and shall be construed in accordance with the laws of California applicable to contracts entered into and to be wholly performed therein (without giving effect to any conflict of laws principles under California law). The parties agree that any action, suit or proceeding based upon any matter, claim or controversy arising hereunder or relating hereto shall be brought solely in the state courts of or the federal court in the State of California and County of Los Angeles; any process in any action, suit or proceeding arising out of or relating to this agreement may, among other methods permitted by law, be served upon either party by delivering or mailing the same in accordance with paragraph 12(c) hereof.

(e) Without limitation of any other rights and remedies of the other partner, if either partner fails to fulfill any of its material obligations hereunder, then the other partner may, at its election, suspend its obligations hereunder for a number of days equal to the number of days between the date on which the other partner failed to fulfill its material obligations under this agreement and the date on which the other partner actually fulfills such material obligation(s). If any such failure exceeds sixty (60) days, in addition to its other rights and remedies, the injured partner may terminate this Agreement by written notice to the other partner and upon such termination the injured partner shall have no obligations to the other partner hereunder except with respect to Profit Share.

(f) This Agreement shall not be construed against either party as the drafter, it being agreed that this Agreement has been drafted jointly by the parties.

(g) This document may be signed in counterparts, and may be executed and delivered by facsimile, which when taken together will have the same effect as if signed in its original by both parties.

(h) Neither party hereto may assign this Agreement without the express written consent of the other party.

Very truly yours,

TONY ROSE

FILM PRODUCTIONS

By: _____
An Authorized Signatory

ENTERTAINMENT COMPANY
By: _____
An Authorized Signatory

XYZ ENTERTAINMENT
By: _____
An Authorized Signatory

FILM PRODUCTION PARTNERSHIP AGREEMENT

This Partnership Agreement ("Agreement) is made and entered into effective this DATE, MONTH, YEAR by the following individuals, NAME AND ADDRESS, and NAME AND ADDRESS referred to in this Agreement as the "Partners" until incorporation occurs.

The Partners wish to set forth, in a written agreement, the terms and conditions by which they will associate themselves in the Partnership.

NOW, THEREFORE, in consideration of the promises contained in this Agreement, the Partners affirm in writing their association as a partnership in accordance with the following provisions:

1. **Name and Place of Business:**

The name of the partnership shall be called NAME (the "Partnership"). Its principal place of business shall be ADDRESS, until changed by agreement of the Partners, but the Partnership may own property and transact business in any and all other places as may from time to time be agreed upon by the Partners.

2. **Purpose:**

The purpose of the Partnership shall be to establish the primary partners in the production of a Screenplay / Script, whether Film, Television Movie, or Docudrama of a factual or fictitious account of the events and lives of the NAME OF SCREENPLAY. The Partnership may also engage in any and every other kind or type of business, whether or not pertaining to the foregoing, upon which the Partners agree.

3. **Term:**

The Partnership shall commence as of the date of this Agreement and shall continue until terminated as provided herein.

4. Capital Accounts:

A. The Partners shall make an initial investment of work hours (in lieu of capital), contemporaneously with the execution of this Agreement, as follows:

Partners and Capital

    NAME: TITLES AND CAPITAL and NAME: TITLES AND CAPITAL ; by NAME (All Copyrights owned by NAME) and solicitation of investors, whether individuals, or groups of individuals how named, including major and independent film studios - HOW MUCH Invested.

    NAME: Executive Producer and Producer: Solicitation of investors, whether individuals, or groups of individuals how named, including major and independent film studios - No Dollars Invested.

In addition to each Partner's share of profits of the Partnership, as set forth in Section 5, each Partner is entitled to an interest after the "initial first rights payment" in the assets of the Partnership acquired within the Partnership by mutual consent.

The Book, Treatment and Script are the property of and owned by NAME . - COMPANY NAME has been DBA'd as an individually owned company by NAME to produce films.

B. For all purposes of this Agreement, the Partnership net profits and each Partner's capital account shall be computed in accordance with generally accepted accounting principles, consistently applied, and each Partner's capital account, as reflected on the Partnership federal income tax return as of the end of any year, shall be deemed conclusively correct for all purposes, unless an objection in writing is made by any Partner and delivered to the accountant or accounting firm preparing the income tax return within one (1) year after the same has been filed with the Internal Revenue Service. If an objection is so filed, the validity of the objection shall be conclusively determined by an independent certified public account or accounting firm mutually acceptable to the Partners.

5. Profits and Losses:

Until modified by mutual consent of all Partners, the profits and losses of the Partnership and all items of income, gain, loss, deduction, or credit shall be shared by the Partners in the following proportions:

6. Partner and Shares

NAME : Seventy Percent (70%)
NAME : Thirty Percent (30%)

Upon NAME receiving advances or payments ($150,000.00) for the sale of the book rights, the treatment, and the script, NAMES percentage shall escalate to fifty percent (50%) and NAMES percentage shall be fifty percent (50%) and all payments, royalties and residuals shall be split thereafter Fifty/Fifty between the partners. (see initial first payment rights)

7. Time, Advance and Salaries:

A. Until otherwise decided by unanimous agreement of the Partners, the relationship will continue as long as royalties and other revenues are generated through the production and/or filming of a Dramatic/Musical Teleplay of a Screenplay. Each Partner shall nonetheless be expected to devote such time and attention to Partnership affairs as shall from time to time be determined by agreement of the Partners.

B. Advances or Payments:

    (1) Film Offering Memorandum - ($50,000,000)

    (2) Investment Fund (Investors)

    (3) Development and/or Production Deal

    (4) Selling the Book Rights

(5) Selling the Treatment

(6) Selling the Screenplay/Script

Upon signing a deal or receiving payment(s) from any of the above, excluding the treatment, NAME shall receive an "initial first payment rights" of One Hundred and Fifty Thousand Dollars ($150,000.00) for providing the story, book rights, treatment, initial script and film offering memorandum.

For co-writing the treatment, an additional Ten Thousand Five Hundred Dollars, ($10,500.00) shall be paid to NAME.

For co-writing the treatment, NAME, will receive Five Thousand Two Hundred and Fifty Dollars, ($5,250.00), paid to NAME by NAME, per a separate agreement between NAME and

For writing the Script/Screenplay, NAME, will receive Two Thousand Five Hundred Dollars, ($2,500.00), paid to NAME by NAME, per a separate agreement between NAME and NAME .

C. In addition, upon signing a major or independent film deal and being greenlit with a budget of twenty million dollars or more to produce FILM NAME or a similar title, NAME shall receive one million five hundred thousand dollars ($1,500,000) as the Executive Producer/Producer, creator, developer, and copyright owner of the PROJECT NAME. (This is subject to change and being pro-rated.)

D. (A) In addition, upon signing a major or independent film deal and being greenlit with a budget of twenty million dollars or more to produce Hangin Tough! The Story of New Kids On The Block and Maurice Starr or a similar title, NAME shall receive Five Hundred Thousand ($500,000) or Twenty Percent (20%) whichever is higher as the Executive Producer/Producer of PROJECT project. (This is subject to change and being pro-rated.)

Salaries: Both partners shall agree on suitable salaries on or before the development deal or initial investment is made.

8. **Books and Records of Account:**

A double set of the Partnership books and records shall be maintained at the principal office of the Partnership and each Partner shall have access to the books and records at all reasonable times.

9. Future Projects:

The Partners recognize that future projects for the Partnership depend upon many factors beyond present control, but the Partners wish to set forth in writing and to mutually acknowledge their joint understanding, intentions, and expectations that the relationship among the Partners will continue to flourish in future projects on renegotiated terms and conditions, but there shall be no legal obligations among the Partners to so continue such relationship in connection with future projects.

10. Incorporation, Titles, Responsibilities and Credits:

A. Upon incorporating, NAME shall be an Executive Producer in charge of creative, and product development and NAME shall be an Executive Producer, in charge of creative, business and budgeting affairs. Both will have an equal say in day-to-day affairs, including development strategy, and spending.

B. Screen Credits: Primary Screen Credits include:

> Executive Producer and Producer:
> Executive Producer and Producer:
> Story By:
> Screenplay By:

11. Transfer of Partnership Interests:

A. Restrictions on Transfer. None of the Partners shall sell, assign, transfer, mortgage, encumber, or otherwise dispose of the whole or part of that Partner's interest in the Partnership, and no purchased or other transferee shall have any rights in the Partnership as an assignee or otherwise with respect to all or any part of that Partnership interest attempted to be sold, assigned, transferred, mortgaged, encumbered, or otherwise disposed of, unless and to the extent that the remaining Partner(s) have given consent to such sale, assignments, transfer, mortgage, or encumbrance, but only if the transferee forthwith assumes and agrees to be bound by the provisions of this

Agreement and to become a Partner for all purposes hereof, in which event, such transferee shall become a substituted partner under this Agreement.

B. Transfer Does Not Dissolve Partnership. No transfer of any interest in the Partnership, whether or not permitted under this Agreement, shall dissolve the Partnership. No transfer, except as permitted under Subsection 10.A above, shall entitle the transferee, during the continuance of the Partnership, to participate in the management of the business or affairs of the Partnership, to require any information or account of Partnership transactions, or to inspect the books of account of the Partnership; but it shall merely entitle the transferee to receive the profits to which the assigning Partner would otherwise be entitled and, in case of dissolution of the Partnership, to receive the interest of the assigning Partner and to require an account from the date only of the last account agreed to by the Partners.

12. **Death, Incompetency, Withdrawal, or Bankruptcy:**

Neither death, incompetency, withdrawal, nor bankruptcy of any of the Partners or of any successor in interest to any Partner shall operate to dissolve this Partnership, but this Partnership shall continue as set forth in Section 3, subject, however, to the following terms and conditions:

A. Death or incompetency: In the event any Partner dies or is declared incompetent by a court of competent jurisdiction, the successors in interest of that Partner shall succeed to the partnership interest of that Partner and shall have the rights, duties, privileges, disabilities, and obligations with respect to this Partnership, the same as if the successors interest were parties to this Agreement, including, but not limited to, the right of the successors to share in the profits or the burden to share in the losses of this Partnership, in the same manner and to the same extent as the deceased or incompetent Partner, the right of the successors in interest to continue in this Partnership and all such further rights and duties as are set forth in this Agreement with respect to the Partners, the same as if the words "or his or her successors in interest" followed each reference to a Partner; provided, however, that no successor in interest shall be obligated to devote any service to this Partnership and, provided further, that no successors in interest shall be treated as holding a passive, rather than active, ownership investment.

B. Payments upon Retirement or Withdrawal of Partner

(1) Amount of Payments. Upon the retirement or withdrawal of a Partner, that Partner or, in the case of death or incompetency, that Partner's legal representative shall be entitled to receive the amount of the Partner's capital account (as of the end of the fiscal year of the Partnership next preceding the day on which the retirement or withdrawal occurs) adjusted for the following:

(a) Any additional capital contributions made by the Partner and any distributions to or withdrawals made by the Partner during the period from the end of the preceding fiscal year to the day on which retirements withdrawal occurs;

(b) The Partner's share of profits or losses of the Partnership from the end of the preceding fiscal year of the Partnership to the day on which the retirement or withdrawal occurs, determined in accordance with generally accepted accounting principles, consistently applied; and

(c) The difference between the Partner's share of the book value of all of the Partnership assets and the fair market value of all Partnership assets, as determined by a fair market value appraisal of all assets. Unless the retiring or withdrawing Partner and the Partnership can agree on one appraiser, three (3) appraisers shall be appointed -- one by the Partnership, one by the retiring or withdrawing Partner, and one by the two appraisers thus appointed. All appraisers shall be appointed within fifteen (15) days of the date of retirement or withdrawal. The average of the three (3) appraisals shall be binding on all Partners.

(2) Time of Payments. Subject to a different agreement among the Partners or successors thereto, the amount specified above shall be paid in cash, in full, but without interest, no sooner than three (3) business days and no later than twelve (12) months following the date of the retirement or withdrawal.

(3) Alternate Procedure. In lieu of purchasing the interest of the retiring or withdrawing Partner as provided in subparagraph (1) and (2) above, the remaining Partners may elect to dissolve, liquidate and terminate the Partnership. Such election shall be made, if at all, within thirty (30) days following receipt of the appraisal referred to above.

13. Procedure on Dissolution of Partnership
Except as provided in Section 10.B (3) above, this Partnership may be dissolved only by a unanimous agreement of the Partners. Upon

dissolution, the Partners shall proceed with reasonable promptness to liquidate the Partnership business and assets and wind-up its business by selling all of the Partnership assets, paying all Partnership liabilities, and by distributing the balance, if any, to the Partners in accordance with their capital accounts, as computed after reflecting all losses and gains from such liquidation in accordance with each Partner's share of the net profits and losses as determined under Section 5.

14. Title to Partnership Property

If for purposes of confidentiality, title to Partnership property is taken in the name of a nominee or of any individual Partner, the assets shall be considered to be owned by the Partnership and all beneficial interests shall accrue to the Partners in the percentages set forth in this Agreement.

15. Leases

All leases of Partnership assets shall be in writing and on forms approved by all the Partners.

16. Controlling Law

This Agreement and the rights of the Partners under this Agreement shall be governed by the laws of the State of Arizona.

17. Notices

Any written notice required by this Agreement shall be sufficient if sent to the Partner or other party to be served by registered or certified mail, return receipt requested, addressed to the Partner or other party at the last known home or office address, in which event the date of the notice shall be the date of deposit in the United States mails, postage prepaid.

18. General

This Agreement contains the entire agreement of the Partners with respect to the Partnership and may be amended only by the written agreement executed and delivered by all of the Partners.

19. Binding Upon Heirs

This Agreement shall bind each of the Partners and shall inure to the benefit of (subject to the Sections 10 and 11) and be binding upon their respective heirs, executors, administrators, devisees, legatees, successors and assigns.

HOW TO BE A FILM PRODUCER

TONY ROSE

IN WITNESS WHEREOF, the Partners have executed this Agreement the date first above written.

_____
NAME
Executive Producer, NAME

_____
Executive Producer, COMPANY NAME
President, NAME

HOW TO BE A FILM PRODUCER

FILM - TELEVISION - THEATRICAL - INTERNET - INTELLECTUAL PROPERTIES

PARTNERSHIP AGREEMENT

This Agreement of General Partnership entered into as of the _____ day of _____, 20__. by and among NAME of _____ NAME of _____ (hereinafter referred to collectively as "Partners" and individually as "Partner").

1. Name and Purpose. The Partnership shall be carried on under the name of NAME OF PARTNERSHIP The Partnership has been formed for the purpose of:

(a) Owning, developing, distributing, commercially exploiting, and otherwise dealing in film, theatrical, television, internet, and other such intellectual properties for the consumer entertainment and multimedia market and industries. All property and interests in property owned by the Partnership shall be deemed owned by the Partnership as an entity, and no Partner, individually, shall have any ownership of such property or interest owned by the Partnership. Each of the Partners irrevocably waives, during the term of the Partnership and during any period of its liquidation following any dissolution, any right that it may have to maintain any action for partition with respect to any of the assets of the Partnership.

(b) Any music soundtrack or music publishing properties developed in conjunction with any of the foregoing shall be owned by the Partners separately from the Partnership, on a 50/50 basis, with each Partner assuming responsibility for the production of one-half of the associated recordings. Under such a scenario, each Partner will assign to the other Partner a 15% interest in the related publishing interest of such assigning Partner, and each Partner will agree to devote 10% of his respective publishing income related thereto toward covering overhead costs associated with maintaining/managing the publishing portfolio.

(c) The Partnership may engage in any and all other activities as may be necessary, incidental, or convenient to carry out the business of the Partnership as contemplated by this Agreement.

2. Place of Business. The principal office of the Partnership shall be located at _____ or at such other place as shall be agreed upon by the Partners from time to time. The Partners shall execute and file any doing business or assumed or fictitious name certificate or certificates or any similar documents required by law to be filed in connection with the formation and operation of the Partnership.

3. Term. The Partnership shall commence as of the date of the agreement as set forth above, and shall continue to operate in the partnership form of business until such time as the Partners determine to form a California Limited Liability Company ("CalLLC"), unless earlier terminated as provided in this Agreement. The Partners shall form and be the initial members and managers of the CalLLC as soon as it is commercially feasible and advisable to do so. Once the CalLLC is formed, the operating agreement of the CalLLC shall be as close an approximation of this Partnership Agreement as possible, containing the same provisions as are contained in this Partnership Agreement with terminology reflecting that of a limited liability company, but in all substantive effects the Partners intend that this Partnership Agreement shall be deemed to reflect their intent for the CalLLC regarding their relationship to one another and to third parties.

4. Capital Contributions. Each of the Partners has contributed one dollar ($1) to the capital of the Partnership. An individual capital account shall be established and maintained for each Partner who shall receive an interest in the Partnership, and shall be credited with the amounts of his Capital Contributions to the Partnership from time to time. The capital account of each Partner shall also be credited with the amount of net profits allocated to such Partner and shall be charged with the amount of any distribution to such Partner and any net losses allocated to such Partner. A Partner shall not be entitled to interest on his Capital Contribution, or to withdraw any part of his capital account, or to receive any distribution from the Partnership, except as specifically provided herein. As used in this Agreement, the reference to a Partner's interest in the Partnership shall refer to the ratio of such Partner's Capital Contributions to the aggregate of all the Partners' Capital Contributions. The terms net profits and net losses shall mean the net profits and losses of the Partnership as determined for federal income tax purposes by the accountant servicing the Partnership account.

5. Profits and Losses from Operations. Net profits from operations in each year shall be allocated among the Partners in equal proportions. Until such time as the Partners determine to accept investments from third parties, the Partners shall share in all Partnership profits and losses on a 50/50 basis, with each Partner being entitled to 50% of the profits and losses. Subsequent to formation of a CalLLC, the Partners agree to seek and accept investments from third party investors up to an amount which correlates to a one-third ownership interest in the LLC, with each Partner (then an LLC Member) agreeing to a one-third ownership interest, respectively, in (and one-third entitlement to the profits and losses of) the CalLLC at such time.

6. Distribution of Profits. The Partnership, and later the CalLLC, (in either form of business and for purposes of this paragraph hereinafter referred to as "company") shall distribute profits and set aside funds as follows:

(a) Ten percent (10%) of the company profits shall be contributed to a general expense account that the Partners shall have joint access to (i.e., both Partners must approve and sign off on any disbursements from this account), and which account shall be used to cover company expenses

(b) All amounts due to NAMES shall be disbursed by the company to them on a monthly basis (less 10% for overhead and 10% for return costs associated with charge-backs from distribution, etc).

(c) Payments to be made to third-party investors in the CalLLC may only be made if authorized by both NAMES. Said third party investor payments, if any are due and payable, shall be made on a quarterly basis

7. Additional Funds. Following the formation of the CalLLC, the Partners shall seek one or more third party investors to invest in the CalLLC or a project or property of the CalLLC, as determined by the Partners. The Partners agree that at such time they shall mutually decide to permit dilution of their respective ownership interests in equal amounts for purposes of permitting such third party investor(s) to acquire an ownership interest(s) in the CalLLC; but at no time shall the Partners permit any one or more third party investor(s) to own a greater than 49% ownership interest in the CalLLC.

8. Management. Each Partner shall have an equal vote in all Partnership decisions (and once it is formed, CalLLC decisions). This includes but is not limited to the following:

(a) Script approval on scripts that are co-produced by NAMES, except that NAME shall have creative autonomy over the dialogue of the specific scripts from books originating from biographies authored by NAME, provided that in any event NAMES shall share ultimate creative control in the context of overarching story and final approval of all scripts.

(b) The hiring of third party screenwriters, if any, to assist with screenplay editing, ghost-writing or any other agreed upon role. Any such third party screenwriter shall be hired strictly and solely on a work-for-hire basis, and paid at market rate with an understanding that:
  (i) all official credit shall stay solely within the discretion of NAMES,
  (ii) any and all agreements will contain a confidentiality clause where resume/CV credits or press discussion of the said works are concerned and any other communications- written or oral- where question of the credited writers of said screenplays might be questioned from public promotions, reviews, etc of the said works might be concerned.

(c) Production budget approval and executive production sign-off on all projects of the Partnership (and CalLLC once formed), with the objective being for NAMES to retain creative control of all projects undertaken, except in instances when a third party director is hired and given creative control.

(d) Decisions to (i) engage personnel, attorneys, accountants, or such other persons as may be deemed necessary or advisable; (ii) to open, maintain, and close bank accounts, and to draw checks and other orders for the payment of money; (iii) to borrow money and to make, issue, accept, endorse, and execute promissory notes, drafts, bills of exchange, loan agreements, and other instruments and evidences of indebtedness, and to secure the payment thereof by mortgage, hypothecation, pledge, or other assignment of, or arrangement of, security interests in all or any part of the property then owned or thereafter acquired by the Partnership; (iv) to take such actions and incur such expenses on behalf of the Partnership as may be necessary or advisable in connection with the conduct of the affairs of the Partnership; and (v) to enter into, make, and perform such contracts, agreements, and other undertakings as may be deemed necessary or advisable for the conduct of the affairs of the Partnership.

(e) No Partner, acting alone, shall have any authority to act for, or to undertake or assume any obligation, debt, duty or responsibility on behalf of, any other Partner or the Partnership except as expressly provided in this Agreement.

(f) Each Partner shall be reimbursed promptly by the Partnership for all third party costs and expenses authorized by this Agreement or by agreement of the Partners.

9. **Right of First Refusal.**
(a) No Partner may sell or negotiate to sell his entire Partnership Interest to a third party without notification to the other Partner and compliance with the process set forth in this section. In no event may a Partner sell more than 2.5% of that Partner's interest in any 6-month period, and the Partners in the aggregate shall not transfer to any third party more than 5% of the total of their combined ownership interests in the company at any time during the first five-year period of their association together as a Partnership and/or CalLLC.

(b) A Partner shall not pledge, cause a lien to be placed against, or encumber his Partnership interest in any way, nor shall a Partner sell or in any other way transfer his Partnership interest without first offering said interest for sale on the same terms to the Partnership and the other Partners by a writing addressed and delivered to each of the other Partners. The Partnership and the Partners shall have a period of 15 days to notify the selling Partner of its or their intention to purchase the interest offered for sale pursuant to the terms of such offer. If the Partnership or one or more of the Partners timely elect to purchase the selling Partner's interest (which election shall be made on behalf of the Partnership by a majority in interest of Partners other than the selling Partner), then within 15 days after receipt by the Partnership of such offer to sell, the Partnership or one or more of the Partners shall purchase said interest at the price and upon the terms at which said interest is offered for sale. If the election is not made by the Partnership or one or more of the Partners within said 15-day period, then the offering Partner may sell his

Partnership interest so offered for sale to a third party; provided, however, that said interest shall not be sold at a lower price or on more favorable terms than the price and terms set forth in the notice sent by the Partner in accordance with this paragraph without first reoffering said interest for purchase by the Partnership in accordance with this paragraph.

10. Transfer of Partnership Interest.

(a) Permitted transfers. Notwithstanding anything to the contrary contained in this Agreement, during the life of a Partner, he may transfer his Partnership interest by gift, either in trust or outright, to or for the benefit of his spouse and/or any of his descendants, including any descendant whose relationship to the Partner is created by birth or adoption. Thereafter, the transferee shall become a Partner with all the interest, rights, and duties previously held by the transferor except that the non-transferring Partner shall assume all creative control and decision-making authority over the Partnership.

(b) Prohibited transfers. Except as otherwise provided in paragraphs 7 and 10(a) above, a Partner shall not sell or in any other way transfer his Partnership interest during his lifetime without first complying with paragraph 8 or 10 above.

11. Restriction on Partners. *N*o Partner, without the consent of all other Partners, shall:

(a) Assign, transfer, pledge, compromise, or release any claim of the Partnership except for full payment, or arbitrate, or consent to the arbitration of, any of its disputes or controversies;

(b) Use the name, credit, property of the Partnership for any purpose other than a proper Partnership purpose,

(c) Do any act detrimental to the Partnership business or which would make it impossible to carry on that business.

12. Independent Activities. Each Partner may engage in whatever non-Partnership activities he chooses, whether the same are competitive with the

Partnership or otherwise, without having or incurring any obligation to offer any interest in any such activities to the Partnership or any party hereto. Neither this Agreement nor any activity undertaken pursuant hereto shall prevent any Partner from engaging in such activities, or require participation in such activities by the other Partners, and as a material part of the consideration hereof each Partner hereby waives, relinquishes, and renounces any such right of or claim to participation in any such activities.

13. Non-Liability.
(a) No Partner shall be liable to the Partnership or to any other Partner for losses or liabilities arising from the conduct of any employee or agent of the Partnership; provided, however, that such losses or liabilities do not arise from willful misconduct or gross negligence by such Partner.

(b) No Partner nor the Partnership shall be responsible or liable for any indebtedness or obligation of any other Partner incurred either before or after the execution of this Agreement, except those responsibilities, liabilities, debts and obligations hereafter undertaken or incurred on behalf of the Partnership under or pursuant to the terms of this Agreement, or assumed in writing by the Partnership and the Partners, and each Partner hereby indemnifies and agrees to hold the other Partner harmless from all such obligations and indebtedness except as aforesaid.

(c) The Partners shall perform their duties under this Agreement with ordinary prudence and in a manner characteristic of businessmen in similar circumstances. However, no Partner shall have any liability whatsoever to the Partnership or to any other Partner for loss caused by any act or by the failure to do any act if the loss suffered by the Partnership arises out of a reasonable mistake in judgment of the Partner, or if the Partner, in good faith, determined that the action or lack of action giving rise to the loss was in the best interests of the Partnership or if the action or lack of action giving rise to the loss was based on the advice of counsel; provided, however, that such exculpation from liability shall not apply to any liability for loss caused by any act or by the failure to do any act which arises out of the gross negligence or willful neglect of the Partner.

(d) The Partnership shall indemnify and hold harmless each Partner, and each partner, employee, agent or associate of each Partner, against any and all claims, actions, demands, costs, expenses (including reasonable attorneys' fees), damages, losses, and threats of loss, as a result of any claim or legal proceeding related to the performance or nonperformance of any act concerning the activities of the Partnership; provided, however, the party against whom the claim is made or legal proceeding is brought is entitled to exculpation under the provisions of Section 4.5 above.

14. Amendments. Amendments to this Agreement, other than amendments to reflect additional Capital Contributions and the admission of new Partners, shall become effective only if in writing and approved by all the Partners.

15. Arbitration. Any controversy or claim arising out of or relating to this Agreement, or to the interpretation, breach, or enforcement thereof, shall be submitted to three arbitrators and settled by arbitration in California in accordance with the rules then obtaining of the American Arbitration Association. Any award made by a majority of such arbitrators shall be final, binding, and conclusive on all parties hereto for all purposes, and judgment may be entered thereon in any court having jurisdiction thereof.

16. Books and Records. The books and records of the Partnership shall, at the cost and expense of the Partnership, be kept or caused to be kept by the Partnership and maintained at the principal place of business of the Partnership, shall reflect all Partnership transactions, and be appropriate and adequate for conducting the Partnership's business. The books shall be kept on either the cash or accrual method of accounting as to Partners shall determine. Each Partner, at its own expense, shall have the right at all times to inspect the books and records of the Partnership during business hours at the principal place of business of the Partnership. All funds of the Partnership shall be deposited in its name in an account or accounts maintained with such banking institutions as may be designated by the Partners on behalf of the Partnership. The funds of the Partnership shall not be commingled with the funds of any other person.

17. Fiscal Year. The fiscal year of the Partnership shall end on December thirty-first.

18. Termination of the Partnership. The Partnership shall be terminated and dissolved upon the vote of a majority in interest of the Partners. Upon the termination of the Partnership as herein provided, a full and general accounting shall be taken of the Partnership business, and the affairs of the Partnership shall be wound up. The Partners shall wind up and liquidate the Partnership by selling the Partnership assets and, after the payment of the Partnership liabilities and the expenses and fees incurred in connection with such liquidation, distribute the net proceeds therefrom in accordance with their respective Partnership ownership interests.

Unless otherwise required by law or by court order and subject to the provisions of this Agreement, the Partnership business shall not terminate upon the occurrence of any event causing dissolution of the Partnership. Any successor by the operation of law to a surviving Partner's interest, including, by way of example and not by way of limitation, a personal representative, an heir or legatee, a guardian, a receiver, or a trustee in bankruptcy, shall be deemed an assignee having the rights and obligations which an assignee of such Partner's interest would have.

19. Notices. All notices, consents, and other instruments hereunder shall be in writing and mailed by certified mail return receipt requested, postage prepaid, and shall be directed to the parties hereto at the addresses set forth above, or at the last addresses of the parties furnished by them in writing to the Partnership. Notices to any successor in interest shall be mailed in the same manner to the last known address of such successor.

20. Severability. If any provision of this Agreement or the application thereof to any person or circumstance shall be determined to be invalid or unenforceable, the remaining provisions of the Agreement or the application of such provision to persons or circumstances other than those to which it is held invalid or unenforceable shall not be affected thereby and shall be valid and enforceable to the fullest extent permitted by law.

21. Governing Law. All questions with respect to the construction of this Agreement, and the rights and liabilities of the parties, shall be determined in accordance with the provisions of the laws of the State of California.

22. Captions. The captions in this Agreement are for convenience only and shall not limit or define the text hereof.

23. Binding Effect. This Agreement shall inure to the benefit of and be binding upon the parties hereto and their respective next of kin, legatees, administrators, executors, legal representatives, successors, and permitted assigns.

24. Complete Agreement. This Agreement constitutes the complete and exclusive statement of the agreement between the Partners and replaces and supersedes all prior agreements, by and among the Partners or any of them. This Agreement supersedes all prior written and oral statements and no representation, statement, or condition or warranty not contained in this Agreement shall be binding on the Partners or have any force or effect whatsoever. It is agreed that neither Partner has rendered any services to or on behalf of either the other Partner or the Partnership and that no Partner shall have any rights with respect to any services which might be alleged to have been rendered.

IN WITNESS WHEREOF the parties hereto have executed this Agreement as of the day and year first above written.

_____
NAME

_____
NAME

HOW TO BE A FILM PRODUCER

Six

HOW TO BE A BOOK PUBLISHER

WHAT IS A BOOK PUBLISHER

Book publishers take responsibility for all aspects of book publication. Their aim is to attract good authors and publish books that achieve commercial success. Depending on the size of the publishing company, the book publisher may carry out all aspects of publication, or may delegate part of the work to editors, designers and marketing specialists.

Profile

Some publishers concentrate on broad categories, such as fiction or non-fiction. Others specialize within those broad sectors, publishing non-fiction books on art, business or science, for example. The choice of subject may be based on tradition if the publishing company has a long history. Newer publishing houses base their lists on market conditions, modifying their publishing programs in line with market demand. Large publishing companies with a wide range of titles appoint a number of publishers, each with responsibility for a different category.

Authors

Book publishers may commission books that fit the profile of the publishing company. Or, they may review book proposals from authors or their agents. In larger companies, publishers delegate the detailed review of book proposals to commissioning editors, using their reports to make final decisions on whether to publish. Publishers prepare contracts that set out the requirements for the book and the payments the author will receive.

Editing and Design

When authors have completed their manuscripts, publishers review the text to ensure that it meets the requirements set out in the contract in terms of content, quality and length. Publishers manage the manuscript editing, design and production process, using a team of editors, proofreaders, graphic designers and printers. They provide schedules for each stage of the process, working backwards from the planned publication date.

Commercial Arrangements

Publishers may look for opportunities to sell copies of the book to book stores, schools and colleges, libraries, special-interest groups and book clubs. They also aim to sell overseas rights to other companies that will translate the text and publish the book in their own territories. They negotiate terms that give the publisher and author shares of the income from various groups. Typically, publishers offer authors a pre-publication advance on royalties from book sales and authors earn further royalties once sales revenue covers the advance. Sales revenue is based on the actual revenue the publisher receives, not the cover price of the book, because publishers give booksellers discounts of up to 50 percent. The income the publisher receives covers costs, including authors' royalties, production, distribution and overhead costs.

Promotion

To build sales of the book, publishers plan and manage a promotional program. They work with marketing and design professionals to create advertisements, direct marketing campaigns and other communications material. They publish book excerpts online, arrange interviews with authors and encourage authors to write opinion pieces for publication or participate in promotional events, such as book fairs, seminars and book store signings.

WHAT IS POD BOOK PUBLISHING?
POD is an acronym for Print On Demand. Print On Demand publishing is a method of producing books in specific quantities needed to meet ongoing bookstore or book buyer orders. The customer ordering the book creates the demand for a single copy. A single copy of that book is then printed on demand, perfect bound with a full color laminated cover, and shipped to the customer or the bookstore ordering the POD book. POD is a process for publishing books only as they are needed.

WHAT IS TRADITIONAL BOOK PUBLISHING?
A traditional book publishing company buys the rights to an author's manuscript. Buying rights from the author is how book publishers have traditionally acquired books. Usually an agent, representing the author, negotiates the deal with the book publisher and in return gets a percentage of any monies earned from the sale of the author's book. Part of the arrangement includes payment of an advance by the book publisher to the author to secure the book deal. In return, the author, working with an in-house editor, is expected to finish writing the book in an allotted time - which is often years away. The advance is deducted by the book publisher from any royalties the author receives from the sale of the book.

Royalties are based on a mutually agreed upon percentage of sales. The author does not receive any royalties until the advance is paid back in full. The book publisher budgets funds to promote and market the book - this amount varies greatly depending on the marketability of the book. The author is often strongly encouraged to hire a book publicist and to work aggressively to promote their book. The book publisher has the final say on every aspect of the author's book, from editorial content to cover design to the number of books in the first printing. The book publisher makes the determination, based on declining sales, as to when to allow a book to go out of print - this could be as short as a year or even less.

Some traditional publishing houses are putting their out of stock or backlist titles into commercial print on demand systems so the book isn't technically out of print and the book's rights will never revert back to the author.

Each day, agents and book publishers receive a staggering number of inquiries and manuscripts. Ultimately, less than 1% of authors seeking to be published traditionally are successful. Thousands of authors and their books are rejected daily.

BOOK PUBLISHING AGREEMENT (1)

Agreement, entered into as of this _____,201___ between company name (hereinafter referred to as the ("publisher"), located at name and located at name. (hereinafter referred to as the ("author"),

Whereas, the author has created a manuscript/book tentatively titled *name*

Whereas, the publisher wishes to publish a book by the author; and

Whereas, the parties wish to have said publication performed subject to the mutual obligations, covenants, and conditions herein.

Now, therefore, in consideration of the foregoing premises and the mutual covenants hereinafter set forth and other valuable considerations, the parties agree as follows:

1. **GRANT OF RIGHTS.** The author grants, conveys, and transfers to the publisher in that published work titled and/or tentatively titled name, exclusive rights as follows:

(a) to publish, distribute, and sell the work in the form of a mass market paperback/commercial paperback or trade paperback. Including books on cd, spoken word audiotapes, computer disc, ebooks and the internet.

(b) in the territory of the entire world, and universe.

(c) in all languages; and for the term of the copyright.

2. **DELIVERY OF THE MANUSCRIPT.** on or before the date of month 201, the author shall deliver to the publisher a complete manuscript of approximately 40,000 words, which shall be reasonably satisfactory in form and content to the publisher and in conformity with any outline or description attached hereto and made part hereof. The material shall include the additional materials listed in paragraph 3 including index.

3. **ADDITIONAL MATERIALS.** The following materials shall be provided by the author. Photos, illustrations (if any), cover outline, computer disc and safety disc, as needed.

4. **PERMISSIONS.** The author agrees to obtain all permissions that are necessary for the use of materials copyrighted by others (if any). The permissions shall be obtained in writing, and author shall make a good faith effort to provide permissions (if any) as quickly as possible.

5. **DUTY TO PUBLISH.** The publisher shall publish the completed work within six months (month and date, 201) of the delivery of the manuscript. Failure to so publish shall give the author the right to terminate this agreement ninety days after giving written notice to the publisher of the failure to make timely publication. If publisher publishes the work during the ninety-day period after such written notice has been received from author or unless author has failed to deliver the manuscript and all additional materials, then the publisher shall retain all rights to the work under this agreement.

6. **ROYALTIES.** The publisher shall pay the author the following royal- ties: eight (8%) percent of the net price on the first 10,000 books sold; ten (10%) percent of the net price on the next 10,000 sold; and twelve (12%) percent of the net price on all copies sold thereafter in the united states of america after initial production and manufacturing costs. These royalty rates shall be discounted only in the following circumstances: books sold outside of the united states of america, book clubs, mail order or direct response advertising (which does not include online ordering from publisher's website), shall be reduced to half the regular royalty rate. Higher than normal discounts to wholesalers or retailers, reading circles, and organizations outside the regular bookselling channels to be reduced to one percent of the royalty for each percent in excess of a fifty-five (55%) percent discount or no royalty at all if the book is sold at less than the publisher's manufacturing cost. Promotional copies and author's copies are royalty free. All copies sold shall be cumulated for purposes of escalations in the royalty rate. Copies sold shall be reduced by copies returned in the same royalty category in which the copies were originally sold.

The royalty rate for other forms of the work shall be: five (5%) percent for cd's; five (5%) percent for cassette tapes; five (5%) percent for computer disc software; five (5%) percent for e-books, five (5%) percent for aol and other services related to the internet.

7. **SUBSIDIARY RIGHTS.** All subsidiary and licensing rights shall be owned and controlled by the publisher. Licensing of subsidiary rights include abridgments, book clubs, reprints by another publisher, first and

second serializations, foreign or translation rights, syndication, advertising, commercial uses, films, plays, radio shows, television, and audio book-to-tape rights, microfilm and all computer uses.

Author shall receive ten (10%) percent of all advances received from subsidiaries and licensing of the work, by the publisher, less manufacturing cost, and excluding film, television, video book rights, theatrical music book/play rights, and spoken word audiotapes.

Author shall receive ten (10%) percent of all advances and royalties received from the licensing of film, television and video book rights, theatrical music book/play rights, and spoken word audiotapes.

Licensing income shall be divided as specified less attorney fees.

Licensing income shall be collected by the publisher and remitted to the author within sixty days of receipt.

8. **ACCOUNTINGS.** Commencing as of the date of publication, the publisher shall send a statement to the author every six months. (publisher maintains two accounting periods, which end june 30 and december 31 of each calendar year - each referred to as an accounting period). At the close of each accounting period, the publisher shall, within sixty days (60), send a royalty statement to the author showing for that period and cumulatively to date the number of copies printed and bound, the number of copies sold and returned for each royalty rate, the number of copies delivered free for publicity purposes, the number of copies remaindered, destroyed, or lost, the royalties paid to and owed to the author, other income earned by author and licensing income. A reserve account will be set up against book returns for four (4) accounting periods following the first publication of the work and shall in no event exceed fifteen percent (15%) of royalties due to the author.

9. **PAYMENTS.** The publisher shall pay the author or author's designee all royalty income due author under this agreement in u.s. dollars, pursuant to paragraph 8 within ninety (90) days of the close of each accounting period.

10. **RIGHT OF INSPECTION.** The author shall upon the giving of written notice, have the right to inspect the publisher books of account to verify the accounting once a year. If errors in any such accounting are found

to be to the author's disadvantage and represent more than five (5%) percent of the payment to the author pursuant to the said accounting, the cost of the accounting shall be paid by the publisher.

11. **COPYRIGHT AND AUTHORSHIP CREDIT.** The publisher shall, as an express condition of receiving the grant of rights specified in paragraph 1, take the necessary steps to register the copyright on behalf of the author and publisher (50% author / 50% publisher) and shall place the copyright notice in the author's name on all copies of the work. The author shall receive authorship credit as follows: written by – name.

12. **WARRANTY AND INDEMNITY.** The author warrants and represents that she is the sole creator of the work and owns all rights granted under this agreement, that the work is an original creation, and that the material has not been previously published, (except for those materials for which permissions have been obtained pursuant to paragraph 5), that the work does not infringe any other person's copyrights or literary property, nor, to your knowledge, does it violate the rights of privacy of or libel, other persons. The author agrees to indemnify the publisher against any final judgement for damages (after all appeals have been exhausted) in any lawsuit based on an actual breach of the foregoing warranties. In addition, the author shall pay the publisher reasonable cost and attorney's fees incurred in defending such a lawsuit. The author makes no warranties and shall have no obligation to indemnify the publisher with respect to materials inserted in the work at the publisher request. Notwithstanding any of the foregoing in the event a lawsuit is brought which may result in the author having breached his warranties under this paragraph, the publisher shall have the right to withhold and place in an escrow account ten percent of sums payable to the author pursuant to paragraph 11, but in no event may said withholding exceed the damages alleged in the complaint.

Each party to this agreement shall give prompt notice in writing to the other party of any claims.

No compromise or settlement of any claims shall be made or entered into without the prior written approval of publisher and author.

13. **ARTISTIC CONTROL.** The author and publisher shall consult with one another with respect to the title of the work. In the event of disagreement after consultation, the publisher shall have final power of decision over all the foregoing matters. No changes shall be made in the completed manuscript of the work by persons other than the author, except

for reasonable copy editing, unless the author consents to such changes. Publisher shall provide the author with galleys and proofs which the author shall review and return to the publisher within ten (10) days of receipt. If the cost of the author alterations (other than for typesetting errors) exceeds ten (10%) percent of the cost of the typography, the publisher shall have the right to deduct such excess from royalties due author hereunder. Author shall provide publisher a list of names to be supplied excerpts for reviews.

14. **FREE COPIES.** The author shall receive five (5) free copies of the work as published, after which the author shall have the right to purchase additional copies at the best available discount price.

15. **REVISIONS.** The author agrees to revise the work on request by the publisher. If the author cannot revise the work or refuses to do so absent good cause, the publisher, shall have the right to have the work revised by a person competent to do so. Author shall deliver the revised manuscript to publisher postmarked thirty (30) days after receipt from publisher. The author is not responsible for the costs to the publisher for such revisions.

16. **SUCCESSORS AND ASSIGNS.** This agreement may be assigned by the publisher without the written consent of the author. The author, however shall retain the right to assign payments due hereunder without obtaining the publisher consent. This agreement shall be binding on the parties and their respective heirs, administrators, successors, and assigns.

17. **INFRINGEMENT.** In the event of an infringement of the rights granted under this agreement to the publisher, the publisher and the author shall have the right to sue jointly for the infringement and, after deducting the expenses of bringing suit, to share equally in any recovery.

18. **PROMOTION.** The author consents to the use of her name and portraits, or pictures for promotion and advertising of the work, provided such use is dignified and consistent with the author's reputation.

19. **REVERSION OF RIGHTS.** If the work goes out of print in all publisher's editions, author shall have the right to request that publisher reprint or cause a licensee to reprint the work. Publisher shall have twelve (12) months after receipt of any such written request from author to comply, unless prevented from doing so by circumstances beyond publisher's control. If publisher declines to reprint the work as described above, or if publisher

agrees to reprint the work but fails to do so within the time allowed, then author may terminate this agreement upon sixty (60) days' notice in writing. Upon such termination, all rights granted under this agreement, except the rights to dispose of existing stock, shall revert to author, subject to all rights which may have been granted by publisher to third parties under this agreement, and publisher shall have no further obligations or liabilities to author except that author's earned royalties shall be paid when and as due. The work shall not be deemed out of print within the meaning of this section so long as the work is available for sale either from stock in publisher's, distributor's or licensee's warehouse, or in regular sales channels and is listed in the publishers catalog.

20. **OPTION.** The publisher shall have the option on the author's next book..

21. **ARBITRATION.** All disputes arising under this agreement shall be submitted to binding arbitration and shall be settled in accordance with the rules of the american arbitration association. Judgement upon the arbitration award may be entered in any court having jurisdiction thereof.

22. **ATTORNEYS' FEES.** In any action on this agreement, including litigation and arbitration, the losing party shall pay all attorneys' fees and costs incurred by the prevailing party.

23. **NOTICE.** Where written notice is required hereunder, it may be given by use of traceable mail addressed to the author or publisher at the addresses given at the beginning of this agreement and shall be deemed received five (5) days after mailing. Said addresses for notice may be changed by giving written notice of any new address to the other party.

24. **ENTIRE AGREEMENT AND MODIFICATIONS.** This agreement represents the entire agreement between the parties. All modifications of this agreement must be in writing and signed by all parties.

25. **GOVERNING LAW.** This agreement shall be governed by the laws of the state.

HOW TO BE A BOOK PUBLISHER

In witness whereof, the parties have signed this agreement as of the date first set forth above.

_____   _____
NAME   DATE:

_____   _____
NAME   DATE:

BOOK PUBLISHING AGREEMENT (2)

AGREEMENT between [XYZ] Publishing LLC ("Publisher") and [John Doe] ("Author").

The parties to this Agreement wish to publish the hardcover edition of Author's book of nonfiction essays ("the Book"). The two parties agree as follows:

1. Author shall deliver to Publisher an original book.

2. Author grants to Publisher the exclusive rights to print, publish, distribute, sell and license the rights to any and all editions and/or formats of the Book, in whole or in part, in the English language throughout the world.

2a. Author grants to Publisher the non-exclusive right to Electronic versions of the Book. (Electronic versions shall be defined as online and digital reproductions and displays of the verbatim text and illustrations of the Book, or excerpts, for promotional purposes only. This grant of rights shall in no event be deemed to be a grant of electronic-book or audio-recording rights, which are reserved by the Author.)

2b. These rights shall be granted to the Publisher for a period of five (5) years from date of this agreement.

3. The Author vows that the work is his; that the Book will not infringe upon the personal rights of or give rise to any claim by any third party, including, without limitation, claims in defamation, privacy, copyright, or trademark; and that the Author has the authority to grant us the rights granted in this agreement. Publisher will have no obligation to publish any part of the Book, which in its opinion would infringe upon such rights of any third party.

4. Publisher will make no changes or alterations to the Book without the Author's permission. The Author will have approval over the design, format and style of the Book, including text, graphic material and dust jacket art. In all matters of design, format and style, Publisher will, in consultation with the Author, present graphic materials to the Author, who will have the right to approve such materials and such approval will not be unreasonably withheld.

5. The Author will have approval over the promotion of the Book. That is, he will decide when/if he tours and where, and how. The Author will have the right to approve how the Book will be described in publicity materials.

6. Publisher agrees to pay to the Author as an advance against and on account of all monies accruing to him under this Agreement, one dollar per copy in the initial print run, which will be no lower than 3000 and no higher than 8000 copies.

Payment will be made according to the following schedule: $......due within one month of signing this agreement The remainder due upon publication.

Acceptance of this advance ensures on the Author's part that he will deliver a complete Book and participate fully in the publication and promotion of the Book.

6a. Publisher shall pay Author 50% of net receipts ("Net Receipts") as defined below. Publisher shall be entitled to retain a reasonable reserve for returnable copies of the book. Net Receipts shall mean 100% of all gross sums received by or credited to Publisher from sales of the books and from licensing of any domestic rights in the books, less the direct costs ("Direct Costs"). Direct Costs shall mean the costs actually incurred by Publisher in connection with the paper, printing and binding of the Book and galleys, of shipping the Book and galleys, or preparing and mailing publicity materials, or promotional expenses, but shall not include the cost of Publisher's overhead or the salaries of Publisher's employees.

7. All sums of money due the Author under this Agreement shall be paid to the Author, and the receipt of the said funds shall be a good and valid discharge of all such indebtedness.

8. Publisher will do everything they reasonably can to give the Author updates, when he requests them, concerning the Book's sales and general progress. Every six months following first publication the Book, Publisher will provide Author with a statement of monies received from sales of the Book along with payment of any monies then due to Author under Paragraph 6.

9. All rights to the Book not expressly granted to us here will remain, always, with the Author. The Author can sell television rights, film rights, billboard rights, plush toy and key chain rights—all without the approval of the Publisher. Publisher has only the rights described in Paragraphs 2, 2a, and 2b.

10. If there is a disagreement between the two parties arising out of this agreement, it will be resolved in good faith through an arbitrator in CITY to be selected by the parties. The arbitrator's decision may be entered in any court having jurisdiction.

No arbitration can be commenced and neither Author nor Publisher can be found to be in breach of this Agreement unless they have been given written notice identifying the breach and a thirty-day opportunity to cure it.

11. This agreement is subject to the laws of the State of _____.

12. The Author shall have the right upon written request to examine the books of account of the Publisher insofar as they relate to the Book; such examination shall be at the cost of the Author unless errors of accounting amounting to five percent (5%) or more of the total sum paid to the Author shall be found to his disadvantage, in which case the cost shall be borne by the Publisher. The examination will be done by the Author's representative or accountant.

13. Should the Publisher default in complying with the terms of this Agreement and does not rectify such default within 30 days, all rights shall revert to the Author.

14. Should the Book be out of print at any time and the Publisher fails to reprint within six months, all rights granted herein shall revert to the Author. The existence of an electronic or print-on-demand edition shall not mean the Book is in print.

15. Upon publication, Publisher shall send # OF COPIES free copies to Author.

16. This Agreement may be assigned by Publisher as part of the sale or transfer of all or substantially all of Publisher's business or is part of a merger or consolidation of Publisher with another company. This agreement may also be assigned by Publisher to any subsidiary or affiliate or any company or entity under controlled by it. The performance of the terms of this Agreement is personal to Author and may not be assigned. Otherwise, the provisions of this Agreement shall be binding upon and shall inure to the benefit of the parties, their respective successors, legal representatives, and assigns.

17. This Agreement reflects the entire understanding between the parties and it may not be changed except in writing signed by both of us.

Signed: _____

WHAT IS ELECTRONIC OR DIGITAL PUBLISHING

Electronic publishing (also referred to as e-publishing or digital publishing) includes the digital publication of e-books, digital magazines, and the development of digital libraries and catalogues.

Electronic publishing has become common in publishing. It is also becoming common to distribute books, magazines, and newspapers to consumers through tablet reading devices, a market that is growing by millions each year, generated by online vendors such as Apple's iTunes bookstore, Amazon's bookstore for Kindle, and books in the Google Play Bookstore. Market research suggests that half of all magazine and newspaper circulation will be via digital delivery by the end of 2016 and that half of all reading in the United States will be done without paper by 2017.

Although distribution via the Internet, also known as online publishing or web publishing when in the form of a website is nowadays strongly associated with electronic publishing, there are many non-network electronic publications such as Encyclopedias on CD and DVD, as well as technical and reference publications relied on by mobile users and others without reliable and high speed access to a network. Electronic publishing is also being used in the field of test-preparation in developed as well as in developing economies for student education, partly replacing conventional books, because it enables content and analytics combined for the benefit of students.

Electronic publishing is becoming increasingly popular in works of fiction. Electronic publishers are able to provide quick gratification for late-night readers, books that customers might not be able to find in standard book retailers (erotica is especially popular in e-book format, and books by new authors that would be unlikely to be profitable for traditional publishers.

While the term "electronic publishing" is primarily used today to refer to the current offerings of online and web-based publishers, the term has a history of being used to describe the development of new forms of production, distribution, and user interaction in regard to computer-based production of text and other interactive media.

ELECTRONIC PUBLISHING PROCESS

The electronic publishing process follows a traditional publishing process but differs from traditional publishing in two ways: 1. It does not include using an offset printing press to print the final product and 2. It avoids the distribution of a physical product. Because the content is electronic, it may be distributed over the Internet and through electronic bookstores. The consumer may read the published content on a website, in an application on a tablet device, or in a PDF on a computer. In some cases, the reader may print the content using a consumer-grade ink-jet or laser printer or via a print on demand system.

Distributing content electronically as apps has become popular due to the rapid consumer adoption of smart phones and tablets. At first, native apps for each mobile platform were required to reach all audiences, but in an effort toward universal device compatibility, attention has turned to using HTML5 to create web apps that can run on any browser.

The benefit of electronic publishing comes from using three attributes of digital technology: XML tags to define content, style sheets to define the look of content, and metadata to describe the content for search engines. With the use of tags, style sheets, and metadata, this enables re-flowable content that adapts to various reading devices or delivery methods.

Because electronic publishing often requires text mark-up to develop online delivery methods, the traditional roles of typesetters and book designers have changed. Designers must know more about mark-up languages, the variety of reading devices available, and the ways in which consumers read. However, new design software is becoming available for designers to publish content in this standard without needing to know programming, such as Adobe Systems' Digital Publishing Suite and Apple's iBooks Author. The most common file format is e-pub, used in many e-book formats, which is a free and open standard available in many publishing programs. Another common format is folio, which is used by the Adobe Digital Publishing Suite to create content for Apple's iPad tablets and apps.

ELECTRONIC PUBLISHING AND COPYRIGHT

Copyright laws are currently tailored to printed books. Electronic publishing brings up new questions in relation to copyright. E-publishing may be more collaborative, often involving more than one author, and more accessible, since it is published online. This opens up more doors for plagiarism or theft.

Some publishers are trying to change this. For example, Harper Collins limited the number of uses that one of its e-books can be lent in a public library. Others, such as Penguin, are attempting to incorporate the elements of the e-book into their publications instead.

EBOOK LICENSING AGREEMENT (1)

This Agreement is made and entered into effective this _____ day of _____ 201__ by COMPANY NAME AND ADDRESS (Licensor) and COMPANY NAME AND ADDRESS (Licensee).

WHEREAS, Licensee wishes to license books on an exclusive basis the ebook rights to certain books to be named in schedule A.

The parties hereto agree as follows:

TERM
The term of this Agreement ("Term") shall be five (5) years, commencing upon execution of agreement by both parties, but no later than 7 days from signed and dated acceptance by Licensor.

TERITORY
The territory for which Licensee is licensing the rights to books is World-wide.

GRANT OF RIGHTS
Licensor hereby grants to Licensee on an exclusive basis, the e-book rights to certain books that will be named in schedule A.

(a) Secure the digital distribution of the Books.

(b) Use the name, voice, and or likeness of writers in conjunction with the use of the Books.

(c) Use any artwork created for use with the Books

LICENSOR'S OBLIGATIONS
Upon execution of the Agreement, Licensor shall furnish Licensee with the following materials:

(a) All documentation providing proof of ownership of Books.

(b) A list of Books set forth on "Schedule A" which is attached to the Agreement. In the event, additional Books become subject to this

Agreement, "Schedule A" may be amended from time to time with discussion and further advances.

(c) Digital files of all Books. Each Book delivered hereunder shall be subject to Licensee technical approval before being commercially used.

(d) Artwork corresponding to all Books if available.

CONSIDERATION:

(a) Digital Distribution: Licensee shall pay to Licensor a sum equal to 50% (percent) of Net Revenues, derived from the sale of e-books hereunder.

(b) Licensee will pay a recoupable advance of Thousand Dollars ($) per book for a five-year licensing agreement.

(c) Advances for the e-book rights to the books will be wired to licensors account upon both parties signing this agreement.

(d) Licensor will invoice Licensee for any set-up fees pertaining to transferring book files for seven books ($) _____.

The term NET REVENUE will be the proceeds remaining after payment of all royalties / publishing due to licensor and any persons engaged in connection with the creation of the books identified on Shedule A (iv) and any other fees, or monies due and or payable with respect to the artwork, medadata, trademarks, and logos provided by licensor to Licensee, All delivery fees and processing cost borne by Licensee will be recouped from book(s) proceeds. Licensor will pay writer royalties from income received by Licensee.

ACCOUNTING:

(a) Within sixty (60) days following the close of each calendar quarter ("Accounting Period") Licensee shall send to Licensor a statement setting forth in detail the royalties payable to Licensor for the preceding Accounting Period. Licensee shall only be required to account and pay with respect to amounts actually received by Licensee. In the event the amount shown due by an accounting to Licensor that is due under this Agreement is less than

Fifty Dollars ($50.00), the obligation to pay such amount shall be carried over to the next accounting period when the aggregate amount due to Licensor is Fifty Dollars ($50.00) or more, at which time such amount shall be paid.

(b) Upon sixty (60) days prior written notice to Licensee, a certified public accountant on Licensor's behalf, shall have the right, once each year, during ordinary business hours, to inspect and audit such of Licensee business books and records solely regarding the Masters in this agreement as may reasonably be necessary for Licensor to verify the accuracy of any royalty statement rendered by Licensee within the eighteen (18) month period immediately preceding the date of the inspection. The information contained in a royalty statement shall be conclusively deemed correct and binding upon Licensor, resulting in the loss of all further audit rights with respect to such statement, unless specifically challenged by written notice from Licensor within eighteen (18) months from the date such royalty statement was delivered by Licensee. Licensor and its auditor shall keep all information learned as a result of such audit in strict confidence. The cost of such an audit will be borne by Licensor and audits shall not interfere unreasonably with Licensee business activities. However, if errors in any such accounting are found to be to the Licensor's disadvantage through Licensee accounting error and represent more than five percent (5%) of the payment to the Licensor pursuant to the said accounting, the cost of the accounting shall be paid by Licensee.

WARRANTIES AND REPRESENTATIONS:

Licensee
(a) warrants and represents that it has the full right, power and authority to enter into and fully perform this Agreement and is not subject to any obligation or disability which will or might prevent or interfere with Licensee keeping and performing all the agreements and conditions to be kept or performed hereunder.

(b) will at all times indemnify and hold Licensor harmless from and against any and all third party claims, damages, liabilities, costs and expenses arising out of any breach by Licensee of any warranty made by Licensee herein.

Licensor

(a) warrants and represents that it has the right and power to enter and fully perform the exclusive Agreement to make the commitments it makes herein and has obtained all necessary licenses, permissions and consents necessary for Licensee to perform its obligations hereunder.

(b) warrants and represents that it has all necessary rights, licenses, permissions and consents in and to the Licensed Content, Meta Data, and other materials to authorize the use by Licensee of such Licensed Content, Meta Data, and other material under this Agreement/ No Licensed Content, Meta Data or other materials furnished to Licensor hereunder or the use of them by Licensee. If used in the manner authorized by Licensor hereunder and not in violation of any restrictions or limitations identified by Licensor hereunder or hereafter, will violate any law or infringe upon any rights of any third party.

(c) will, at all times, indemnify and hold Licensee and Licensee directors, shareholders, employees, agents, and representatives harmless from and against any and all third party claims, damages, liabilities, costs and expenses arising out of any breach by Licensor of any warranty made by Licensor herein.

MISCELLANEOUS

This Agreement contains the entire understanding of the parties hereto relating to the subject matter hereof and cannot be changed or terminated except by written instrument signed by both parties hereto.

(a) This Agreement has been entered in CITY AND STATE, and the validity, interpretation and legal effect of this Agreement shall be governed by the laws of the STATE, applicable to contracts entered into and to be wholly performed therein with respect to the determination of any claim, dispute or disagreement that may arise out of the interpretation, performance or breach of the Agreement.

(b) If any provision herein shall be deemed or declared unenforceable, invalid or void by a court of competent jurisdiction, the same shall not impair any of the other provisions contained herein which shall be enforced in accordance with their respective terms.

HOW TO BE A BOOK PUBLISHER

This Agreement shall not become effective until executed by both parties.

Licensee
By_____
    An authorized signatory

Licensor
By_____
    An authorized signatory

_____
Print authorized signatory name

_____
Print authorized signatory name

_____
Phone number / Email

_____
Phone number / Email

Fed Tax ID #_____

SCHEDULE A

HOW TO SELF-PUBLISH AN EBOOK

The whole e-book market is rapidly evolving, and a lot of self-publishing companies are offering e-book deals bundled into their print book publishing packages.

TIPS

- **It's gotta be good**: The same rule applies to self-published e-books as it does to print books. You have to start with a good product if you have any hope of selling it.

- **Create an arresting cover**: When it comes to e-books, everything starts with the cover image. Creating an eye-catching, professional-looking cover that also looks good small (it has to stand out as a thumbnail image, since it's being sold online) is easier said than done, but it can really make a difference in terms of sales. Ideally, you should hire a graphic designer who has some experience creating book covers. From a production standpoint, an e-book cover is easier to create than a cover for a print book (you just need a JPEG with decent resolution), but it shouldn't look out of place among traditionally published e-books. I can't tell you how many bad self-published covers are out there.

- **Price your e-book cheaply**: You should sell your e-book for $5.99 or less. According to research done by Smashwords, an online e-book publishing and distribution platform for authors, publishers, agents, and readers, $2.99 to $5.99 yields the most profit for self-published authors, and although 99 cents will get you more downloads, it's a poor price point for earning income (see Smashwords' presentation on pricing here). On the other hand, Lulu, one of the bigger online self-publishing operations, says that authors who price their e-books in the 99-cent to $2.99 range "sell more units and earn more revenue than those in any other price range."

It's important to note that Amazon's 70 percent royalty for authors only applies to Kindle books priced between $2.99 and $9.99; otherwise, the rate kicks down to 35 percent). As for going free, well, Smashword data indicates that free e-books get about 100 times more downloads than priced e-books.

- **Avoid any outfits that don't let you set the price**: This is one of the cardinal rules of self-publishing an e-book. You must be able to control the pricing of your e-book. If you want to sell it for 99 cents, then you should be able to sell it for 99 cents.

- **Marketing is all about creating awareness for your e-book**: I don't have any secret marketing tips to offer, but what I can say is that you can't sell a book if no one knows it exists. Most of book marketing is simply about creating awareness and you need to do that however you can, whether it's through social media or blogging or passing out fliers on a street corner.

E-BOOK PUBLISHING OPTIONS

Here are the three big questions to bear in mind with e-book creation: first, what is the easiest and most cost-efficient way to produce an e-book? Second, where will it be distributed? And third, how much of a cut do you get? With those in mind, let's take a look at some of the more high-profile options available currently. I'm limiting it to these options because I want to keep this as simple as possible.

AMAZON KINDLE DIRECT PUBLISHING (KDP)

This is Amazon's e-book publishing platform, and if you think you're going to sell a lot of e-books, you might figure out a way to upload your file (book) directly to KDP and avoid using any sort of middleman or e-book "aggregator" that takes a cut of the profits. If you're a true DIY person, you can create your own cover (though if you're not a professional designer, it's better to hire a pro) and format your e-book from a Word file using free software tools such as Mobipocket eBook Creator or Calibre. Mobipocket Creator allows you to create an e-book with a table of contents and convert it into Amazon's proprietary e-book format, AZW (MOBI, the file output by the program, is the same as AZW). You can start with a Word file, which then gets converted to HTML, then MOBI. Check out the Mobipocket eBook Creator guide at the company's Web site

If you don't want to go the total DIY route, you can pay someone a few hundred dollars (or less) to format your e-book for you, but you'll still need to come up with a cover. J.A. Konrath, who's had a lot of success in the self-published e-book space and has written an excellent primer called "How to Make Money on eBooks," recommended Rob Siders at 52novels.com. You can also try Ray Fowler at rayfowler.org. And Smashwords' founder Mark

Coker maintains "Mark's List," which is a list of low-cost e-book formatters and cover designers with pricing starting at about $50. You can get the list via instant autoresponder by e-mailing list@smashwords.com.

Amazon offers a 70 percent royalty rate for authors, but some rules apply (see the complete list of terms). This is the same royalty that Apple offers iPhone/iPad app developers and authors who sell e-books via its iBookstore store. You can upload your e-book directly to the iBookstore, but you have to fill out an application and it's a bit of a process. That's why authors tend to use an "aggregator" like Smashwords or Lulu to get into the iBookstore (see complete list of Apple-approved aggregators here). Even though the iPad supports most of the leading e-book stores (Amazon's Kindle, Barnes & Noble's Nook, Kobo), getting into the iBookstore is becoming more important as Apple continues to sell millions of iPads, iPhones, and iPod Touches.

That said, Amazon is offering incentives to authors to offer their works exclusively on Amazon. This program is called KDP Select and it comes with some key perks. Here's what Amazon has to say:

KDP Select is a new option that features a $6 million annual fund dedicated to independent authors and publishers. If you choose to make a book exclusive to the Kindle Store for at least 90 days, the book is eligible to be included in the Kindle Owners' Lending Library and you can earn a share of the fund based on how frequently the book is borrowed. In addition, by choosing KDP Select, you will have access to a new set of promotional tools, starting with the option to offer enrolled books free to readers for up to 5 days every 90 days. Authors and publishers can enroll a single title, their whole catalog or anything in between within KDP Select.

The Kindle Owners' Lending Library allows Amazon Prime members to "check out" your e-book for free (members can only check out one eligible title per month). Obviously, being able to offer your book for free to thousands -- or potentially millions of customers -- increases the odds you'll "sell" more books. And what's nice is that even though people may not be paying to download your book, you're still getting paid -- and pretty well, according to Amazon.

"Every time a customer borrowed an independently published book in March [2012], the author earned $2.18," said Russ Grandinetti, vice president of Kindle Content, in a recent press release. "That's more than many authors earn when their books are sold."

I can't tell you how long Amazon will continue offering this deal -- and what future payout rates will be -- but I do know plenty of indie authors who are choosing the KDP Select option and not publishing on other platforms because they think it makes the most sense both in terms of number of sales (or downloads) and earnings. Kindle still has the largest market share with about 60 percent of the e-book pie (Nook is at around 25 percent, Apple 15 percent, and others are left to pick up the crumbs).

Of course, not everybody feels KDP Select is the way to go. Smashwords' Coker, who's also the author of the free e-book "Secrets to Ebook Publishing Success" (it's worth checking out), thinks authors should shy away from KDP Select and has written an article explaining why.

Needless to say, Coker has a vested interest in you not going exclusive with Amazon. But he's also well-regarded in the indie book world.

SMASHWORDS

Smashwords, one of the e-book pioneers and largest distributors of self-published e-books, with more than 125,000 titles from over 40,000 authors, is very much a DIY operation. You bring your Word file and cover image, upload it into the company's "Meatgrinder" tool, and in a matter of minutes, you create your e-book in just about every format you'd want. You can then sell that e-book on Smashwords.com or have the company distribute it to most of the major e-book sellers, including Barnes & Noble's eBookstore, Apple's iBooks, Sony, Kobo, and Baker & Taylor's Blio and others. Smashwords also has deals in place for having its authors' e-books distributed to libraries.

As for the Kindle, well, Smashwords says it's still waiting for Amazon to update its KDP intake systems so it automatically can ingest Smashwords titles as other retailers do (the 200 or so titles that Smashwords has loaded into KDP have been loaded manually). Amazon encourages authors to upload directly through KDP, so I wouldn't count on this happening anytime soon.

Smashwords offers a free style guide for formatting your e-book. Although Smashwords encourages authors to keep things simple, you can still create a professional-quality e-book with Smashwords that includes a linked table of contents, NCX navigation, and custom paragraph styling. A couple of years ago, I created an acceptable-looking e-book in about 30 minutes after making some tweaks (usually they involve spacing between chapter breaks) and reprocessing my file three times. If you follow Smashwords' guidelines, you can end up with a professional-quality "reflowable" e-book that looks as good as what many of the big publishers are putting out and reads well on any screen size.

Smashwords prides itself on not charging you for creating your e-book and taking only a small cut of author's royalties (see Smashwords' overview).

Though the cut is small, it's still a cut, but that's the price you're paying for the convenience of having your book distributed on a wide array of platforms and having Smashwords track your sales.

Coker has chided me a bit for disparaging the middleman. He's quick to point out that a good middleman partner (distributor) saves you time, helps you reach retailers you can't reach, and helps you centrally and efficiently manage distribution and metadata updates (change your price or book cover and the change propagates out to all retailers).

Lastly, it's worth noting that Smashwords provides free ISBNs. I'm not going to get into a full on discussion of ISBN, which is "a unique identifier" associated with your e-book, but most companies provide a free ISBN for your e-book or roll the price up into a package. Smashwords has a good quick guide to e-book ISBNs that you should take a look at.

Some distributors are more transparent than others about disclosing exactly what cut they take from your sales. Smashwords considers itself especially transparent. As soon as you upload your book, you get a dynamic pie chart that estimates how the pie is split at each price point across the different sales channels.

Smashwords operates its own e-book store, where authors earn 85 percent of the net sale (what's left after credit card fees are deducted). That works out to between 60 and 80 percent of the list price, depending on the book's price (for more info on author earnings and payment schedules, see Smashwords' FAQ).

For books distributed by Smashwords to its retail network of the Apple iBookstore, Barnes & Noble, Sony, Kobo, Diesel and Baker & Taylor's Blio, the author earns 60 percent of the list price, the retailer takes 30 percent and Smashwords earns 10 percent. The cuts work essentially the same for overseas sales, though in countries that impose VAT taxes, the VAT often comes out of the purchase price before the percentages are applied.

As far as international sales go, Coker says they're growing rapidly. Apple's in 32 countries already and Amazon, Kobo, B&N and Sony are all expanding their global operations. Coker says that 45 percent of its Apple iBookstore sales are from outside the U.S.

"Authors should think globally from day one," Coker says. He predicts that the market outside the U.S. for indie English-language e-books will soon be larger than the U.S. market. Indie book growth is slowing in the U.S., he says, but fledgling international e-book markets are on the cusp of entering their exponential growth phases.

BOOKBABY.COM

BookBaby, the sibling of CD Baby (Brian Felsen is the president of both operations), has a slightly different business model from some of its competitors. Instead of taking a cut of your royalties, it makes you pay a fee of $99 upfront, then charges you a yearly fee of $19 per title you have in its system. It also offers print publishing services.

I haven't used BookBaby yet, but I spoke to a customer service representative at length and was impressed with her responses. When I asked about what advantages BookBaby had over Smashwords, she didn't knock her competitor.

"Smashwords is great," she said. "But BookBaby is for someone who wants a little more hand-holding through the process."

Smashwords' Coker concurs and told me that he's sent people who wanted more hand-holding to BookBaby.

Of course, you'll have to pay a bit more to get that hand-holding. There's a Premium package that runs $199, as well as cover design services (the customer service rep recommended going with the $279 Deluxe option).

BookBaby offers distribution with all the major e-book sellers and offers an Author's Accounting Dashboard to track and analyze sales data.

In all, BookBaby seems like one of the better indie e-book operations out there. If you only sell a few books, that $99 entry fee (or $199 if you go with the premium package) may not seem like such a great deal. But if you sell a lot, you'll quickly recoup your investment.

BARNES & NOBLE'S PUBIT

Barnes & Noble's PubIt self-publishing operation offers similar features to Amazon's KDP, but the two platforms do have their differences. Barnes & Noble has set the PubIt royalty rate for authors at 65 percent of the sale price for titles priced $2.99 and higher. The rate falls to 40 percent if you choose to go lower than $2.99 or higher than $9.99, with B&N setting 99 cents as the lowest allowable price and $199.99 as the highest. (For books priced under $2.99 or over $9.99, you actually earn more by distributing your book to B&N through Smashwords, which pays 60 percent list for all prices 99 cents and up.

B&N's 65 percent is close to Amazon's 70 percent royalty, but not quite as high (Amazon also has pricing restriction to get its highest rate). PubIt includes a free conversion tool that takes your Microsoft Word, TXT, HTML, or RTF files and automatically converts it to an EPUB file, which you then upload to Barnes & Noble's eBookstore (alternatively, of course, if your e-book is already an EPUB file, you can just upload it directly through PubIt). Barnes & Noble allows you to preview how your content will look on one of Barnes & Noble's e-reading devices using the Nook emulator.

Barnes & Noble says that going forward it will offer some unique features and is looking for ways to tie-in the Nook's in-store Wi-Fi streaming features and feature local self-published authors in stores specific to each location.

LULU

When you publish a print book at Lulu -- and a lot of people do -- you also have the option of just publishing an e-book. Lulu e-books are distributed to Apple's iBookstore, Lulu.com, and Barnes & Noble (Nook).

The main benefit Lulu offers in the e-book realm is that it's one of the designated aggregators for Apple's iBookstore.

It appears that Lulu doesn't charge you anything to create an e-book (it offers an EPUB conversion tool and eBook Creator Guide), but like some competitors it offers fee-based premium services.

Lulu has greatly improved its royalty terms in last 18 months. As far as I can tell from its royalty calculator tool, Lulu takes a 10 percent cut of your net earnings from Apple's iBookstore and B&N's Nook Book Store. That's good.

It's hard to say what advantages Lulu has over competitors like Smashwords but at least the royalty rates appear to be the same. Weirdly, I found the Lulu Web site to be straightforward yet convoluted at the same time. For instance, I couldn't figure out whether Lulu distributes your e-book to any retailers beyond Lulu.com, Apple, and Barnes & Noble. From what I saw on the site, it appears they don't.

BOOKTANGO

Author Solutions, one of the largest self-publishers in the U.S., has entered the DIY e-book market with Booktango. Whether Booktango should be called an "e-book generating app" or "self-publishing platform" is hard to say, but it basically provides a free and simple way to upload your manuscript, edit it for proper formatting, then automatically serve it up to various e-book stores, including Kindle, Nook, Kobo, and iBooks.

On the surface, Booktango, which bears the "beta" tag, looks fairly slick and should improve as the company adds more features. The ability to have

WYSIWYG formatting capabilities is nice (even on the iPad) and you can either upload a cover image of your own choosing or design one using some provided templates. All in all, it looks like a perfectly decent way to get your e-book formatted and distributed to all the major e-book stores quickly. Like its competitors, Booktango also manages your e-book sales -- it rolls them all up into one account -- and you can have your royalties sent directly to your checking account.

Booktango is free to use, but the company is working off a freemium model and provides additional fee-based services, such as copy editing, custom cover design, and marketing packages.

Booktango's Web site advertises a "100 percent royalty," which is misleading considering you get that rate only from the e-books you sell on the Booktango Web site and Booktango charges a fee for each book you sell (30 percent of the list price -- the same as Amazon). For other outlets, Booktango takes 10 percent of your net profits, resulting in a "90 percent royalty," which is also misleading because the net profit in its sample royalty rates seems smaller than it should be. Honestly, Booktango's royalty rates don't look too good and can't match its competitors' rates.

However, in an effort to attract authors Booktango is offering a true 100 percent royalty rate until July 4. And the Web site says that if you publish an e-book with Booktango by July 4, you'll retain that 100 percent rate for the life of that book. That means if you make a sale through Booktango's e-book store, you'll get the full amount of the sale (I'm not sure if credit card fees are deducted or not). You'll also get the full 100 percent net of the sale when selling through other e-booksellers (Apple, Amazon, and others will take their 30 percent cut, of course).

Since the service is so new I can't vouch for it, but Booktango's limited-time 100 percent royalty offer certainly has some appeal.

IBOOKS AUTHOR

A lot of people ask me about creating children's books or other types of graphically rich books and e-books. I can't say I'm an expert in this area, but when you're dealing with graphics and images, the self-publishing equation becomes more difficult and expensive (formatting costs tend to go up as you add more images). However, Apple's trying to change all that with iBooks Author, which allows you to build multitouch interactive e-books that you can upload and sell in the iBookstore and view in the iBooks2 app on the iPad, iPhone, and iPod Touch.

The software program is a free download for Mac owners and using it is not so different from creating a PowerPoint presentation. It's not perfect, but overall it's pretty impressive, and Apple will undoubtedly continue improving it with updates.

You work from a selection of templates and can add multitouch widgets to include interactive photo galleries, movies, 3D objects, and more. When you're done, you then have to fill out an application to create an account before you can upload your creations to the iBookstore or iTunes U (Apple has billed iBooks Author as a multifaceted tool for creating everything from textbooks to cookbooks to picture books, and anything else you can think of).

If you can't find a template you like, there are already third-party vendors, including ibooksauthortemplates.com, selling additional templates. (Yes, Apple's spurred another cottage industry).

When iBooks Author launched, some people were upset by the fact that your project can only live in Apple's e-book ecosystem and nowhere else. So it goes. At the moment, the iPad is far and away the best-selling tablet and represents arguably the biggest market for graphically rich color e-books, not to mention the best way to view them (particularly on the new iPad's Retina display). Yes, Amazon has sold a lot of Kindle Fires and the Barnes & Noble's Nook Color and Nook Tablet have found their way into a lot of homes. But the iPad's still king, and Apple's calling the shots here.

I don't have a problem with that and think it's great that Apple offers iBooks Author for free. But the one thing that does bother me is Apple's failure to provide a free ISBN for your e-book. Instead, it tells you to get your own and provides a link to Bowker's Identifiers Services page. Bowker's charges $125 for a single ISBN or 10 for $250. The price drops to single digits when you buy thousands of ISBNs as other self-publishing outfits do. (You can buy a single ISBN for less than $125, but I'd prefer not get into all that). In short, it's patently absurd that Apple's making its authors pay $125 for ISBN number, and I think it's deterring a lot of people from publishing an iBook directly with Apple.

Apple's the exclusive publisher here. It needs to provide free ISBNs to its authors. If Smashwords can afford to do it, so can Apple.

CreateSpace, iUniverse, Xlibris, AuthorHouse, and other POD self-publishing outfits

Most of the large print-on-demand self-publishing operations offer some sort of e-book conversion service and distribution -- and sometimes it gets bundled into a print-publishing package (these companies usually charge a few hundred dollars for converting your e-book). In some cases, this can work out OK for authors who don't care about extracting as much money as they can from each sale and don't want to work with a separate company to create an e-book once they've uploaded their PDF file for their print book. For those who don't think they'll end up selling a lot of copies of their e-book, this can be a fine arrangement, but just beware that in many cases you can't set your own price and more money is being taken out of your net profits than should be. Again, you should strongly consider avoiding companies that don't let you set your own price.

SCRIBD

Scribd.com offers one of the fastest and easiest ways to get an e-book or even a short story up on the Internet, though Scribd isn't a serious player yet as far as e-book sales go. After you create an account, you simply create a PDF of your book with the cover image embedded in the first page of the PDF and upload the PDF to Scribd.

Its online software quickly converts your document into a file that can be viewed on a PC, iPad, or other portable devices. You can also choose to allow people to download your file for viewing.

Scribd has added HTML5 coding, so your document can easily be read on the iPad via the Safari browser (this allows you to use Apple's finger-based, pinch-and-spread touch zoom controls). Currently, the majority of documents posted to Scribd are free to view or download (it's a great way to post samples of your work), but you can sell your work on Scribd as well. (If you want to see an example, I posted a free excerpt of my own book to Scribd. Alas, I should have made my cover larger so it didn't have a white border, but so it goes).

IN SUMMARY

To be clear, there are other ways to go about self-publishing your e-book. For example, I haven't talked about such outfits as Ingram Digital, Overdrive, or LibreDigital, because they're geared toward larger publishing or self-publishing operations rather than individuals. To help focus your decision-making process, I've tried to stick to what I consider the important players right now.

I should also say that everybody comes to the self-publishing process with a different agenda -- and a different book --and some e-book self-publishing options will appeal to you based on the type of book you have (aside from the iBooks Author reference, this article is slanted to publishing more text-based e-books rather than books with lots of illustrations or graphic images, such as children's books). For those who are publishing an e-book as an experiment or "just to get it out there" and who are less concerned with making money and extracting every last dime out of a sale, aggregators offer a convenient solution to get your book in a variety of e-book stores and roll up your sales into one single record that you can easily track (most companies pay out earnings from e-books within 60 to 90 days; Amazon is 60).

It's also worth noting that you can mix and match and go direct with Amazon (KDP), uploading your own file and managing your account, and then use an aggregator such as Smashwords for additional distribution to other e-book stores. At this point there are no hard and set rules and, as I said in the beginning, the e-book market is very fluid, seeing significant changes almost every month. Remember, Google is your best friend for the finer parts of self-publishing, such as converting a Word file to a PDF.

E-BOOK PUBLISHING CONTRACT (2)

This Assignment is effective as of DATE, MONTH, YEAR and is between the following parties:

NAME (the "Author")_____ and COMPANY (the "Publisher") _____
PUBLISHERS ADDRESS _____
AUTHORS ADDRESS _____

The parties agree as follows:

1) THE AGREEMENT IS DATED as recorded on the email submission between NAME indicated in the online submission (hereinafter referred to as the Author), and NAME hereinafter referred to as the Publisher.
2) This Agreement is entered into in good faith. The email submission in the proper format from the Author indicates acceptance to the terms described in this Agreement by all parties named in this Agreement.
3) Author agrees to grant the Publisher the exclusive license to electronically produce, sell, and promote electronic versions (commonly known as "eBooks" or "Electronic Books") of NAME OF TITLE hereinafter known as The Work, worldwide in the English language.
The Author retains the right to publish and excerpt all or portions of the Work for promotional use on her personal Internet website, with no restriction upon length of time the excerpt(s) may be posted.
4) The Author represents that The Work is her original work or that she is sole living copyright owner of The Work, and that she has the exclusive right to grant all rights here-in. The Author retains all rights in The Work not granted specifically to the Publisher for the purposes of publication, promotion and distribution in this document or other agreements signed by both parties.
5) The Author agrees to secure permission for use of any copyrighted materials incorporated in Author's original work, and which is included in the electronic Work covered by this Agreement.
6) Publisher agrees to secure permission for use of any copyrighted material that will be added to the electronic Work covered by this Agreement, and ensures that these added elements will not infringe on existing copyrights or the rights of others.

7) Publisher holds Author harmless from litigation resulting from breach of warranty or other fault of the Publisher.

8) Hard copy excerpts or anthologies from the Work will not be permitted without Author's approval. This Agreement does not permit any hard copy rights, other than the right of each consumer to print a single paper copy for permitted personal use and not for resale. Hard copy rights may be negotiated in a separate agreement.

9) Publisher may not assign this electronic publication agreement to another publisher without the Author's express written consent.

10) Publisher agrees to pay Author an advance of 500 USD upon receipt of The Work.

11) Publisher shall recoup the advance of $ USD and shall receive a further profit of $ USD from initial sales of The Work prior to the payment of royalties to Author. Thereafter, Publisher agrees to pay Author a royalty fee representing a 50% share of the net profit from sales. The net profit is calculated after publishing costs have been deducted, including any advances paid the Author and costs of promotion. Publisher agrees to provide Author full details of their royalty calculations. Royalty payments shall be made quarterly and shall be mailed or sent electronically no later than the 15th day of the month following the end of a calendar quarter.

12) Author agrees to allow the Publisher to perform certain minor script editing (abridgment of the text, sentence restructuring, correcting spelling and grammar errors, etc.) without significantly changing the meaning.

13) Author has the right to modify the final presentation following publication. Modification requests must be presented to the Publisher in the form of a letter or e-mail transmission.

14) Author may request a sales audit at any time with a limit of one per calendar year. Should the sales audit prove the Publisher's figures are accurate, Author will bear the cost of a reasonable auditing fee. Should the sales audit prove the Publisher's figures are inaccurate, Publisher will bear the cost of a reasonable auditing fee and promptly pay the Author the correct amount of royalties due, per the auditor's finding's.

15) Upon the Author's death, royalties shall be paid to the Author's legal heir(s) and shall continue for the duration of the copyright, and not beyond. All rights shall revert to the Author in the event of the dissolution of the Publisher due to bankruptcy.

16) Publisher has the license to publish, promote, and distribute the Work, as an electronic book only, the full term of the Work's copyright, provided that rights have not reverted to the Author under the terms of this contract.

Use of excerpts of the work in promotional materials shall be permitted to the Publisher without consultation with the Author.

17) Publisher will endeavor to produce eBooks in a manner which reflects state-of-the-art industry standards, as these standards evolve.

18) Any changes in this Agreement must be in writing and signed by both parties.

LITERARY AGENCY AGREEMENT (1)

NAME Literary Agents will be the author's sole representative to advise and negotiate sales of all kinds for all of the author's literary material and its subsidiary rights in all forms and media and for all future uses throughout the world. The agency may appoint co-agents for subsidiary rights management, including but not limited to foreign and film rights.

If the agency declines to handle a property, the author shall be free to do as he or she pleases with it without obligation to the agency.

The agency is irrevocably entitled to deduct 15% commission on all income earned through the agency for author's writing services. For foreign and film rights, the agency may deduct 20%, which includes 10% for co-agents. All commissions received by the agency will not be returnable for any reason.

If a potential buyer for the author's literary work or writing services approaches the author, they will be referred to the agency.

The author must approve all offers and sign all agreements negotiated on the author's behalf. NAME Literary Agents will be named as the agency of record in all agreements the author signs on all projects that the agency represents.

The agency shall receive on author's behalf all money due to the author from agreements signed through the agency's efforts. This includes all sales for which negotiations begin during the term of this agreement, and all changes and extensions in those agreements, regardless of when they are made or by whom.

The agency will remit all money and statements due to the author within 10 working days of receiving them.

The agency may respond to mail and email received on the author's behalf unless it is personal, in which case the agency will forward it to the author promptly. The author will notify the agency promptly if there is a change in the author's phone number, email or address.

The agency will pay for all expenses that arise in selling the author's work, except photocopying the work; mailing it abroad; buying galleys and books; and legal assistance. The author must approve all expenses of more than $50 per occurrence.

If an idea originates from the author and the agency does not develop it with the author, the rights to the idea or any basic variation on it belong to the author. However, if another writer approaches the agency with the same idea or a similar idea, the agency is free to represent that project.

If the idea for a project originates from the agency, only the agency retains the rights to the idea or any basic variation on it. The agency may represent a project competitive to the author's project, provided that author and agency agree that it doesn't lessen the agency's ability to represent the author's work.

The author realizes that it may take years to sell a book, and the agency agrees to try as long as the agency believes it is possible. The agency will notify the author promptly when it can no longer help on a book. Then the author may do as he or she wishes with it without obligation to the agency.

If a problem arises about the agency's efforts or the agency/author relationship, the author will contact the agency, and the agency will conscientiously try to solve the problem with fairness to both parties. A problem that can't be solved will be resolved with a mediator or arbitrator chosen by both parties.

Either party may end this agreement with 60 days' notice by registered mail. However, the agency will be entitled to receive statements and commissions on all rights on properties on which the agency makes the initial sale, whether or not the agency represents the author on the sales of these rights.

This agreement is binding on authors and agency's respective personal and business heirs and assigns, and will be interpreted according to STATE law.

The author is free to sign this agreement and will not agree to a conflicting obligation. The author will sign two copies, and each party will have one. Both party's signatures are needed to change this agreement.

Both parties sign this agreement with the hope that it will symbolize a mutual long-term commitment to the development of the author's career and to sharing the rewards of this growth.

Date _____

Social Security Number _____

My Signature _____

My Name _____

Birth Date _____

Street Address _____

City, ST, ZIP _____

Home Phone /2nd Phone (Work or Cell) _____

Fax _____

E-mail _____

Website _____

How I was referred to you _____

Agent's Signature _____

LITERARY AGENT AGREEMENT (2)

This Representation Agreement (the "Agreement") is made and entered into as of the date last written below between AGENCY NAME ("Agency") and NAME (Author)on the following terms and conditions:

1. AGENCY: Author appoints Agency as Author's sole and exclusive Agency to advise, arrange and negotiate for the publication, sale, license or any other disposition in any language, media, form or format the nonfiction content, commencing with the project (the "Work") currently entitled: [Title of Project]

2. PERFORMANCE: Agency will endeavor in good faith to secure the best possible offers for the Work in a professional and efficient manner and, absent other agreements made hereafter, bear all related costs of the representation. Agency has the right to choose the agent in its employ to aid in placement, and may work with independent sub-agents in specific rights categories at its discretion. Agency will always offer its best advice and suggestions for the improvement, marketing and disposition of the Work. Author agrees to carefully consider in good faith all advice given. Author agrees that if a potential buyer approaches Author directly for Author's literary Work or writing services, any such potential buyer will be referred to Agency for negotiation.

If Author has or does create additional nonfiction works prior to the sale of the Work and during the term of this Agreement (including as renewed), Author shall offer such to the Agency for review and possible representation; however, Agency is not obliged to accept any such additional works for representation. If Agency declines such further representation within 60 days of notification of any such additional work, Author is free to take any such works elsewhere without obligation to Agency. Any such new work on which Agent agrees to assume representation shall be subject to the terms of this Agreement.

Upon the sale of the Work or any other work for which representation is assumed hereunder, Author agrees to give Agency first right of refusal on Author's next non-fiction work.

If either party approaches the other with an idea for a work other than the Work, but the parties do not agree to or do not proceed diligently and satisfactorily to Agency to jointly develop the idea, it shall belong to the party first presenting it and such party is free to develop the idea as he/she/it sees fit. If Agency presents the idea to Author, even though Author may prepare a written manifestation of the idea or otherwise have spent time to develop the idea, it belongs to Agency if the parties do not agree to jointly develop the idea. The parties agree that the sharing of any such ideas shall be confidential and protected from disclosure to third parties without the consent of the originator of the idea.

3. COMPENSATION: Author agrees to pay Agency and Agency has the right to deduct as commission the following listed percentages of all monies received related in any way to the Work, with the sole exception of fees for speaking engagements in which Agency did participate in booking:

(a) Fifteen percent (15%) of all income earned from the domestic sale or placement of the Work in any form or format from rights granted to the publisher;

(b) Twenty percent (20%) of all income earned from any foreign, electronic, digital, sponsorship, special sales, merchandise, dramatic, film, performance or other ancillary or secondary right related to the Work. This covers the expense in shipping and selling books overseas, as well as travel costs typically incurred in the placement of secondary rights. An additional five percent (5%) of gross income may be required by a sub-agent if one is used; and Agency is entitled to the commission percentages set forth in paragraphs 3(a) and 3(b) for the legal life of the Work on all agreements substantially pertaining to or made possible by the Work, whether they arise from an agreement initiated or negotiated by Agency or anyone else, including Author. Agency is entitled to the commission percentages set forth in paragraphs 3a and 3b for the legal life of the Work on all agreements pertaining to the Work when Keller Media directly engages in the placement or negotiations of said agreements.

4. TERM OF AGENCY: While book proposals represented by this Agency often sell within 90 days of presentation to publishing houses, the timing of sale can depend on a variety of factors, including, without limitation, how long it takes the Author to prepare the best possible proposal; the optimal season of presentation of the Work for sale; the subject matter; the quantity of similar content being proposed concurrently by third parties; and world events. Agency agrees to work on Author's behalf as long as it believes a sale is possible, and notify Author in writing if no sale seems likely; Author agrees to allow Agency such reasonable time to sell the Work. If Agency believes that it is not likely to make a sale or if Author fails to meet Author's agreed time frame for completion of the Work or parts thereof or otherwise creates an unsatisfactory working relationship, Agency may terminate this Agreement upon written notice to Author at the address set

forth below for Author and Author shall be free to sell or license the Work directly or through others without obligation to Agency.

If the Agency successfully places any right to the Work while this Agreement is in effect, Agency will be the "Agency of Record" on the contract with the publisher or other third party and is thus entitled to compensation as outlined in 3 above and to participate in the placement of all secondary rights extant within the Work not granted to the publisher or first licensor.

If within three (3) months of cessation of this Agreement a publisher to whom the Work had been submitted by the Agency notifies Author or Agency that it desires to contract publication of the Work, this Agreement shall be reactivated and Agency shall be entitled to all rights provided hereunder, including, without limitation, the right to receive commissions.

5. RECEIPT AND DISBURSAL OF FUNDS: All third parties acquiring rights to the Work or any other work covered by the terms of this Agreement in any form or format shall be directed and authorized by Author to remit Author's advance or upfront lump sum payments to Agency. Receipt of all such payments by Agency shall be deemed receipt by Author. All such funds are placed in an Author's Trust account held by the Agency at Chase Bank. Within ten (10) business days after any such monies have been received by Agency, it shall remit the funds to Author less Agency's then unpaid and owing commissions. Author agrees that any Author-Licensor or Author-Publisher contract for the Work or any other work covered by this Agreement shall incorporate the obligation that such advance or upfront payments be made directly to Agency; thereafter whenever possible, licensors shall be instructed to send Agency's portion hereunder of any royalty and other payments due Author paid directly to Agency and the Author's portion hereunder of any royalty and other payments due Author paid directly to Author.

6. EXECUTION OF AGREEMENTS: Agency will not enter into agreements on behalf of the Work without Author's approval. No agreement for sale of a Work shall be valid without Author's signature unless Author has expressly provided permission for Agency to sign by proxy (usually only applicable for the sale of translation/foreign rights.) This Agreement may be digitally or facsimile signed and in counterparts, each of which together shall be deemed one and the same document.

7. INDEMNIFICATION: Author hereby warrants ownership to all the rights related to the Work and other works governed by this Agreement and represents that Author is authorized to dispose of them and represents and warrants that all manuscripts are original, are free from any plagiarism,

slander or libelous content or intent, and do not give advice or make statements that are not supportable and may, if followed, cause harm to others or property. Author will keep an original copy of the manuscript in Author's possession and declares that there are no liens or pending legal action against the Work or any other work subject to this Agreement. Author accepts full and complete responsibility for the results of the authorized disposition of the Work or any other work subject to this Agreement by any third parties. Author shall defend, indemnify, and hold Agency and its employees, subcontractors, and corporation harmless from any and all liabilities, losses, claims, demands, costs (including attorneys' fees and expenses) and any other expenses arising from or in connection with any breach or claimed violation of any of the representations or warranties set forth in this paragraph 7.

8. PREVIOUS EXPOSURE: Prior to or upon signing this Agreement, Author will provide Agency with a complete list of publishers, if any, located anywhere in the world who have seen the Work or any other work subject to this Agreement or a proposal for the Work or any other work subject to this Agreement in any form.

9. NO WARRANTIES: Author acknowledges that Agency does not purchase literary properties and cannot guarantee or warrant a sale of the Work or any other work covered by the terms of this Agreement. Author acknowledges that other works may exist in the marketplace which may be similar to the Work, and that neither the Agency nor its employees, successors or assigns can bear any responsibility for the existence of such competing works. Agency has the right to represent similar content as long as the representation does not directly interfere with the efforts made on behalf of the Work. At the Author's option, works submitted for representation can be registered with the United States Copyright Office, although it is customary for the publisher to obtain copyright on behalf of the author when the work has become a viable commercial property as a result of a legally binding contract. Author agrees to notify Agency if and when such copyright is obtained.

10. ENFORCEMENT: In the event that a dispute should arise for breach, enforcement or interpretation of this Agreement, the parties agree to resolve such dispute by binding arbitration administered by JAMS, Inc. or ADR Services, Inc. Santa Monica or Los Angeles, California, at the election of the party first filing for relief and subject to the applicable rules of the selection arbitration tribunal. Prejudgment remedies may be sought in the Los Angeles Superior Court, with the parties hereby consenting to such exclusive court jurisdiction. The prevailing party in any dispute arising out of or relating to this Agreement, whether in arbitration or court, to procure prejudgment relief

or confirmation of any arbitration award or on appeal shall recover from the other party his/her/its reasonable attorneys' fees, costs and expenses, including those charged by the arbitration tribunal and arbitrator. This Agreement shall be governed by the laws of the State of California except its conflict of laws principles.

11. GENERAL TERMS: The parties hereto are independent contractors of one another and, except as expressly set forth herein, they are not agents or representatives of the others, and in no event an employee of the other. Due to the personal nature of Author's services, this Agreement is not assignable or transferrable by Author, however, Author's heirs and assigns shall be bound to pay Agency any fees due hereunder as if Author were alive. This Agreement constitutes the entire agreement between the parties, superseding all prior discussions, understandings, and agreements. No waiver or indulgence of any breach hereof shall be deemed a waiver of any other breach. In the event any part of this Agreement is deemed unenforceable or invalid, the remainder of the Agreement shall remain enforceable and in effect. Paragraph titles are inserted for convenience only, and are not to be used to construe the provisions. This Agreement shall be interpreted according to its fair meaning and intent and not against the drafter of all or any provisions hereof. This Agreement cannot be canceled, altered or amended except in writing and signed by both parties.

The undersigned represent and warrant that they have read and fully understand the terms of this Agreement and agree to be bound thereby and that this Agreement.

_____   _____
Author   Date:

_____   _____
Agent   Date:

PARTNERSHIP AGREEMENT FOR BOOK FAIRS AND FESTIVALS

Objective: To form a partnership between TLC and ACI in the production and success of the Book Fair & Art Festival

I. Points of Agreement

Co-Sponsorship: TLC and ACI will co-sponsor the Book Fair & Art Festival on *This Date* _____. This would involve promotions including: direct mail, e-mail/social networking messaging, newsletters, website advertising, printed materials and any other promotion vehicle for the events. Sponsorship will be exclusive to TLC and ACI for *date and year*

- TLC is a non-profit organization chaired by _____.
- ACI / Book Fair and Art Festival are companies / corporations owned by NAME.
- This agreement in no way suggests that either company / corporation is owned by the other and concludes that each entity is a separate company / corporation chaired by and owned by _____.
- The Book Fair and Art Festival lends its name to TLC / to use, promote, publicize and advertise until the Book Fair and Art Festival, dated_____, is over and a new agreement between TLC and ACI is reached.

Remuneration: TLC and ACI will equally share (50%-50%) residual revenue from all sponsorships, booth sales, ticket sales, merchandise sales, seminar sales, - author, entertainer, speaker, promotional sales – book signing sales, book display sales, program book ad sales, commissary / concession (tshirts, etc. sales) and all other sales after expenses. Remuneration to be paid to ACI by the TLC accountant five days after all agreed upon expenses have been met and outstanding financial commitments are received.

The name of the bank and type of account(s) to be used, will be mutually agreed upon.

II. Schedule of Events
Date of Event
For this event, TLC and ACI out of all revenue:
- Will provide staffing and manage the Book Fair & Art Festival.

- Will pay for costs including but not limited to; security, booth registrations, setup of booths, hiring a decorator, volunteer expenses, program books, signage and venue.
- Will comply with applicable use agreement terms that TLC has with the venue.
- Will barter advertisements and seek earned media.
- Will send a direct mail piece to solicit companies for the event. Some sponsors require paper proposals and packages. Where appropriate and expedient all solicitations will be sent electronically.
- Will announce the event in all of its collateral and calendars associated with the Book Fair & Art Festival.
- Will assist in advertising the Book Fair and Art Festival through media outlets including but not limited to Sponsors: the Business Journal and the Informant, that may provide significant pro-bono/traded press.
- TLC and ACI will receive a consultant fee in the minimum amount of $300.00 per week for coordination/production work for the Book Fair and Art Festival per approved budget.

ACI will Email nationally to the book trade industry, including, authors, publishers, self-publishers, libraries, distributors / wholesalers, the general public and the national media.

A. Either party may cancel this Agreement, or an extension of it, for cause by giving 30-days' notice to the other, with ACI to be paid fees earned for work completed and reimbursement for costs incurred to the date of termination in the regular prescribed manner. This specifically includes: Willfully breaching or neglecting the duties required to be performed under this Agreement; Committing clearly dishonest acts; or Engaging in acts of disruption or violence.

B. All out of pocket expenses such as standard office charges, printing, postage, office supplies, fax fees, association related travel expenses, etc… will be approved by the (TLC) President & Chair. Per approved budget.

All out of pocket expenses such as standard office charges, printing, postage, office supplies, fax fees, association related travel expenses, etc… will be approved by the (ACI) President/CEO. Per approved budget.

C. Estimates/expenses for services not included in this contract per approved budget shall be provided to the (TLC) President & Chair and approval obtained, in advance of any project involving compensation beyond out of pocket expenses and outside the budget.

D. ACI is not responsible for any delinquency, bankruptcy or other failure to pay by TLC.

E. This agreement is a one-year contract or the length of time till the ending of the Book Fair and Arts Festival and all remuneration to ACI has been paid in full, renewable by mutual consent and a letter. The length of the term and dollar amount is contingent upon achievement of desired results.

F. Because ACI is an independent and not an employee of TLC, TLC will not:
- withhold Social Security and Medicare taxes from ACI's payments or make such tax payment on ACIs behalf
- make state or federal unemployment contributions on ACI's behalf,
- or withhold state or federal income tax from ACI's payments.

G. ACI will pay all applicable taxes related to the performance of services provided by ACI under this contract. This includes income, Social Security, Medicare and self-employment taxes.

H. ACI will also pay all unemployment contributions related to the performance of services under this contract. ACI will reimburse TLC if TLC is required to pay such taxes or unemployment contributions if it pertains to ACI.

I. Neither ACI nor ACI's employees are eligible to participate in any
employee pension, health, vacation pay, sick pay or other fringe benefit plan of the TLC.

III. Other Services

ACI retains the right to produce other book fairs in other cities and states and produce a book fair within 300 miles of STATE and perform services for other business as long as ACI and TLC determine said work does not constitute conflicts of interest for the Book Fair and Art Festival has not received a letter from TLC accepting a "first rights of refusal" to produce a book fair with ACI within the two-week period of ACI sending out a letter stating its intentions to produce a book fair.

IV. Assistants

ACI may employ assistants for the Book Fair & Art Festival as TLC deems appropriate to fulfill contractual services. Payment by TLC of any professional services will be contingent upon prior written approval of a request to utilize such professional services to TLC.

V. Equipment and Supplies

ACI will do its best to find the services to provide any equipment, tools and supplies necessary for the Book Fair & Art Festival to perform the contractual services. Payment by TLC for equipment, tools and supplies will be contingent upon prior written approval of a request for equipment, tools, and supplies to the TLC.

VI. Disputes

If a dispute arises, the parties will try in good faith to settle it through mediation conducted by a mediator to be mutually selected.

The parties will share the costs of the mediator equally. Each party will cooperate fully and fairly with the mediator and will attempt to reach a mutually satisfactory compromise to the dispute. If the dispute is not resolved within 30 days after it is referred to the mediator, it will be arbitrated by an arbitrator to be mutually selected.

Judgment on the arbitration award may be entered in any court that has jurisdiction over the matter. Costs of arbitration, including lawyers' fees, will be allocated by the arbitrator.

VII. Successors and assignees

This Agreement binds and benefits the heirs, successors and assignees of the parties.

VIII. Notices

All notices must be in writing. A notice may be delivered to a party at the address that follows a party's signature or to a new address that a party designates in writing. Notice shall be deemed given upon receipt. A notice may be delivered:
- in person
- by certified mail, or
- by overnight courier.

IX. Governing law

This Agreement will be governed by and construed in accordance with the laws of the State of........

X. Waiver

If one party waives any term or provision of this Agreement at any time, that waiver will be effective only for the specific instance and specific purpose for which the waiver was given. If either party fails to exercise or delays exercising any of its rights or remedies under this Agreement, that party retains the right to enforce that term or provision at a later time.

XI. Severability

If any court determines that any provision of this Agreement is invalid or unenforceable, any invalidity or unenforceability will affect only that provision and will not make any other provision of this Agreement invalid or unenforceable and such provision shall be modified, amended or limited only to the extent necessary to render it valid and enforceable.

XII. Ownership and confidentiality of records, papers and information

A. TLC shall make available to ACI any and all documents and/or information necessary or useful for ACI to perform its duties under this Agreement.
B. TLC shall have final authority to determine what documents and/or multi-media content may or may not be used for this project.
C. ACI shall not during the term of this Agreement, or any extension thereof, impart any information relative to the business and affairs of TLC to any agency, institution, governmental or business entity, or individual, except to those employees or ACI's, of TLC and others who are authorized or directed by TLC to receive such information.
D. All original materials prepared by the ACI in connection with performance of services under this Agreement including, without limitation; TLC shall own all its financial and corporate records together with any work or other papers, which may be used to develop those records by ACI.
E. Termination: TLC shall furnish thirty (30) days prior written notice of termination to ACI if the termination of this Agreement is for cause. No compensation shall be due to ACI for such thirty (30) day period if termination by TLC is for cause. If ACI terminates this Agreement for cause, it is entitled to compensation for the remainder of the contract. Cause is defined as, and includes: willfully breaching or neglecting the duties required to be performed under this agreement; committing clearly dishonest acts and/or engaging in acts of disruption or violence.

XIII. Entire agreement

A. This Agreement contains the entire Agreement between the parties, and all its terms are contractual and not merely recitations. Any waivers or modifications to this Agreement must be in writing and signed by both parties.

B. If any court or body of competent jurisdiction finds any portion of this Agreement invalid, the invalidity of that portion of the Agreement shall not affect the balance of the Agreement.

XIV. Miscellaneous provisions

A. Section titles or captions contained in this Agreement are inserted only as a matter of convenience and for reference and in no way define or limit, extend or describe the scope of this Agreement or the intent of any of its provisions.
B. The parties agree to execute all documents that may be necessary to carry out the intent purposes of this Agreement.
C. At the option of the parties, disputes arising from or connected with this Agreement may be resolved by mediation, initiated by a party giving written notice to the other. Any Agreement reached through mediation shall be binding on both parties. Each party to any mediation shall bear its own costs.
D. No modification or waiver of any of the terms of this Agreement shall be valid unless reduced to writing and executed with the same formality as this Agreement. Failure by either party to enforce the rights hereunder shall not be construed as waiver of such right. Any waiver, including a waiver of default, in one instance, shall not constitute a continuing waiver in any other instance.
E. Any notice to either party may be delivered personally, by mail, or by fax.

This Agreement contains the entire agreement between the parties, and all its terms are contractual and not merely recitations. Any waivers or modifications to this Agreement must be in writing and signed by both parties.

At the option of the parties, disputes arising from or connected with this Agreement may be resolved by mediation, initiated by a party giving written notice to the other. Any agreement reached through mediation shall be binding on both parties. Each party to any mediation shall bear its/his/her own costs.

IN WITNESS WHEREOF, the signatories below have the authority to execute this Agreement and have done so on the day and year below.

ACI / BOOK FAIR AND ART FESTIVAL
NAME
ADDRESS

Dated: _____

By: _____

TLC
NAME
ADDRESS

Dated: _____
By: _____

SCHEDULE A

For the purposes of this Agreement, ACI will assist TLC with the tasks outlined below to provide successful economic, management and participant outcomes for the Book Fair and Art Festival accordingly:

Administration Services – Co-Management of the Book Fair and Art Festival Steering Committee Members whose responsibilities include but are not limited to:

- Sales and Ticketing - TLC
- Registration, Credentials, Booth Assignments, Website – TLC
- Sponsorship Compliance – JOINT
- Volunteer Coordination/Greeters/Staff Communications on and off site, - TLC / ACI
- Entertainment Coordination, Seminars, Authors, Prayer Breakfast, Staging, etc - TLC / ACI
- Public Relations & Marketing, Photography, - JOINT
- Day Care – TLC
- Youth Activities – TLC
- Activities for the men and women – TLC
- Tucson & Out of State Coordination – TLC
- Signage – TLC
- Chair Meetings and Develop and Manage Report Requirements - TLC
- Develop Strategic Plan/Action Plan – JOINT
- Conduct Limited Research and Develop Market Analysis – TLC
- Work with Exhibit Management Team – TLC
- Develop Event Timelines - TLC / ACI
- Where Appropriate, Negotiate Contracts - TLC / ACI
- Pre, Day Of and Post Conference Planning and Oversight - TLC / ACI
- Proofing and Editing Documents - TLC / ACI
- Establish Reporting Guidelines - TLC

Performance metrics - TLC

The following metrics should be used to measure the success and progress of this project.
- Past results
- Industry benchmarks or averages
- Set goals and requirements
- Desired improvements of quality or cost
- Behavior based
- Increases attendance or clientele
- Number of website visitors, length of stay, depth of navigation, number of clicks
- Number of calls received
- Number of complaints
- Change in customer behavior/buying patterns
- Attendee's satisfaction level
- Cost-based
- Conversion rate (proportion of customers who perform a specific action)
- Cost per sponsor and booth vendor cost per sale
- Return on Investments (ROI)
- Production costs

TONY ROSE

**Historic List of The Sponsors
For the Book Fair and Art Festival**

Book Fair Joint Venture Agreement

THIS AGREEMENT MADE and entered as of the _____ day of _____, _____, by and between City Book Fairs, Art Festivals and Book Pavilions, Inc., a STATE corporation having an office at _____ (hereinafter referred to as "CBF"), and_____, a _____[state] [corporation, limited liability company], having an office at _____ ("Local Partner") (both of the foregoing individually or collectively, as the case may be, sometimes referred to herein as the "Venturers").

WITNESSETH:
In consideration of the mutual covenants set forth herein, and intending to be legally bound and for other good and valuable consideration, the parties hereto hereby agree as follows:

ARTICLE I – THE JOINT VENTURE

Section 1.1 *Joint Venture Purpose*. CBF and Local Partner hereby enter into and form a joint venture (herein called the "Venture") for the limited purposes and scope set forth herein. The business and affairs of the Venture shall be conducted solely under the name _____ Book Fair & Art Festival ("Book Fair"). The purpose of the Venture shall be to produce, market, and commercially profit from Book Fair. The principal place of business in the Book Fair local market shall be at _____ [location].

More specifically, the purpose of the Book Fair shall be carried out by promoting reading, encouraging writing, and heightening an awareness of education, literacy and the arts in _____'s [location] multi-diverse communities, and will:
1. Honor the book publishing industry and artists on a citywide level in the form of a two day literary and art celebration;
2. Provide a format for local and national authors and artists to meet their reading and buying public;

3. Encourage literacy, education and the arts among children, young adults and adults in the urban and rural communities in and around the City of _____ [location];
4. Showcase the work of independent publishers, self-publishers and artists who may not necessarily have the forums available to them on a national scale;
5. Offer educational seminars, workshops and panels to authors and writers who are interested in the many facets of the book publishing industry including: self-publishing their manuscripts, ebooks, international licensing and social networking; and
6. Enable a diverse selection of literary work and art to be seen as an important part of _____'s [location] history and culture.

The Book Fair will celebrate small press books, independent publishers, self-publishers and mainstream publishers with an interest in multi-cultural literature. The genres will include: non-fiction, fiction, children's books, teenage, how-to, self-help, biographies, poetry, audio/spoken word, magazines, comics, e-books, fan fiction, romance, urban, and other selected or permitted genres. The potential attendees will consist of children of all ages, as well as adults who love books and art, resulting in a positive day for everyone, including those who work within the book publishing and art industries.

The Book Fair will also be promoted as a great vehicle for publishers, self-publishers and authors to showcase their existing title(s) or introduce their new book(s) by exhibiting and book signing them. There will be an Authors' Stage for them to present to a large and diverse audience and a meet-and-greet VIP reception. The book fair's program format will include: booth and table exhibitors; self-published / independent published author and celebrity author book signings, national and local talent performances; seminars, workshops and panels that cover social networking, marketing, promotion and book writing. There will also be author readings; fine art displays; spoken word poetry and cultural dance performances. For those authors who cannot attend, the Venture will promote and market their title(s) at the NCCBF book display showcase and in the _____ Book Fair Journal which will be handed out to the attendees. The Book Fair be open to the public and will be intended to attract bookstore owners, authors, artists, publishers, librarians, educators, major book publishing houses, celebrity authors, agents and news media personnel with an interest in the arts.

Section 1.2 *Term*. The term of this Agreement shall commence as of the date set forth above in the preamble and will expire on _____, unless otherwise terminated as set forth in Article IV.

Section 1.3 *Project Success*. Following the completion of a given Book Fair, the Venturers will evaluate the level of success the event, and the following metrics will be used to measure the success level and progress of this project.

1. Past results;
2. Industry benchmarks or averages;
3. Set goals and requirements;
4. Desired improvements of quality or cost;
5. Behavior based;
6. Increases attendance or clientele;
7. Number of website visitors, length of stay, depth of navigation, number of clicks;
8. Number of calls received;
9. Number of complaints;
10. Change in customer behavior/buying patterns;
11. Attendee's satisfaction level;
12. Cost-based;
13. Conversion rate (proportion of customers who perform a specific action);
14. Cost per sponsor and booth vendor cost per sale;
15. Return on Investments (ROI); and
16. Production costs.

Section 1.4 *CBF Fee*. Local Partner agrees and acknowledges that: (i) CBF has expended considerable time and resources in building the NCCBF brand; (ii) CBF has developed considerable expertise in producing and organizing events of the kind contemplated under this Agreement, and (iii) CBF has developed relationships with and has access to companies, individuals and resources critical to the success of the Venture. In view of the foregoing and for the opportunity to enter this Agreement with CBF, Local Partner agrees to pay CBF the sum of $_____, subject to the Terms of this Agreement.

ARTICLE II Management

Section 2.1 *General Management*. Express as specifically provided otherwise, the overall management and control of the business and affairs of the Venture shall be vested in the Venturers collectively. Except where herein

expressly provided to the contrary, all decisions with respect to the management and control of the Venture must be approved by the Venturers and shall be binding on the Venture and all of the Venturers. Among the specific responsibilities to be shared by the Venturers are the following:
1. Determination of location and date of Book Fair;
2. Sponsorship Compliance;
3. Volunteer Coordination/Greeters/Staff Communications on and off site;
4. Entertainment Coordination, Seminars, Authors, Prayer Breakfast, Staging, etc;
5. Public Relations & Marketing, Photography (to defray costs, the Venture will seek to barter; advertisements and seek earned media);
6. Develop Strategic Plan/Action Plan;
7. Develop Event Timelines;
8. Where Appropriate, Negotiate Contracts;
9. Pre, Day of and Post Conference Planning and Oversight;
10. Announce the Book Fair event in all of their respective collateral and calendars associated with the Book Fair; and
11. Proofing and Editing Documents.

Section 2.2 *Specific Local Partner Duties*. Notwithstanding the foregoing, in conducting the joint venture, Local Partner shall assume the following duties and shall have the authority and power reasonably necessary to carry out these duties, subject to veto by CBF:
1. Sales and Ticketing;
2. Youth Activities;
3. Activities for the men and women;
4. _____ & Out of State Coordination;
5. Signage;
6. Chair Meetings and Develop and Manage Report Requirements;
7. Day Care;
8. Registration, Credentials, Booth Assignments, Website;
9. Work with Exhibit Management Team;
10. Conduct Limited Research and Develop Market Analysis; and
11. Establish Reporting Guidelines.

Section 2.3 *General Local Partner Duties*. In addition to the specific tasks stated in Section 2.2., Local Partner shall implement or cause to be implemented the ordinary and usual business and affairs of the Venture which take place in the Local Partner's local geographic area, in accordance with and limited by this Agreement, unless expressly reserved by CBF to itself.

These include, but are not necessarily limited to the following:
1. Coordinating and implementing the advertising, promotional and marketing plan approved by CBF;
2. Sending direct mail pieces to solicit companies for the event (some sponsors require paper proposals and packages) and, as appropriate and expedient, sending electronic solicitations;
3. Utilizing e-mail/social networking messaging, newsletters, website advertising, printed materials and any other promotion vehicle for the events; and
4. Obtaining and coordinating the services of all local independent contractors, necessary or appropriate to carry out the Book Fair; obtaining any equipment, tools and supplies necessary for the Book Fair.

Section 2.3 *CBF Specific Duties*. CBF will email publicity material nationally to the book trade industry, including, authors, publishers, self-publishers, libraries, distributors / wholesalers, the general public and the national media.

Section 2.4 *CBF Major Decisions*. All Major Decisions are to be made by or are subject to the authority of CBF. If to be implemented by the Local Partner, any such decision requires the prior written approval of CBF (written approval may be in the form of electronic communication), upon no less than 5 business day written notice by Local Partner to CBF requesting approval. Major Decisions include the following:

1) Hiring an accountant, attorney or other professional necessary or appropriate to carry out the business of the Venture;

2) Entering into a commercial lease related to the operation of the Venture or Book Fair or any agreement or arrangement for the furnishing to or by the Venture of space;

3) Financing for the Venture;

4) Any single transaction involving the expenditure of Venture funds exceeding $_____ or the aggregate expenditure of $_____ over any _____ week period;

5) Determining the maximum and minimum working capital requirements of the Venture; and

6) Adjusting, settling, or compromising any claim, obligation, debt, demand, suit, or judgment against the Venture.

ARTICLE III ALLOCATIONS, DISTRIBUTIONS, ACCOUNTING, AND CONTRIBUTIONS

Section 3.1 *Profit and Loss Allocation*. The Venturers agree that CBF shall own sixty percent (60%) of the undivided interest in the Venture and the Local Partner shall own forty percent (40%) of the undivided interest in the Venture (hereinafter referred to as the Distribution Percentage Interests). The Venturers agree that they shall share in the profits or losses of the Venture and in all distributions of income of the Venture in the same proportions as their respective Distribution Percentage Interests. For accounting and federal, state, and local income tax purposes, all income, deductions, credits, gains, and losses of the Venture shall be allocated to the Venturers in proportion to their respective Distribution Percentage Interests.

Section 3.2 *Revenue*. The revenue of the Venture shall include all income generated directly from the operation of the Venture. Possible anticipated sources of revenue from the Venture include, and are not necessarily limited to: sponsorships; booth sales; ticket sales; merchandise sales; seminar sales; author, entertainer, speaker, promotional sales; book signing sales; book display sales; program book ad sales; and commissary/concession (tshirts, etc. sales). CBF shall receive a consultant fee in the amount of $_____ per week, and Local Partner shall receive a consultant fee in the amount of $_____ per week for coordination/production work for the Book Fair in each given year that the Book Fair is held, per approved budget.

Section 3.3 *Costs*. The costs of the Venture shall include only those expenses that are direct costs for the operation of the Venture. Anticipated costs include, but are not necessarily limited to, the following: security, booth registrations, setup of booths, hiring a decorator, volunteer expenses, program books, signage, venue, insurance, accounting and legal fees.

Section 3.4 *Distribution*. Net income received by the Venture shall be distributed to the Venturers, in proportion to their interest in the Venture, within five days after all agreed upon expenses have been met and outstanding financial commitments have been received. Notwithstanding the expiration of the Agreement or the conclusion of any particular Book Fair in any given year, the Venturers shall conclude all necessary and appropriate business to reconcile the business and financial affairs of the Venture, including the payment of debts of the Venture and the receiving of revenue due the Venture, as efficiently and expeditiously as commercially reasonable. Further, all monies contributed by parties to this joint venture and all monies received as revenues from the Venture or otherwise shall be treated and regarded as, and are declared to be, trust funds for the performance of the operation and not for any other purpose until all obligations of the parties to this joint undertaking shall have been paid, otherwise discharged, or provided for by adequate reserves. Any reserves shall likewise be treated as trust funds until they serve the purpose for which they were created.

Section 3.5 *Bank Account*. Subject to the control of CBF, the Venturers shall establish a separate bank account in the name of the joint venture, and all Venture income shall be deposited into the bank account and all Venture expenses shall be paid from this bank account. Upon the direction of CBF, Local Partner will open a bank account in the Local Partner's city; and, any such bank account must have a branch office in the vicinity of CBF's office. To be valid, all drafts or checks issued in connection with this Joint Venture Agreement must be signed by a representative of CBF.

Section 3.6 *Capital Account for Accounting Purposes, Capital Contributions*. Each Venturer shall have a capital account to which its share of the profit or loss of the Venture shall from time to time be credited or charged. Withdrawals from said account and other distributions *(whether or not of capital)* to the Venturers shall be made in proportion to their Distribution Percentage Interests. No interest shall be payable on the capital contributions or accounts of the Venturers, notwithstanding that the amounts thereof may not be equal. The initial capital contribution of the Local Partner shall be $_____$. The initial capital contribution of CBF shall be $_____$. The Venturers may contribute additional capital to the Venture in such amounts and at such times as they mutually agree.

Section 3.7 *Financial Records*. Accurate financial records shall be kept by the Venturers of all transactions pertaining to Venture business. CBF shall have primary responsibility for determining the financial system to be used, and for keeping the official accounting records. The accounting system shall ensure timely and accurate record-keeping. The Venture's financial records shall be kept in accordance with good accounting principles and procedures applied in a consistent manner, and the Venturers will keep statements, receipted bills, and invoices, and all other records covering all collections, disbursements, and other data in connection with the Venture. These records shall be open for inspection by the Venturers at all times. Each Venturer shall receive an annual financial report including a balance sheet and a profit and loss statement together with tax returns (state, federal, and local) as soon as reasonably practicable after the close of the Venture's fiscal year.

CBF shall have the right to appoint with mutual agreement at the expense of the Venture, an accountant for the purpose of controlling on behalf of Venture the revenues generated in accordance with this joint venture agreement. This representative shall be provided with access to all financial reports, accounting summaries, bank reports, and other documents relating to the joint operation and necessary to the preparation of reports for _____ as to the daily operations including income and expenditures in connection with the Venture.

Section 3.8 *Tax Returns*. The Venturers shall prepare or cause to be prepared a partnership form 1065, which must be submitted to the Venturers for their approval prior to filing, and which must be filed with the appropriate federal, state and/or tax authorities on behalf of the joint venture regarding this transaction; and a form K-1 for each Venturers. The tax and fiscal years for the Venture shall be the calendar year.

ARTICLE IV TERM AND TERMINATION

Section 4.1 *Prohibition of Termination*. The Venture shall commence on the date set forth in Section 1.2 and shall continue until terminated in accordance with the provisions of this Article IV. No Venturer shall have the right, and each Venturer hereby agrees not to dissolve, terminate, or liquidate, or to petition a court for the dissolution, termination, or liquidation of the Venture except as provided in this Agreement.

Section 4.2 *Post Book Fair Termination or Pre-Book Fair Termination*. Following the operation and conclusion of a Book Fair in any given year under this Agreement, either party may terminate this Venture upon one hundred twenty (120) days' notice to the other party at any time or times without regard to fault or default on the part of the other party. Or, prior to the expenditure of funds by the Venture for a Book Fair in any given year, either party may terminate this Venture upon one hundred twenty (120) days' notice to the other party at any time or times without regard to fault or default on the part of the other party. Or, upon the mutual agreement of the Venturers, the Venture may be terminated.

Section 4.3 *Default*. (a) A default shall occur in the event that a Venturer (hereinafter referred to as the Defaulting Venturer):

1) Fails in any respect to make capital contributions required to be made by it pursuant to this Agreement, and the other Venturer shall not have paid the whole of such deficiency within thirty (30) days of notice of such default as provided for herein, or if any Venturer otherwise materially fails to comply with or violates any of the provisions of this Agreement, and such failure or violation continues for a period of thirty (30) days after notice of such failure or violation is given by the other Venturer; or

2) Institutes proceedings to be adjudicated a voluntary bankrupt, or consents to the filing of a bankruptcy proceeding against it, under the Federal Bankruptcy Act or any other similar federal or state law; or

3) Shall have entered against it a decree or order of a court having jurisdiction adjudging it a bankrupt or insolvent under the Bankruptcy Act or any other similar applicable federal or state law; or

4) Shall have entered against it a decree or order of a court having jurisdiction for the appointment of a receiver, liquidator, or trustee or assignee in bankruptcy or insolvency. If this Venture is terminated or dissolved due to default by either Venturer, the non-defaulting Venturer shall have the option to acquire from the defaulting Venturer, all of the defaulting Venturer's interest in the Venture for an amount equal to the balance of the defaulting Venturer's capital account as of the date of such dissolution or termination, including the defaulting Venturer's unwithdrawn share of profits and losses of the Venture as of such date, less the sums necessary for repayment of any indebtedness of the Venture to the defaulting Venturer or any affiliate thereof.

Section 4.4 *Dissolution upon Event of Dissolution*. The Venture shall not be wound up and terminated by the occurrence of an Event of Dissolution unless the remaining Venturer shall so decide. The term Event of Dissolution as used hereunder shall mean: the dissolution or termination of any partnership or corporation which is now or which shall hereafter become a Venturer.

Section 4.5 *Obligations Prior to Termination or Dissolution*. The termination of the Venture, whether pursuant to Section 4.3 or 4.4 hereof, shall in no way affect the obligation of the Venture, any of the Venturers, or any other signatory hereto as to acts or omissions which may have occurred prior to the effective date of termination hereof, and such obligation shall continue until a final determination by a court or courts of proper jurisdiction of the matter or matters at hand.

Section 4.6 *Prohibition Regarding Encumbrances etal*. Local Partner may not, without the prior written consent CBF, mortgage, pledge, sell, assign, hypothecate, or otherwise encumber, transfer, or permit to be transferred in any manner or by any means whatever, whether voluntarily or by operation of law, all or any part of its interest in the Venture.

ARTICLE V REPRESENTATIVE

Section 5.1 *Selection of Representatives:* To facilitate the handling of all matters and questions in connection with the performance of this joint venture by CBF and Local Partner, each of the Venturers shall appoint a representative with full and complete authority to act on its behalf in relation to any matters in connection with, arising out of, or relative to any matter involving the operation of the Venture. Each Venturer shall give the other written notice of its choice of a representative.

Section 5.2 *Change of Representative*. Either party may at any time change its representative by furnishing to the other a notice and duly executed appointment of a new representative or alternate, but until the appointment and provision of the notice, the actions of the representative or alternate shall be conclusively binding on the respective parties.

Section 5.3 *Actions of Representative:* The representatives of CBF and Local Partner shall meet from time to time, as required, to act on necessary matters pertaining to the Venture. No representative shall be liable to the Venturers by reason of his acts as a representative, except in the case of his gross negligence or actual fraudulent or dishonest conduct. The meetings described in this section may occur in person or by telephone or electronic communication

ARTICLE VI MISCELLANEOUS

Section 6.1 *Notices*. All notices, demands, or requests provided for or permitted to be given pursuant to this Agreement must be in writing. Notices may be provided by certified postage pre-paid United States mail, by overnight courier utilizing a major service such as Fedex, by personal delivery to a Venturer, or by fax or electronic transmission provided that documentary evidence of receipt is produced and available. Notice by personal delivery, fax, or electronic transmission shall be deemed given upon evidence of receipt; by U.S. Mail, shall be deemed given 3 business days following deposit in the U.S. Mail; and by overnight courier service, shall be deemed given 2 business days following drop-off with the courier service. Notice shall be addressed to the party at the address set forth for each in the Preamble. Any party may change its address for purposes of notification by written notice to the other Venturer.

Section 6.2 *Governing Law*. This Agreement and the obligations of the Venturers hereunder shall be interpreted, construed, and enforced in accordance with the laws of the State of Arizona.

Section 6.3 *Whole Agreement*. This Agreement contains the entire agreement between the parties hereto relative to the formation of a venture and any actions thereunder. No variations, modifications, or changes herein or hereof shall be binding upon any party hereto unless set forth in a document duly executed by or on behalf of such party. If a party waives any term or provision of this Agreement at any time, that waiver will be effective only for the specific instance and specific purpose for which the waiver was given. If either party fails to exercise or delays exercising any of its rights or remedies under this Agreement, that party retains the right to enforce that term or provision at a later time.

Section 6.4 *Successors and Assigns et al*. Subject to the restrictions on transfers and encumbrances set forth herein, this Agreement shall issue to the benefit of and be binding upon the undersigned Venturers and their respective successors, and assigns. Notwithstanding the foregoing, it is understood and agreed that the services of _____ ("Key Person") are essential to this Agreement and that he/she shall personally oversee and be involved with conducting all key aspects of Local Partner's responsibilities and activities set forth in the Agreement. In the event that there is any change in business form, management or organization of Local Partner or there is any other occurrence (such as death, disability, or otherwise) which materially frustrates the involvement of Key Person in the Venture, as described herein ("Transpiring Event"), CBF may elect to terminate the Agreement by service of written notice to Local Partner. If a Transpiring Event occurs, CBF may consider – in its sole discretion – proposals by Local Partner to satisfactorily address the personnel needs occasioned by the loss or unavailability of the Key Person, as an alternative to terminating the Agreement, but in no event shall such consideration be deemed to eliminate or diminish CBF's termination rights.

Section 6.5 *Rights and Remedies*. The rights and remedies of the Venturers hereunder shall not be mutually exclusive, i.e., the exercise of one (1) or more of the provisions hereof shall not preclude the exercise of any other provision hereof. Each of the Venturers confirms that damages at law may be an inadequate remedy for a breach or threatened breach of this Agreement and agrees that, in the event of a breach or threatened breach of any provision hereof, the respective rights and obligations hereunder shall be enforceable by specific performance, injunction, or other equitable remedy, but nothing herein contained is intended to, nor shall it, limit or affect any rights or rights at law or by statute or otherwise of any party aggrieved as against the other for breach or threatened breach of any provision hereof, it being the intention by this paragraph to make clear the agreement of the Venturers that the respective rights and obligations of the Venturers hereunder shall be enforceable in equity as well as at law or otherwise. If any court determines that any provision of this Agreement is invalid or unenforceable, any invalidity or unenforceability will affect only that provision and will not make any other provision of this Agreement invalid or unenforceable and such provision shall be modified, amended or limited only to the extent necessary to render it valid and enforceable.

Section 6.6 *Assignment*. Neither this agreement nor any interest of either of the parties herein, including any interest in monies belonging to, or which may accrue to, the joint venture, or any interest in the joint accounts or in any property of any kind employed or used in connection with the operation, may be assigned, pledged, or transferred without the prior written consent of the Venturers, except that CBF may assign this Agreement to a subsidiary company owned or controlled by CBF or of which CBF may be an affiliate, or to a company owned or controlled by any owner of CBF.

Section 6.7 *Disputes*. If a dispute arises, the parties will try in good faith to settle it through mediation conducted by a mediator to be mutually selected. The parties will share the costs of the mediator equally. Each party will cooperate fully and fairly with the mediator and will attempt to reach a mutually satisfactory compromise to the dispute. If the dispute is not resolved within 30 days after it is referred to the mediator, either party may elect to have the matter arbitrated in binding arbitration, however, the party electing arbitration shall bear all costs of arbitration.

Section 6.8 *Independent Companies*. The Venturers agree and confirm that neither is the employee, subsidiary or affiliate of the other, and that each is dealing with each other as independent entities and no parent, subsidiary, or affiliate of any Venturer shall have any duty, responsibility, obligation, or liability to the other Venturer under this Agreement or in any manner pertaining herein or hereunder. CBF is responsible for paying its own employees, and for complying with the tax, worker's compensation, and any other employment obligations related thereto; and Local Partner is responsible for paying its own employees, and for complying with the tax, worker's compensation, and any other employment obligations related thereto. Except as otherwise expressly and specifically provided in this Agreement, no Venturer shall have any authority to act for, or assume any obligations or responsibility on behalf of, any other Venturer or the Venture. Nothing herein shall be construed to create a general partnership between the parties or to authorize either party to act as general agent for the other party, or to permit either party to bid for or to undertake any other contract for the other party.

Section 6.9 *Borrowing Money*. Neither party shall have the right to borrow money on behalf of the other party or to use the credit of the other party for any purpose, except as specifically agreed between the Venturers.

Section 6.10 *Other Business*. Except for the rights of the Venturers as set forth herein, nothing in this Agreement shall be deemed to restrict in any way the freedom of either Venturer to conduct any other business or activity whatsoever at any location.

Section 6.11 *Non-Compete*. During the term of this agreement and for a period of _____ months/years immediately after termination of this agreement, Local Partner will not directly or indirectly own, manage, be employed by or engaged by or subcontracted by, operate, or control any other book fair or closely similar event business within 300 miles of _____ [location], unless CBF gives its prior written consent. During the term of this Agreement and for a period of one_____ year immediately after termination of this agreement, Local Partner will not directly or indirectly call upon or solicit any sponsor of the Venture, or a person or firm referred by NCCBF, with the intention of diverting or attempting to divert such sponsor to competing venture of the Venture or NCCBF. Subsequent to the aforementioned one year period, and for the one year period next subsequent thereto, if Local Partner has an interest in producing, sponsoring or operating a book fair event in the _____ area or within a 300 mile radius thereof, Local Partner shall first offer the applicable venture, collaboration, affiliation or partnership business opportunity to CBF (i.e., right of first refusal).

Section 6.12 *Proprietary Information.* Local Partner will not at any time, during or after the term of this agreement, directly or indirectly divulge or otherwise disclose Proprietary Information of CBF (or any of its affiliates) or the Venture to anyone other than an employee of CBF or Local Partner. For purposes of this Agreement, Proprietary Information shall mean, by way of illustration and not limitation, all information (whether or not patentable and whether or not copyrightable) owned, possessed or used by the CBF or the Venture, including, without limitation, any invention, formula, vendor information, customer information, apparatus, equipment, trade secret, process, research, report, technical data, know-how, computer program, software, software documentation, hardware design, technology, marketing or business plan, forecast, unpublished financial statement, budget, license, price, cost and employee list that is communicated to, learned of, developed or otherwise acquired by the Local Partner in the course of Local Partner's participation in the Venture. All books, records, notes, reports, copy, advertising, contracts, orders, drafts, accounts, documents and other information or writings relating to CBF or the Venture or its customers, employees, sales representatives, or agents, whether prepared by Local Partner or otherwise coming into the possession of Local Partner, is and shall remain the exclusive property of CBF or the Venture, as the case may be, and shall be returned to CBF or the Venture, as applicable, upon demand. Local Partner shall report all violations of CBF's trademarks and/or copyrights and other proprietary rights in its Proprietary Information and other works immediately upon discovery of such violations by Local Partner. Local Partner acknowledges that each of the above matters is important and material to the business and success of CBF and agrees that any breach of this section is a material breach of this agreement, from which Local Partner may be enjoined and for which Local Partner shall also pay to CBF all damages (including but not limited to compensatory, incidental, consequential, and punitive damages) which arise from the breach, together with interest, costs and CBF's attorney fees.

Section 6.13. *Cooperation.* The parties agree to execute all documents that may be necessary to carry out the intent purposes of this Agreement.

Section 6.14. *Headings and Titles.* Section titles or captions contained in this Agreement are inserted only as a matter of convenience and for reference and in no way define or limit, extend or describe the scope of this Agreement or the intent of any of its provisions.

Section 6.15 *Trademark and Servicemark.* The parties agree and acknowledge that mark and name _____ Book Fair & Art Festival (the "Brand") shall be owned solely and exclusively by CBF in perpetuity, and neither Local Partner, nor any owner, officer, director, employee, agent, assignee or affiliate thereof shall be deemed to own or control the Brand or shall be entitled to make or file any claim, affidavit, complaint or cause of action which alleges or attests anything to the contrary. Local Partner agrees and acknowledges that nothing in this Agreement shall give Local Partner any right, title, or interest in, or to, the Brand other than the right to participate in the Venture in a manner consistent with this Agreement and as may be expressly granted hereunder. Nothing herein shall be construed as granting Local Partner the right to sublicense, transfer, assign, or authorize others to use the Brand. Local Partner will not enter into any agreement allowing another person or entity to perform any act that Local Partner is prohibited from undertaking under the terms of this Agreement. Local Partner shall ensure that it does not take any action which negatively impacts CBF's reputation or goodwill in the Brand. Local Partner acknowledges that CBF owns all rights, title, interest, and goodwill in and to the Brand and agrees it will do nothing inconsistent with such ownership and that all use of the Brand by Local Partner shall inure to the benefit of and be on behalf of CBF.

IN WITNESS WHEREOF, this Agreement is executed effective as of the date first set forth above.

Citywide Book Fairs, Art Festivals and Book Pavilions, Inc.

By: _____, _____ (title)
_____ [print name]

_____ (*Type Local Partner here*)

By: _____, _____ (title)
_____ [print name]

ABOUT THE AUTHOR

TONY ROSE, PRESIDENT
SOLID PLATINUM RECORDS AND PRODUCTIONS 1979-1995.

Solid Platinum Records and Productions founded by Tony Rose, would become a major independent record label with distribution, production, licensing and music publishing including:

Pavilion/CBS Records (U.S.A.); *CBS Records* (Worldwide); *Reach Out International Records* (Worldwide); *M.J.S. Records* (U.S.A.); *Greyhound Records* (UK); *Virgin Records* (UK); *Virgin Records* (Worldwide); *EMI Music Publishing* (Worldwide); *Virgin Music Publishing* (Worldwide); *Brampton Music Publishing* (UK); *Atlantic Records* (Worldwide); *CNA Records* Roba (Holland & Germany); *Emergency Records* (U.S.A.); *Precision Records* (UK); Music Publishing (Germany, Austria, Switzerland, Belgium, The Netherlands); *Carrerre Records* (UK and France); *The Company of Two P(i)ters* (The Netherlands, Austria, Switzerland, Luxemburg); *Metronome/Polygram Re-cords* (Germany); *Maurice Starr Music Publishing / EMI Music Pub-lishing* (Worldwide); *Danceteria Records* (France); *Unidisc Music Inc.* (World- wide), *Unitunes Music Publishing* (Worldwide).

Tony Rose was born in Roxbury (Boston) Massachusetts and raised in the Whittier Street Housing Projects. He was honorably discharged from the U.S. Air Force after serving in the Vietnam War, and attended the University of Massachusetts, the University of California in Los Angeles and the New England Conservatory of Music, Boston, MA. He was employed as a production assistant at the *Burbank Studios* (**Warner Brothers and Columbia Pictures**), in the accounting and sales division at **Warner/Electra/Atlantic Records** (WEA), as an accounts represent-tative at *Warren Lanier Public Relations* and as an A&R Representative at *RCA Records*, Los Angeles, California.

Rose returned to Boston and along with record producer Maurice Starr became the primary architect of "The Roxbury (Boston) Black Music Scene" a movement that ultimately led to the discovery of the international blockbusters

TONY ROSE

Prince Charles and the City Beat Band, The Jonzun Crew, New Edition and New Kids on the Block. Rose held recording / production deals with Virgin Records, Atlantic Records, Pavilion and CBS/Sony Records

Rose was a successful Executive Producer, Record Producer, Record Company Owner, Personal Manager, Music Publisher, Recording Studio Owner, Recording Engineer, Song Writer and Composer for more than fifteen years. His Solid Platinum Records and Productions was the first African American production company to have a production deal with Virgin Records. Albums produced by Rose, **Gang War** and **Stone Killers** by **Prince Charles and the City Beat Band** reached Gold Album status and shared the charts with Michael Jackson's *Thriller* for six consecutive months in the number one, two and three positions throughout the world; and his legendary **Prince Charles and the City Beat Band** albums **Gang War**, **Stone Killers, Combat Zone** and singles, have accounted for more than Four Million sold worldwide. Rose's many music awards include "Gold" and "Platinum" Albums and "Ampex Golden Reel" Awards for recording and engineering **New Kids on the Block**. Rose, has also penned **Before the Legend – The Rise of New Kids on the Block and ...A Guy Named Maurice Starr – The Early Years,** published August 2008.

In 2009, Charles C. Yancey, The City of Boston and The Boston City Council presented Tony Rose, Maurice Starr and Prince Charles Alexander an **Official Resolution** for their success in the Music / Recording Industry.

In 2010 Tony Rose was named by Pacey C. Foster, Professor of Management, University Of Massachusetts at Boston, author of - **Hip Hop In the Hub: How Boston Rap Remained Underground - The Story of Boston's Hip Hop Community From 1979-2006** - The **GodFather of Boston Rap** for producing, distributing and releasing, on *Solid Platinum Records and Productions* - Boston and New England's - first Rap Records - **Tight Jeans** and **Passion** from the album **Gang War** by Prince Charles and The City Beat Band, and the singles **Sweat It Off** & **Hood Rock** by **Kevin Fleetwood and the Cadillacs of Sound.**

Today, Tony Rose is an **NAACP Image Award Winner for Outstanding Literature,** the Publisher and CEO of **Amber Communications Group, Inc.**, the nation's largest African American Publisher of Self-Help Books and Music Biographies.

www.ingramcontent.com/pod-product-compliance
Lightning Source LLC
Chambersburg PA
CBHW071651090426
42738CB00009B/1491